Religion, Civilization, and Civil War

Religion, Civilization, and Civil War

1945 through the Millennium

Jonathan Fox

LEXINGTON BOOKS
Lanham • Boulder • New York • Toronto • Oxford

LEXINGTON BOOKS

Published in the United States of America
by Lexington Books
An imprint of The Rowman & Littlefield Publishing Group, Inc.
4501 Forbes Boulevard, Suite 200, Lanham, Maryland 20706

PO Box 317
Oxford
OX2 9RU, UK

British Library Cataloguing in Publication Information Available

Library of Congress Cataloging-in-Publication Data

Fox, Jonathan, 1968–
  Religion, civilization, and civil war : 1945 through the new
millennium / Jonathan Fox.
      p. cm.
Includes bibliographical references and index.
  ISBN 0-7391-0744-5 (cloth : alk. paper)
  1. Civil war—Religious aspects—History—20th century. 2. Ethnic
conflict—Religious aspects—History—20th century. I. Title.
BL65.W2F695 2004
201'.72—dc22   2003024514

Printed in the United States of America

♾™ The paper used in this publication meets the minimum requirements of American
National Standard for Information Sciences—Permanence of Paper for Printed Library
Materials, ANSI/NISO Z39.48–1992.

To Pearl Nathan,
a pillar in my life from when I was born.

Contents

Acknowledgments

I would like to thank Ted R. Gurr, without whom this book would not have been possible, both for his insightful advice and criticism and for making the Minorities at Risk data and State Failure so accessible. I would also like to thank the staff of the Minorities at Risk project, especially Michael Dravis, Deepa Kholsa, Anne Pitsch, and Pamela Burke, who helped out with the backup codings, as well as Michael Haxton, Shinwa Lee, and Steve Kurth, who helped out at other stages of the project. I similarly thank all of those who worked on the project since I left in 1997 for providing the updated and improved data that I used in this book. I also thank Monty Marshall and the staff of the State Failure project for their work on the data which has made this research possible. In addition, I would like to thank R. Scott Appleby, Charles E. Butterworth, Eliezer Don-Yehiya, Hillel Frisch, Ollie A. Johnson, Shmuel Sandler, Shlomo Shpiro, William T. Stuart, Bernard Susser, and Jonathan Wilkenfeld, all of whom provided useful advice at various stages of this project. Any errors of fact or interpretation that remain are mine alone. Finally, a portion of this research was supported by the Israel Science Foundation (grant #896/00) and I thank the foundation for its generous support.

Chapter 1

Introduction

The topic of religion, culture, and conflict has been attracting increasing attention by academics, policy makers, and the media. This increased attention is part of a process of a reevaluation of past assumptions that religion was becoming irrelevant. The terror attacks of September 11, 2001, certainly accelerated this reassessment but the reevaluation of the role of religion in conflict, as well as in society and politics in general, began well before then. For example, Samuel Huntington's "Clash of Civilizations" (CoC) theory posits that religious-based identity groups he calls civilizations will be the basis for world conflict in the post-Cold War era. This theory sparked one of the most voluminous debates of the 1990s in the international relations literature.[1] This is but one of many examples of a growing literature on the role of religion in conflict.[2]

Nevertheless, the terror attacks of September 11, 2001, caught the United States and the West by surprise. This highlights the fact that our understanding of the religious causes of conflict is inadequate. Yet much of the discussion on religion and conflict is based on anecdotes, speculation, and opinion and is characterized by the fact that the participants agree on very little. The majority of writings on the topic use this type of ad hoc analysis. A smaller proportion of writings on the topic are theoretical. There are also a very few empirical studies. However, these empirical studies tend to focus on narrow aspects of conflict. Because of this they do not provide enough information to answer more general questions like what is the overall influence of religion on conflict.

Accordingly, this study examines the impact of religion on domestic conflict using two datasets. The first includes all instances of ethnic conflict between 1945 and 2000. The examination of this data includes the impact of religion on rebellion, protest, discrimination, and international intervention. The second includes all ethnic wars, mass killings, and civil wars between 1948 and 2001. Thus, this study includes an evaluation of the impact of religion on multiple forms of conflict for a

1

period of over five decades. This includes the impact of multiple more specific potential religious influences on domestic conflict. These include religious identity, religious legitimacy, religious institutions, religious discrimination, and religious issues. It also examines whether the conflict patterns of some religions differ from those of other religions.

Furthermore, in addition to examining the impact of religion on conflict, this book also tests Samuel Huntington's CoC theory. This is because, as noted above, the debate over this theory is among the most voluminous debates over the impact of religion on conflict in recent decades in the social sciences. While Huntington's formulation of religious identity into civilizations produces a unit of analysis that is not exactly the same as religion, as is discussed in more detail in Chapter 8, it does overlap strongly with religion. More importantly, the level of attention given to this theory in the literature essentially makes any analysis of the role of religion in conflict without an evaluation of the CoC theory incomplete.

For these reasons, this study examines the impact of both religion and civilization on conflict, first separately then in a head-to-head comparison. The results of this analysis not only answer the question of what impact, if any, religion has on domestic conflict, but they also address whether Huntington's concept of civilizations provides a better explanation for domestic conflict than does religion.

In sum, this study provides the most comprehensive and detailed empirical analysis of the impact of religion and civilization on domestic conflict to date. This includes ethnoreligious conflict–those conflicts between ethnic groups who belong to different religions–as well as other forms of religious conflict. This includes an evaluation of what proportion of conflicts are religious as well as the extent of the impact of a number of religious factors on conflict. The overall goal is to analyze every aspect of religion and domestic conflict that it is possible to analyze in order to better understand the larger picture. That is, while the few existing past empirical studies of religion and conflict focus on narrow topics, this study looks at a wide range of topics. This is in order to unearth not only the influence of specific aspects of religion on more specific types of conflict, but also the larger trends in religion's influence on domestic conflict.

Research Design

This study uses data from two separate datasets on domestic conflict as well as additional data on religion and civilization collected by the author. A more detailed description of the specific variables used in this study can be found in Appendix B.

Minorities at Risk

The Minorities at Risk (MAR) dataset includes data on 337 ethnic minorities for the years 1945 to 2000.[3] The unit of analysis for the dataset is the ethnic minority within a state. Thus, the same majority or minority group may appear more than once in the data; however, each pairing of majority and minority groups is unique. For example, the Hindu majority in India appears in this study several times, once for each ethnic minority in India and the Russians appear as a minority in twelve former USSR republics. This also means that some states are not represented in the dataset because they do not contain any ethnic minorities which meet the MAR projects criteria for inclusion (which are discussed below).

The 337 minorities coded in the MAR dataset constitute all ethnic minorities in the world which meet the project's criteria for inclusion. It is important to recognize that the 337 ethnic minorities contained in the MAR dataset constitute only a fraction of the as many as 5,000 ethnic minorities existing worldwide. (Gurr, 1993a: 5-7) These minorities were selected for analysis by the MAR project because they are most likely to be politically active based on two criteria, one of which is sufficient for the group to be included in the dataset. The first is whether "the group collectively suffers, or benefits from, systematic discriminatory treatment vis-a-vis other groups in the state." (Gurr 1993a: 6) The second is whether "the group was the focus of political mobilization and action in defense or promotion of its self-defined interests." (Gurr, 1993a: 7) The use of these criteria has led to some criticism of the MAR dataset as being guilty of selection bias. (Fearon and Latin, 1997) Gurr (2000, 10-13) addresses these criticisms arguing that the MAR dataset is intended to contain all ethnic groups that are politically significant, not an exhaustive list of all ethnic minorities. Furthermore, the project is constantly adding groups based on the suggestions of research assistants as well as outside researchers. Given that the project has been in existence for about two decades it is arguable that this has resulted in an accurate list of groups.

Not all minorities included in the MAR dataset were active for the entire 1945-2000 period. For example, the Russian minorities in the twelve former USSR republics mentioned above did not exist as minorities before the fall of the Soviet Union. Rather, they were part of the Russian majority in the USSR. Furthermore each of these twelve states represents a minority that existed within the former USSR which in the 1990s became a majority within its own state. Thus as political boundaries change, so can the distribution of ethnic majorities and minorities. In addition, some minorities, which always existed within states demographically, become politically active during this period for other reasons. The Scots in the United Kingdom and the Assamese in India are examples of this. Others like the Chams in Cambodia and the Santals in India become politically inactive and are dropped from the codings during this period.

The MAR dataset contains a considerable amount of information on ethnic conflict. In addition to basic variables like the amount of ethnic rebellion and ethnic protest that take place in a given period, it has information on many factors that influence the ethnic conflict process. These include, but are by no means limited to, discrimination, complaints expressed over discrimination, demographic factors, economic factors, the spread of conflict across borders, international intervention, the level of political mobilization of the minority group, and the characteristics of the regime. Thus, it is possible to control for all of these factors, and others, in multivariate analysis. This allows us to isolate the influence of religion on ethnic conflict to the exclusion of all of these factors. It also allows us to assume that any impact religion is found to have on ethnic conflict in these multivariate analyses is a causal impact. That is, these analyses allow us to discover how religion causes or contributes to conflict, rather than just showing that religious conflicts are different.

The supplemental data on religion and civilizations I collected can be divided into two categories. The first category is identity variables. These variables contain information on the religious and civilizational identities of the minority and majority groups in each of the 337 ethnic conflicts in the MAR dataset.[4] They also show which conflicts are between groups of different religions (ethnoreligious conflicts) and different civilizations (civilizational conflicts). The second type of variable was collected only with regard to the impact of religion on conflict for a subset of 105 ethnoreligious minorities who were politically active during the 1990s.[5] These variables measure the impact of specific religious factors on conflict. These factors include religious discrimination, complaints expressed over religious discrimination, demands for more religious rights, religious legitimacy, religious institutions, and whether religion is relevant to the conflict.

The nature of the dataset has several implications for this portion of the study. First, it is limited to the same unit of analysis as the MAR dataset: the ethnic minority within a state. This eliminates all cases of domestic conflict within the same ethnic group. For our purposes, this is especially relevant to conflicts between secular and religious elements within a state. For example, while the MAR data contains information on the Berber minority in Algeria, it completely ignores the civil war that has been going on there since the early 1990s. This is because the Berbers are an ethnic minority but the civil war is between Islamic fundamentalists and the government, all of whom are part of the Arab majority in Algeria.

Second, in order for the more specific information on religious factors to be as compatible with the MAR dataset as possible, it is best collected in a similar manner. That is, the religion variables were modeled after the ethnicity variables used by the Minorities at Risk project. While this can potentially complicate the data collection process, in this case it did not. However, it does influence the structure of the religion variables.

Third, that the unit of analysis is the ethnic minority greatly complicates the analysis. That is not to say that the issue of religion and conflict is not complicated in and of itself. Be that as it may, a number of nonreligious factors can complicate ethnic conflict. These include, but are by no means limited to, discrimination directed against the ethnic minority, a desire for autonomy by the ethnic minority, linguistic and cultural differences between the ethnic minority and the dominant group, and the level of ethnic conflict among similar groups elsewhere, otherwise known as contagion or diffusion. Thus, in order to discover the impact of religion on ethnic conflict, we must control for all of these factors.

State Failure

The State Failure (SF) dataset includes major episodes of "state failure" which "is a new label that encompasses a range of severe political conflicts and regime crises exemplified by events of the 1990s in Somalia, Bosnia, Liberia, Afghanistan, and Congo-Kinshasa."[6] Thus, this study focuses only on the most intense of conflicts.

This study uses data from three sections of the state failure dataset, those concerning revolution, ethnic war, and mass killings.[7] Revolutionary wars are defined as "episodes of violent conflict between governments and politically organized groups (political challengers) that seek to overthrow the central government, to replace its leaders, or to seize power in one region. Conflicts must include substantial use of violence by one or both parties to qualify as wars." (Gurr, Harff, and Marshall 1997) Ethnic wars are defined as "episodes of violent conflict between governments and national, ethnic, religious, or other communal minorities (ethnic challengers) in which the challengers seek major changes in their status." (Gurr, Harff and Marshall 1997) Mass killings are defined as

> the promotion, execution, and/or implied consent of sustained policies by governing elites or their agents–or in the case of civil war, either of the contending authorities–that result in the deaths of a substantial portion of a communal group or politicized non-communal group. In genocides the victimized groups are defined primarily in terms of their communal (ethnolinguistic, religious) characteristics. In politicides, by contrast, groups are defined primarily in terms of their political opposition to the regime and dominant groups. Geno/politicide is distinguished from state repression and terror. In cases of state terror authorities arrest, persecute or execute a few members of a group in ways designed to terrorize the majority of the group into passivity or acquiescence. In the case of geno/politicide authorities physically exterminate enough (not necessarily all) members of a target group so that it can no longer pose any conceivable threat to their rule or interests. (Gurr, Harff, and Marshall 1997)

The unit of analysis for the State Failure dataset is a conflict year. Each year during which a particular type of conflict was occurring in a particular state is coded separately, including partial years in which the conflict began or ended. In addition to the variables specifically coded for the purposes of this study, which are discussed below, an additional modification was made to the data. First, there are several cases where the State Failure dataset codes conflict by several groups against the state together as a single entry. This study separates them into separate cases.[8] Second, many of the cases in the three categories overlap. For the tests performed on the entire dataset, the overlapping cases were removed from the study.[9] As a result, 683 years of ethnic war, 249 years of mass killings, and 449 years of revolutionary war were coded. Taking overlapping cases into account, this totals 1,106 conflict years between 1948 and 2001.

Unlike the MAR dataset, the SF dataset does not contain many control variables. Accordingly, the analyses of the SF dataset are of necessity bivariate. This means that while we can determine how many conflicts in a given year or a given category are religious, we cannot address the issue of causality. The supplemental data on religion and civilizations for the SF dataset is also more limited than the supplemental data for the MAR dataset. This is because only identity variables are available. Despite all this, the SF dataset is useful because it covers a wide range of violent conflict for the 1948 to 2001 period.

Implications for This Study

While the SF and MAR datasets have drawbacks individually, combining the two into a single study overcomes most of these drawbacks. The primary drawback of the MAR data is that it focuses on ethnic conflict to the exclusion of all other types of domestic conflict. The SF dataset, however, includes data on all types of violent domestic conflict. Similarly, the SF dataset has two major drawbacks. First, only bivariate analyses with violent conflict as the dependent variable can be performed on the dataset. Second, the SF dataset can only examine the impact of religious identity on conflict and not the impact of more specific religious factors. The MAR dataset, in contrast, has considerable depth and multivariate analyses are possible on a number of dependent variables including ethnic rebellion, ethnic protest, discrimination, and international intervention. It also contains information of religious factors other than identity. Thus, what is missing in the MAR data is covered by the SF and what is missing in the SF dataset is covered by the MAR data.

However, there remain two drawbacks which the combination of the two datasets does not cover. First, we cannot perform multivariate analyses on any type of conflict other than ethnic conflict. Second, we cannot analyze the impact of religious factors other than religious identity on nonethnic conflict. While it would have been preferable if this were otherwise, the nature of the data currently available makes this unavoidable. In any case, the combination of these two datasets allows for the most comprehensive analysis of the topic to date.

A final difference between the SF and MAR that should be noted concerns the nature of conflict which they cover. The SF data covers only the most violent of conflicts, usually involving a number of deaths. While the MAR dataset includes such conflicts, it also includes nonviolent conflicts that take place in the political arena. This includes cases like the Baha'i in Iran who engage in no violence but suffer from high levels of discrimination. They also include politically active minorities like the Scots in the United Kingdom who try to attain their political goals through peaceful means. Such depth is necessary for the multivariate analyses performed on the MAR data because when one asks when and why violent conflict occurs, one also asks when and why it does not occur. Thus, cases in which there is no violence are necessary to the analysis. As the examination of the SF dataset is a bivariate analysis, these extra cases are not necessary.

Also, it should be noted that when examining the impact of civilization on conflict, we only examine identity. However, this poses no difficulty because the CoC theory focuses on identity to the exclusion of all other factors.

A full listing of all the cases in both datasets is available in Appendix A. A full listing of the variables used in this study is available in Appendix B.

There is an additional limitation on this study which is common to all such empirical studies, that this study is limited to what can be measured. That is, this study ignores all factors which are too intangible to be measured. This problem is illustrated by a well-known story where a man sees another man searching for something near a lamppost and a dialogue ensues:

First man: What are you doing?
Second man: I lost my glasses and have been searching for them here under this lamppost for several hours.
First man: Why is it taking so long to find the glasses?
Second man: Probably because I lost them over there in the dark.
First man: Then why are you looking for them over here?
Second man: Because it's light over here and dark over there.

The moral of the parable is that looking in the light doesn't help if your answer lies in the dark. This problem is an unavoidable drawback of large-n empirical studies such as this one. However, this drawback is countered by an advantage over anecdotal studies described by Deutsch (1963: 53):

Introspection, intuition [and] insight [are] processes that are not verifiable among different observers. . . . But even though we can understand introspectively many facts and relations which exist, it is also true that we can understand in our fertile imagination very many relations that do not exist at all. What is more, there are things in the world that we cannot understand readily with our imagination as it is now constituted, even though we may be able to understand them . . . in the future, after we have become accustomed to the presuppositions of such under-standing. We can, therefore, do nothing more than accept provisionally these guesses or potential insights. . . . If we want to take them seriously, we must test them. We can do this by selecting . . . data, verifying them [and] forming explicit hypotheses as to what we expect to find. . . . And we then finally test these explicit hypotheses by confrontation with the data. . . . In the light of these tests we revise our criteria of relevance, we get new and revised data and we set up new methods of testing.

Deutsch's basic point is that the use of human intuition and insight also have their

Chapter 1

limitations. Researchers are often unintentionally biased. They often see what they expect to see, often reinterpreting the facts to suit their theories and emphasizing facts consistent with their theories and downplaying or even ignoring facts which do not fit their theories. They also often fail to see patterns which they do not expect to see. That is, relationships which are counterintuitive are less often revealed through the comparative process. As a result of both of these processes, two researchers looking at the same facts can come to wildly different conclusions. In the literature on most major conflicts this is the rule rather than the exception.

In contrast, quantitative methodology is not subject to these drawbacks. Two researchers examining the same data will get the same results. Thus, while empirical methodology loses something because it cannot accommodate unmeasurable factors and the uniqueness of each individual case, it is more objective than the anecdotal approach and can reveal trends that otherwise would likely not have been revealed.

As will be seen in this book, there are many aspects of religion and conflict which are under dispute, including whether religion and Huntington's concept of civilization have any impact on conflict at all. The anecdotal literature has been unable to resolve these issues. Accordingly a study such as this one is not only warranted, it is necessary. Whatever its limitations, it will be able to provide authoritative answers to questions which the anecdotal literature has been unable to definitively resolve.

Finally, it is important to note that both of these datasets constitute all, or nearly all, of the existing cases of the types of conflict which they measure. This means that the results found in this analysis are real results rather than an estimation based on a sample of a larger population. For this reason, measures of statistical significance measure only the strength of a result, not whether the differences or correlations unearthed by the analysis are real. For example, if exit polls in an election show one candidate one or two percentage points ahead of the others, this is considered statistically a dead heat. This is because the polls represent an estimation of a large population of hundreds of thousands or perhaps millions based on a small sample of voters, say one thousand. There is always a chance that this sample does not exactly represent the population it is intended to measure; thus, measures of statistical significance are important. However, once the votes are counted (leaving issues of how they should be counted aside) if one of the candidate wins by one vote, it is still a victory for that candidate. The results of this study are akin to the final results of an election because we have information on the vast majority, if not all, of the relevant cases.

Overview

The first part of this book examines the impact of religion on conflict. Chapter 2 addresses the existing literature on the topic. This includes a discussion of the debate over whether religion is important at all, the theorized impact of religion on conflict, and previous empirical studies on the topic. Chapter 3 begins the quantitative analysis. It examines whether religious conflicts are different from other conflicts. It also examines whether specific religions are more violent than others. This includes a bivariate analysis of the MAR and SF datasets. Chapter 4 uses multivariate techniques to examine religious causes of conflict using the MAR data. It includes an examination of the religious causes of rebellion, discrimination, and international intervention. Chapter 5 uses both bivariate and multivariate methodology, using the MAR data to examine the impact of religion on ethnic protest.

The second part of the book examines Huntington's CoC theory. Chapter 6 describes the theory and the debate surrounding it. Chapter 7 provides a bivariate analysis of the theory using the MAR and SF datasets.

The final part of the book examines the comparative impact of religion and civilization on conflict. This includes bivariate examinations of the SF and MAR data as well as a multivariate examination of the MAR data.

There are three general conclusions from this analysis. First, while religion influences conflict, it does so only as an intervening variable. That is, factors other than religion are the primary causes of conflict, but religion significantly influences the process of domestic conflict in several different ways. Second, Huntington's CoC theory is not supported by the evidence. Finally, in head-to-head comparisons, religion has a stronger impact on conflict than does Huntington's concept of civilizations.

Conclusions

With 188 tables and figures this book is likely the most exhaustive analysis of the impact of religion and Huntington's concept of civilization on domestic conflict. Every relevant test which can be performed on the SF and MAR datasets is included in this study. This analysis is, therefore, arguably the most comprehensive to date on the impact of religion and civilization on domestic conflict.

Notes

1. For a discussion of Samuel Huntington's CoC theory and the debate surrounding it see Chapter 6.
2. For a detailed discussion of this literature, including the debate over religion's relevance, see Chapter 2.
3. A copy of the MAR dataset as well as a more detailed description of the dataset, the variables in it, and the data collection methods can be found at the MAR website at www.cidcm.umd.edu/inscr/mar.
4. These variables are listed in Appendix A of this book.

5. A copy of these variables can be found listed separately at the MAR website at www.cidcm.umd.edu/inscr/mar.

6. State Failure website at www.cidcm.umd.edu/inscr/stfail. A copy of the data is available at this site.

7.While abrupt regime transitions are included in the dataset, they are not included in this study because they generally represent changes in regimes, not major conflicts.

8.There are episodes of conflict which were broken up. First, the joint Serb and Croat war against the Bosnian government from 1992 to 1995 was broken up into two separate cases, one for Serbs and one for Croats. As a result, four conflict years were added. Second, the Abkhaz and South Ossetian rebellion from 1991 to 1993 in Georgia, broken up into two separate cases, one for Abkhaz and one for South Ossetians. As a result, three conflict years were added. Third, the Shi'i and Kurdish rebellions in Iraq from 1991 to 1998 were broken up into two cases. As a result eight conflict years were added.

9. There are forty conflict years where all three categories overlap. In addition, there are 209 conflict years of mass killings which overlap with ethnic wars, sixty-seven conflict years of revolutionary wars which overlap with ethnic wars, and twenty-one conflict years of revolutionary wars which overlap with mass killings.

Chapter 2

Theories of Religion and Conflict

The relationship between religion and society, politics, and conflict is both one that has been discussed for millennia and one that has been neglected until recently. In the past it was assumed that religion could not be fully separated from society, politics, and conflict, but with the Enlightenment this assumption was challenged in favor of an assumption that religion's influence was becoming a thing of the past. This assumption, in turn, is now itself being questioned.

The purpose of this chapter is to briefly examine what role, if any, religion plays in conflict. This examination includes the comparative, theoretical, and quantitative literature. The larger purpose is to place in context the quantitative analysis in the following chapters of the role of religion in conflict.

Is Religion Important?

The question of whether religion is important in society, politics, and conflict may seem to be a "no-brainer" with the obvious answer of "Yes." However, for much of the twentieth century most branches of the social sciences, at least within Western circles, answered this seemingly simple question with a resounding "No." That is, the dominant paradigms in the social sciences considered religion to be an increasingly epiphenomenal phenomenon, having no relevance in the modern age.

This trend can be traced back to eighteenth- and nineteenth-century scholars and thinkers like Voltaire, Marx, Nietzsche, Freud, Weber, and Durkheim who were among the founders of the social sciences. While their understandings of the role of religion in past times as well as modern times were by no means identical, there are a few common themes that can be found in all of their diverse treatises on the topic. First, religion can only be understood through examining its social context. Second, society was changing from a primitive one based on religion and superstition to a modern one based on science and reason. Third, this was manifesting itself both on the cultural and political-institutional levels. In all, science and reason were thought to be taking the place of religion and superstition in society. They expected that eventually religion would become irrelevant to most aspects of society that mattered.

During the twentieth century this argument became formalized into paradigms within the social sciences. In political science, it became known as modernization theory. This body of theory actually focused on ethnicity but was also applied to religion. In sociology it became known as secularization theory which did specifically focus on religion.

The basic argument of these bodies of theory was that a number of factors inherent in modernity would lead to the demise of primordial phenomena like ethnicity and religion. First, mass education and increasing literacy would help to undermine the hold of religion and superstition on the minds of the masses.

Second, increasing scientific knowledge would replace religion as a basis for our understanding of the world. For example, the concepts of evolution and the big bang provide the explanations for our existence that had previously been filled by Creation stories like that of Genesis.

Third, improved technology provides people with alternatives and options not previously available. For example, modern contraception techniques give people the ability to violate the religious norm of chastity without the risks associated with it in the past. Similarly, modern communications make it more difficult to restrict the ideas to which people are exposed. This makes it more difficult to socialize people into traditional religious societies.

Fourth, urbanization undermines the traditional community where everybody knows each other's business. This removes a basic social mechanism for enforcing religious norms. Ironically, modern cities, with their populations in the hundreds of thousands or millions, decrease the influence of people's neighbors on their behavior. Large population concentrations can give individuals more anonymity and an ability to form a network of like-minded peers to a greater extent than was possible in smaller, more traditional communities.

Fifth, political and social institutions are now based on rational and scientific principles. Modern governments are based on the work of social theorists like John Locke and Rene Rousseau who derive their theories from secular assumptions such as governments are legitimated by the will of the people. This assumption is common to modern democratic theory as well as communist and fascist theory, though the mechanisms for representing the common will differ among these bodies of theory. This stands in stark contrast to the previous theory of legitimacy in which a monarch received his mandate to rule from God and, therefore, could not be challenged by the masses.

Sixth, secular norms based on rationalism are replacing religious norms. This occurs both in the formal legal realm as well as in the cultural realm. The laws that now guide behavior are based on legislation that occurs through a political process and are guided by the secular social theories and scientific knowledge of the modern age. The concept of freedom to choose one's own religion, including the choice to have no religion at all, is enshrined in most Western countries' constitutions. Also, secular ideas like universal human rights provide a secular source for the personal moral guidance once provided by religion.[1]

Private lives and issues are also guided by rationalism. In the past, people with personal problems tended to seek the clergy for help. Today it is more common to seek the help of mental heath care professionals like psychologists, psychiatrists, and social workers. Furthermore, modern programs for training clergy often include instruction in these secular rationalist techniques for dealing with mental health issues.

In all, modernization and secularization theory predicted the eventual demise of religion due to these and other factors inherent in modernization. Yet these paradigms were never dominant in all branches of academics. Rather they were strongest among Western academics who studied the West. In these circles modernization and secularization theory can be described as the dominant paradigms. However, scholars of Middle East politics, for example, tended to be less convinced by these theories as the facts in the region do not fit the predictions of modernization and secularization theory. The supporters of the theory argued that this is because the Middle East, and the rest of the Third World, for that matter, have not sufficiently modernized for the predictions of modernization and secularization theory to take effect.

Thus, modernization and secularization theory are particularly Western. They originate in the work of Western social theorists and they find their strongest support among Western social scientists who study the West. The support among this body of academics for modernization and secularization theory was near universal for most of the twentieth century.

Only around 1980 did Western academics begin to question the assumption that religion was becoming irrelevant. This happened as world events began to convince many academics that religion was still playing an important role in politics and society. The rise of the religious Right in the United States showed religion to continue to be important in what can be called the bastion of modernization and secularization theory. The Iranian revolution showed that the perceived trend of states becoming more secular in the Third World was not an absolute one. The hostage crisis associated with the Iranian revolution showed that the religious politics of Third World states could influence the West. The additional violent Islamic opposition movements, some successful and some not, in countries like Afghanistan, Algeria, and Egypt showed that Iran was not an isolated event. Ethnic conflicts with religious overtones, some of which had previously been considered secular in origin, like the conflicts in Northern Ireland, the former Yugoslavia, and Israel showed that the influence of religion was more widespread and could occur in different contexts. Also, the growing influence of nonviolent fundamentalist movements of many religions throughout the world added further evidence of the fallaciousness of modernization and secularization theory.

These world events convinced many political scientists who began to write on

Chapter 2

issues of religion and politics in the 1980s, but most were not truly convinced that religious violence could be important in the West until the events in Waco, Texas in 1993. (Kaplan, 2002) Few sociologists began to question secularization theory until the mid-1990s.[2] Even in the late 1990s, many sociologists ardently argued that secularization was still occurring.

For example, an entire issue of *Sociology of Religion* was devoted to the debate over secularization theory with articles like "Secularization R.I.P." vying against "Secularization in a Context of Advanced Modernity."[3] The debate in this journal came down to two issues: whether secularization meant people becoming less religious or it meant religion moving from the public sphere to the private sphere and whether either of these processes has been occurring. While many of the authors in the journal still defended secularization theory, the form of secularization theory they defended was nowhere near the absolute assumptions of religion's demise of the previous decades. Rather, more limited arguments prevailed. For instance, Beyer (1999) argued that modernity has caused a decline in religion's influence but that this influence has not disappeared. Dobbelaere (1999) argues that even if people are becoming more religious, modern religions are more worldly and religion is a private choice. Lambert (1999) similarly argues that secularization has occurred in the sense that people are more autonomous from religion but specifically states that religion has not disappeared. Thus, while secularization theory may still survive among sociologists, it no longer is dominant in the field and makes more limited claims of a weakening of religion in the public sphere, and perhaps the private one. However, the claims that religion will become an epiphenomenon have been dropped.

The discipline of international relations, at least among Western academics, has more profoundly ignored religion. Unlike sociology and political science, international relations does not have a theory or paradigm which explains why religion is unimportant. Rather, it is simply assumed with no explanation considered necessary. Furthermore, no reawakening to the importance of religion occurred in international relations during the last twenty years of the twentieth century. A survey of 4 major international relations journals found that only six of 1,600 articles published between 1980 and 1999 considered religion an important influence on international relations. (Philpott, 2002: 69)[4]

The only significant aspect of international relations that dealt with religion even indirectly during the 1990s was the debate over Samuel Huntington's "clash of civilizations" theory which is discussed in detail later in this book. However, one of the signatures of this debate was the effort made by its participants to avoid the term "religion." Terms like "culture," "civilization," and "society" were almost universally preferred over the term "religion." This is representative of a more general trend in international relations that places religion in the context of some other more important phenomenon like culture, institutions, terrorism, or civil society. (Kabalkova, 2000: 682-683) That is, religion, if it must be dealt with by international relations scholars, tends to be dealt with as a subset of some other topic, and when discussing that topic, religion is somehow de-emphasized.

For example, it is a fact that most terrorism since 1980 has been by religiously motivated Islamic militants and most new terror groups since 1980 are militant Islamic groups. (Weinberg and Eubank, 1998; Weinberg, Eubank, and Pedahzur, 2002) Yet the number of academic articles and books which focus on religion as a cause of terrorism of which I am aware, especially those written before September 11, 2001, can be counted on one's fingers.[5] Most theories on the topic deal with secular economic, political, and social explanations. While it cannot be denied that these explanations have merit, it also cannot be denied that religious motivations are an important contributor to terror, yet this seems to be mostly ignored in the literature.

It is too soon to evaluate the impact of the events of September 11, 2001 on the study of terrorism and international relations. However there are some indications that this tendency to ignore religion will continue, at least among some academics. One such indication is the insistence of the Bush administration to call their fight against Al Quaeda the "war on terrorism" and insist that the administration has no grievance against Muslims. While clearly one cannot fairly blame all Muslims for the acts of Usama bin Laden's organization, the acts of terror perpetrated by it were perpetrated by Muslims motivated by their interpretation of Islam. Furthermore, their actions and interpretations of Islam are supported by a significant minority of Muslims worldwide. Thus, the West is, in fact, at war with a subset of Muslims. The argument that the war is with terrorism, which is a tactic, rather than the people who use that tactic, is absurd.

Perhaps one of the greatest ironies of the predictions of religion's demise is that many now believe that modernity has had the opposite effect and has, in fact, caused a resurgence of religion. That is, a number of interrelated processes associated with modernization have caused religion's influence to increase rather than decrease.

First, efforts at modernization in much of the Third World spearheaded by secular governments guided by Western ideologies like liberalism, communism, and socialism have failed to meet the goals of improving the material situation and providing social justice. That these secular Western ideologies are perceived as foreign intrusions further undermines their legitimacy. As a result, these governments are suffering from legitimacy problems, leaving room for locally authentic alternatives for an ideology to govern the state. This includes religious ideologies. (Juergensmeyer, 1993)

Second, modernization has undermined traditional lifestyles and communities, as modernization and secularization theory predicted, but this has led to a religious backlash against modernity rather than the predicted demise of religion. (Sahliyeh, 1990: 9; Haynes, 1994: 34; Thomas, 2000: 816) Third, many individuals have been unsuccessful at adapting to modernity for a variety of reasons. These people tend to feel alienated from the modern secular culture, leaving them open to overtures by religious groups who promise to provide them with the sense of belonging which they lack. (Sahliyeh, 1990)

Fourth, modernity has changed the nature of both religious and political institutions. Both now have the ability to enter more areas of life, thus causing increased tension between the two. (Shupe, 1990: 23-26) Conversely, it has allowed more individuals to influence politics through mass participation. Many of these individuals have used this to bring their religious views into the political arena. (Rubin, 1994: 22-23) That political institutions now allow freedom of religion has given people the ability to choose their own religion. Many argue that this has made religion more popular, as people can find religious alternatives more attractive to them, thus increasing religiosity. (Iannaccone, 1995a, 1995b; Warner, 1993)

Fifth, religious institutions are a common basis for political mobilization. By their nature they include most of the resources necessary for political activities. These include people with leadership skills, physical infrastructure (including a place to meet and offices) and a core group of supporters and activists. They also include less tangible assets like interpersonal and interorganizational networks and legitimacy.(Hadden, 1987a; Harris, 1994; Johnston and Figa, 1988)

Sixth, modern communications technology have allowed religious groups to better coordinate and learn from each other as well as export their ideas to new populations. (Shupe, 1990: 22)

In fact, the rise of religious fundamentalism is often attributed to many of these processes. Explanations for fundamentalism include the reaction to modernity's failures both on the individual and macro levels. These groups use modern mobilization and communication techniques as well as take advantage of the modern political environment. They also criticize the undermining of traditional values and lifestyles and seek to restore them. (Marty and Appleby, 1991; 1993; 1994)

Thus, despite predictions to the contrary, religion is still present and influential in the modern age. However, there are some who argue that this is beside the point because most times we see a religious influence, it is really a manifestation of some more basic social force. That is, it is not religion which is important but rather the social or political force which pulls religion's strings. Marx's claim that the ruling classes use religion to keep the working classes in line, thus making religion the "opiate of the masses," is a classic example of this type of argument which is known as functionalism. According to this body of theory, even if there is evidence that religion has an impact on society, any seeming religious influence on society, politics, and conflict would be simply a facade and, therefore, unimportant.[6]

Clearly, religion is often used by cynical politicians, among others, with non-religious agendas. Nevertheless, it is argued here that religion's role is not limited to this. Rather, in addition to sometimes being a tool of those with alternative motives, religion has an independent influence. The evidence of previous studies discussed later in this chapter as well as the evidence provided in later chapters in this book supports this.[7]

Religious Influences on Conflict

There are numerous and diverse theories which posit some form of religious influence on society, politics, and conflict. While it is not possible within this context to discuss all of them, this section is intended to provide an overview of these theories.

Religious Identity

The argument that identity influences politics and conflict is a common one. The concept of nationalism is based on the assumption that national identity groups want to create a political unit, usually a state, in which they can reside. Numerous theories of conflict and politics posit that when dividing up the economic pie, identity groups, whether they be based on economic class, nationality, race, or religion, join together to improve the result for their group.

Perhaps the most prominent of those who apply this argument to religious identity is Samuel Huntington. His "clash of civilizations" theory, which is discussed in considerably more detail in Chapter 6, posits that in the post-Cold War era most conflict will be between major cultural groupings he calls civilizations. In practice, these civilizations are defined mostly along religious lines. Of his eight civilizations all but one include specific mention of religion in their definitions.[8] (Huntington, 1996a: 45-48) Based on all of this, it is fair to interpret Huntington's arguments as implying that conflicts involving groups of different religions will be more common and intense, and, thus, conflict is more likely between religious identity groups than within them.

Huntington's theory has many critics, who are also discussed in more detail in Chapter 6. Interestingly, many of Huntington's critics who make qualitative arguments that conflict will not be between civilizations still believe that conflict will be based along lines of identity, except that those identities will be national or ethnic. It is undisputed that religion can be a source of these types of identity. Religion is linked to identity in general (Voye, 1999: 280-284; Seul, 1999: 558), ethnic identities (Carment and James, 1998: 68; Little, 1991: xx; Gurr, 1993a: 3), and national identities (Anthony Smith, 1999; 2000). Given this, it is fair to say that the proposition that religious differences contribute to conflict is considerably less in dispute than Huntington's proposition that this will specifically manifest itself through his concept of civilizations.

Thus, both Huntington and many of his critics make arguments consistent with a primordialist view of religion. Primordialism is a type of theory generally applied to ethnicity and nationalism which posits that shared culture leads to strong identity groups which see themselves as having common interests. Because of this, most conflict will be between separate primordial groups with diverging interests. Two major perspectives compete with the primordial perspective as explanations for ethnic and national conflict. The instrumentalist perspective posits that while culturally based identities exist, they only become politically relevant when political entrepreneurs make use of them to further their own political goals. The constructivist perspective holds that group identities are often created in order to further political goals. While these three perspectives were developed mostly to explain national and ethnic conflict, they can and have been applied as explanations for religious conflict. (Hasenclever and Rittberger, 2000)[9]

One thing that these three perspectives, as well as the arguments of Huntington and most of his critics, have in common is the assertion that differences in identity, including differences in religion, are core causes of conflict, though they differ as to the path from identity to conflict. Either identity itself is enough to cause conflict, someone must actively invoke identity, or an identity must be formed for political purposes before conflict will occur. The "civilizations" debate highlights that there is no agreement as to whether religious, national, or ethnic identities will be most important in the post-Cold War era.

It is also clear from the general literature on identity that religion and identity are linked, whatever the level of analysis. Seul (1999: 558) argues that "no other repositories of cultural meaning have historically offered so much in response to the human need to develop a secure identity. Consequently, religion often is at the core of individual and group identity." Little (1991: xx) and Voye (1999) similarly argue that religion can be an important source of group identity. Carment and James (1998: 68) and Gurr (1993a: 3) argue that this is the case for ethnic identity. Anthony Smith (1999; 2000) argues that religion is an important source of national identity and Juergensmeyer (1993; 1995) argues that nationalism and religion serve the same social functions, and Western nationalist ideologies are really just a cover for Christianity. Finally, Philpott (2000) argues that religion was the source of the modern Westphalian state system itself.

Religious Issues and Belief Systems

Religion has always been among the motivations for human behavior. Human beings need some sort of mental or psychological framework in order to help them interpret the information their senses give them. One aspect of this framework is the one that gives meaning and order to the diverse facts and information that we accumulate. One potential source for this is religion. That is, many people use religion to interpret the world for them, to understand their place in the world, and to understand how they should behave in it. It provides us with a sense of what is moral and immoral, right and wrong, and good and evil. Religion also can fill the role of answering what happens to us after death and providing the tools for us to deal with seemingly unbearable tragedies. Thus, religion provides answers for essential questions. Who are we? Where did we come from? Why are we here? What is our place in the world? How should we behave? How do we interpret day-to-day events as well as the ununderstandable?

Clearly religion is not the only source of these essential elements of people's belief systems. Ideologies and other bases for identity like nationalism and ethnicity, among other sources, can also fill this role. Yet religion is undeniably an essential source for many people's belief systems. Thus, religion can provide more than just identity; it can provide an essential and inseparable element of our sense of self. In this way even an atheist might admit that it can truly be a component of our souls.

Given this, for many people it is impossible to separate religion from their motivations. It colors their understanding of political and social events as well as the decisions they make. This encompasses political decisions and the decision to go to war.

One version of this argument is made by Richard Wentz (1987). Wentz argues that humans are more than just biological entities; rather, we are open to possibility of understanding ultimate order and meaning in our existence. In fact we seek such meaning. Religion is one source of this meaning and it allows us to transcend our biological existence and to tell a story about ultimate order and meaning. Thus, religiousness is fundamental to human nature. (Wentz, 1987: 13-21)

Wentz (1987: 35, 53-58, 68-70) uses the metaphor of the "walls of religion" to describe the importance of this phenomenon. People build walls around their belief systems and defend them. These walls are psychological and often shared by entire communities. These walls are the boundary between the order we create to make sense of ordinary existence and chaos. Some people will do anything to preserve this order and, thus, defend their walls at all costs. Thus, anything that is interpreted as a threat to an individual's or group's belief system can provoke a defensive response which is often a violent one. Put in other words, people need the security of absolutes and are willing to fight to defend this security.

It is important to emphasize that the perceived threat to a religious belief system is defined by the defender of that belief system and not the perceived enemy. Thus, the purported attacker may have no intention of engaging in an aggressive act and, perhaps, even no idea that he has done so. Sometimes the mere presence of others who believe differently can be seen as a threat and provoke a violent response. For example, many Muslims believe that it is wrong for any non-Muslim to set foot in the Islamic holy places of Saudi Arabia. Some feel that this includes most, if not all, of the peninsula. The Saudi government enforces this belief with a ban on the display of any non-Muslim religious symbols as well as a ban on public prayer by non-Muslim groups. Thus, what many believe to be nonaggressive acts like wearing the symbol of one's own religion or praying can be potentially perceived as a threat by others and provoke violent conflict, or as in this case, government repression. While this is an extreme example, it is but one of many.

There are a number of other types of events which commonly provoke a defensive response to defend religious belief systems. These include attempts to change or replace the role of religion in society, attempts by minority religions to assert their rights, and attempts to convert group members to another religion. Defensive responses against these types of perceived threats occur even in countries considered secular, enlightened, and tolerant. For example, among Western democracies, Finland, France, Germany, Greece, and Switzerland all in some way restricted proselyting in 2003. Also in 2003, Austria, Belgium, France, Germany, Italy, Spain, Sweden, and Switzerland all had government agencies whose job was to monitor minority religions and sects. Given this amount of government action in tolerant democratic states, it is arguable that at the individual and community levels, perceived threats to religious belief systems are even more common.

Another common challenge is modernity itself. As discussed above, modernity presents a threat to traditional religion in multiple ways and has provoked a defensive response against it which often takes the form of religious fundamentalism. Thus, government policies and individuals seen to represent this type of threat are often attacked. For instance, the teaching of evolution, which challenges the biblical story of creation, is still challenged by fundamentalist groups in the United States. Modern technologies such as birth control which are seen to undermine traditional morality are also opposed. Similarly, abortion is seen by many as murder due, at least in part, to religious motivations. While in Western countries the opposition to abortion is generally limited to legal protest tactics, this opposition has at times become violent.

The defending of religious beliefs is particularly likely to lead to violence for a number of reasons. First, religion is an emotional issue. It involves defending essential elements of people's identities and psyches and is, therefore, not always a rational issue. Second, religion is based on faith and belief in absolutes. It is often not possible to compromise on this type of issue. Third, enemies can be seen as more threatening because they are often perceived as mirror images of one's self who are guided by misguided faith. Thus, the perceived enemies are seen as unwilling to compromise their own faiths and beliefs, leaving violence as the only option. Fourth, many like Girard (1977) argue that violence is an intrinsic element of religion. One of the origins of religion was to place social controls on violence. He argues that ritual violence like animal sacrifices or violent images like the Crucifixion provide a socially acceptable way for people to express their instincts for violence. Thus, as religion is so intimately associated with violence, it is not surprising that violence is often invoked on its behalf.

The path between religion and conflict is not limited to defending religion against its perceived enemies. It also involves another aspect of religious belief systems: the fact that they can motivate people to engage in specified actions. Religions almost invariably include a code of behavior including morals as well as required and prohibited actions. Thus, the more religious a person the more difficult it is to separate religion from his motivations and actions. In fact, a truly religious individual would see his God in all things that happen and behave at all times in the manner he believes his God would want. Clearly all people are not this religious but the principle holds even if religion is only a small portion of someone's belief system.

Religious motivations of this nature are an important element of society politics and conflict. Religious people often feel a need to change the world to make it in more accordance with their religious ideology. Movements to legislate religious values are not uncommon. One example is the movements to ban abortion. Abortion is significantly restricted even in many Western states including Australia, Belgium, Ireland, New Zealand, and Switzerland. Also, governments fund religious education in public schools in the majority of Western Europe. In other regions of the world, like the Middle East, many aspects of religion are commonly legislated as law. Efforts to change the status quo with regard to the legal position of religion in society can be sources of tension and conflict.

Religious motivations can also lead directly to war. Holy war is an aspect of many religions. While the concept of holy war is interpreted differently by different people, even within the same religion, there are few religious traditions which have not at some point in time been used to justify holy war. Even pacifist religions like Buddhism have been interpreted to justify holy war, as has happened recently in Sri Lanka. (Manor, 1994)

Given all of this, religious issues are potentially extremely volatile. They run the risk of invoking defensive responses on multiple sides of the issue. They also involve motivations based on uncompromising belief systems. Furthermore, these types of motivations can involve themselves in seemingly secular issues. Whenever one may ask the question of what is the moral thing to do, religion can potentially be invoked. It can also color people's perceptions of events and how they react to them.

For example, the two United States military interventions in Iraq were seen by the United States government as guided by the secular issues of defending Kuwait against aggression, fighting terrorism, protecting the world against weapons of mass destruction, and freeing an oppressed people from a ruthless dictator. Yet, President George W. Bush calls Iraq a member of the axis of evil, a term with religious connotations. On the other side of the issues, many Muslims see this conflict in religious terms. It is seen as an attack by the Christian world against Muslims and even an attempt by Christianity to gain a foothold in the Muslim world that is close to Islam's holiest places in Saudi Arabia.

Thus, despite the fact that both sides of the conflict are not particularly motivated by religion, it can also be seen as a conflict between religious belief systems. The motivations for it cannot be wholly separated from religion and are certainly seen in a religious light by many. It can also motivate some Muslims to defend their walls of religion through violent terrorist acts. For instance, the presence of U.S. troops on Saudi soil is one of the justifications used by Usama bin Laden for the multiple terrorist attacks by his organization on U.S. targets. In his eyes, he is defending Islam.

More overtly religious issues like the dispute over holy sites in Jerusalem are also intractable issues. If the Palestinian-Israeli peace process fails (assuming it has not already failed) over a single issue, that issue will likely be Jerusalem, a city holy to both Judaism and Islam. Even secular Israelis are generally unwilling to compromise on this issue. Furthermore, there are numerous disputes dating back centuries between various Christian sects over control of the Christian holy sights in Jerusalem. For example, in order to avoid a number of conflicts, a Muslim family living in the Old City of Jerusalem has traditionally held the keys to the outer door of the Church of the Holy Sepulcher since none of the various Christian sects trust the others with them.

Sometimes it is difficult to determine where positive religious motivations for actions end and defensive reactions to perceived threats begin. Often they overlap. Yet both processes are important and among the ways religion can cause conflict as well as influence politics and society.

Elites, Legitimacy, and Institutions

The role of religious elites, legitimacy, and institutions in society, politics, and conflict is a complex one. All three are interrelated with each other. For instance, religious elites tend to control religious institutions and both elites and institutions can significantly influence which individuals and causes will be granted religious legitimacy.

That religion can grant legitimacy to individuals, groups, policies, causes, and actions is rarely if ever disputed. This is true whether whatever is legitimated has religious or secular motivations or origins. Thus, religion can justify actions taken in conflicts, as well as the conflicts themselves, even if the issues involved in the conflict are not particularly religious ones.

Religious institutions have multiple, and sometimes crosscutting, influences on the conflict process. On one hand, based on classic mobilization theory,[10] religious institutions should facilitate mobilization. This is because they include ready-made meeting places. They are part of formal and informal networks of people. They have activists and leaders with organizational skills. They have easy access to the media and often their own media. They also often have a protected status in the sense that governments are less likely to repress or interfere with religious institutions.

However, religious institutions are also associated with supporting the status quo. They often choose to support the government and its policies and not those who oppose it. That is, there are many state religions throughout the world as well as more informal, but no less solid, relationships like those which traditionally existed in Latin America between the Catholic Church and the government.

Gill (1998) documents this trend of the Catholic Church supporting Latin American governments but finds that in some countries this relationship is changing with the Church supporting opposition movements. He argues that the key factor for determining when the Church supports governments and when it supports opposition movements is institutional survival. The Church began to challenge the government in those states where other denominations of Christianity were making inroads among the populace because it was perceived that the Catholic Church was supporting corrupt and repressive governments rather than the interests of its adherents. However, when no such threats of losing its congregations were present, the

Catholic Church continued to support the government in a classic relationship where the government and religious institutions mutually support each other's position in society. Thus, in short, when the Church benefitted from supporting the government it did, but when this support threatened its position with the people it opposed the government.

Fawcett (2000) found a similar relationship between religious institutions and the status quo in South Africa and Northern Ireland. In South Africa the Dutch Reformed Church supported apartheid for many years until the white population began to question its morality. When this occurred, the Dutch Reformed Church changed its policy and became an avid supporter of ending apartheid. Similarly, the religious institutions of Northern Ireland supported the various sides of the conflict between Catholics and Protestants. However, when an agreement seemed imminent and popular, most of them became supporters of the agreement.

Thus, while religious institutions have influence over religious legitimacy, this influence is not absolute. In some cases they must follow what is popular with their congregation in order to remain legitimate and relevant. Thus, the elites who guide these institutions both guide their congregants and are guided by them. Because of this, conflicts which are popular will often gain the support of religious elites and institutions who need to stay within the moral center of their congregation in order to avoid becoming marginalized. In short, religious institutions will support governments as long as they benefit from this support, but when such support undermines their support within the community they will oppose the government in order to remain relevant.

Religious Fundamentalism

Religious fundamentalism is a specific type of belief system. As noted above, one of its defining characteristics is that it is a negative reaction against modernity. Specifically, it is a reaction against what fundamentalists perceive as modernity's undermining of traditional religion, culture, and values. Thus, it is the ideological and social impact of modernity which fundamentalists oppose. Generally, fundamentalists do not oppose advances in technology unless that specific technology undermines traditional values. For example, it is not the computers and the Internet they generally oppose, but rather the fact that the Internet is used for pornography and the spreading of ideas they consider improper. Similarly, it is not television that they oppose but, rather, shows like *Baywatch* which are seen to be immodest.

Thus, the walls of religion, as Richard Wentz calls them, which fundamentalists defend are those that divide traditional society and beliefs from modern secular ideas and culture. They fortify their communities with doctrines and beliefs from the past. In doing so, they seek to protect their community from the evils of modernity and the outside world. They do this through a return to the texts which they generally selectively interpret to justify their actions. In their reinterpretation of religious texts fundamentalists often learn things from them that have never been learned before. That is, while trying to return to the past, fundamentalists often create a new interpretation of their religion that is unique to the modern era.

The new social order they create orders even the intimate zones of life including marriage, family life, sex, child rearing, education, morality, and interpersonal relations. There is no public-private distinction. They focus on the family because the family is the main means of transmitting religion form one generation to the next. They also build clear boundaries between the members of the fundamentalist community and outsiders. The only way to truly enter the community is to join and accept its rules. These values are always enforced within the community and fundamentalists sometimes try to impose them on others. This is one way fundamentalist religions commonly lead to conflict as the rest of society often does not want to live under the religious rules of fundamentalists.

While some may see this as a fundamentalist attack on non-fundamentalists, fundamentalists nearly always see their use of political power and violence as defensive. They see themselves as defending against the incursions of modernity upon the true way. Occasionally the best defense is a good offense, to proactively fight it within the larger society. Thus, religious fundamentalism leads to conflict in the same way as do other religious belief systems. They defend their religion against perceived threats and their religiously motivated actions are sometimes conflictive and/or provoke others.[11]

Political Islam has recently been one of the most visibly violent fundamentalist movements, though certainly not the only one. Islamic terrorist movements have been active since the 1980s. Violent Islamic terrorist and opposition movements have taken place in Egypt, Israel, Algeria, Lebanon, the former Yugoslavia, Chechnya, and Afghanistan, among other places. Usama bin Laden's Al Quaeda organization is a manifestation of this movement on the international stage. All of these groups are interrelated and have formal and informal connections with each other.

More importantly, these Islamic movements are basically reacting to the same things as other fundamentalist movements. They see most Muslim states as too modern and Western and often accuse the governments of these states of being Western puppets. The West is seen as the embodiment of all that is bad in modernity and, therefore, an enemy. Al Quaeda attacks the West, at least in part, due to the fact that it sees the West in general, and the United States in particular, as the only thing stopping them from realizing their goal of creating a pan-Islamic state. In such a state they would be able to create a large community that would be insulated from what they see as the evils of modernity. This pan-Islamic state would also be a good platform from which they could bring Islam to the rest of the world, an essential goal of the Islamic religion.

Thus, Islamic militants are not too different from other fundamentalists. They are reacting to the undermining of traditional religion by modernity. They reinterpret religious doctrine to find an answer to this problem. They seek to create a community where their interpretation of the religion is safe from the threats posed by modernity, as embodied by the West. Finally, they seek to impose their ideals upon others.

Religion and Specific Issues

A large portion of the scholarship on the influence of religion on politics, society, and conflict focuses on more specific topics. For example, many focus on the influence of religion on terrorism. Religion is considered one of many sources of the ideologies which are used to define terrorists' political aims. (Drake, 1998) In fact, "what is distinctive about the international terrorism of the 1980s and 1990s is this combination of politics and religion." (Juergensmeyer, 1997: 17) Hoffman (1995: 272) and Rapoport (1984: 659) take this one step further and argue that religion and nationalism have been the only major justifications for terror this century and before the advent of nationalism, religion was the only justification.[12]

Religious terrorists are also considered different from other types of terrorists for a number of reasons. First, for secular terrorists, violence is a means to an end; for religious terrorists, it can be the end itself. Second, while secular terrorists usually are trying to influence an outside audience, religious terrorists often care about no audience but themselves. Third, while secular terrorists usually see themselves as part of a system they must change, religious terrorists generally see themselves as outside of a system they must replace, allowing greater levels of destruction. Fourth, the religious belief that a messianic event is imminent can justify greater violence than most secular beliefs. Fifth, religious terrorists focus on the past, trying to re-create the conditions believed to exist at the founding time of their religion, while secular terrorists generally focus on creating a new future. Sixth, while secular terrorists can change their ends, religious terrorists are more restricted in this by their doctrines. Seventh, religious concepts of martyrdom make suicide attacks more likely. Eighth, both the timing and targets of religious terrorists usually have religious significance. Ninth, modern secular terror determines its own justifications, means, and limits but in holy terror these things are determined by religious law and foundation myths. Finally, one's religious perspective influences what one considers terrorism. (Hoffman, 1995; Ranstorp, 1996; Rapoport, 1988; 1990; Richard Martin, 1989: 356-357; Kennedy, 1999)

Religion is also linked to most other types of politics and conflict. This includes ethnic conflict (Fox, 2002a), international conflict (Henderson, 1997), international intervention (Fox, 2001e), discrimination against minorities (Little, 1991; 1996a; 1996b), genocide (Fein, 1990: 49), ethnic cleansing (Osiander, 2000: 785), totalitarianism (Osiander, 2000), the origins of the Westphalian state (Philpott, 2000), population growth (Fox, 2001e), conflict resolution (Appleby, 2000; Gopin, 2000), international diplomacy (Johnston and Sampson, 1994), democracy (Midlarsky, 1998; Oommen, 1994; and Fox, 1998: 58-59), the family (Hardacre, 1993), environmentalism (Taylor, 1998), perceptions of the nature of human rights

(Van der Vyver, 1996), public school policy (Wayland, 1997), economics (Kuran, 1991; Rosser, 1993), personal wealth (Schbley, 2000), the politics of specific states,[13] the process of globalization (Beyer, 1994), political culture (Latin, 1978), nationalism (Anthony Smith, 1999; 2000). Some, like Bader (1999) argue that religion influences even those democratic states which supposedly enshrine separation of religion and the state as an aspect of liberalism.

Previous Quantitative Studies of Religion and Conflict

Before proceeding with the quantitative analysis of the influence of religion on conflict, which is a major theme of this book, it is important to discuss previous quantitative studies. The majority of the studies discussed here are based on earlier versions of the MAR dataset, which is one of the two datasets used in this book. The comments in the previous chapter with regard to this dataset apply here except that most of the studies discussed in this chapter are limited to data from 1990 to 1998 and between 267 and 275 cases when all groups are examined and as few as 105 cases when religious groups are examined. Results of studies using other datasets are also included in this discussion.

This examination of the quantitative literature is organized by topic. The first is the question of whether religion is an important issue in conflict. Fox (1997) shows that among the 267 cases of ethnic conflict analyzed 105, a minority of about 39%, are ethnoreligious cases. Of these 105 ethnorelgious cases, only in 12 (11.4 percent) is religion a primary issue, but in another 65 (61.9 percent) it is a secondary issue. Thus, religion is not an issue at all in only 28 (26.7 percent) of these cases. Yet, even in most of these 28 cases other religious factors like religious legitimacy or religious institutions also play a role. Given this, it is fair to say that while most ethnic conflicts are not religious ones, most ethnoreligious conflicts involve at least some religious issues and factors.

Second, the dynamics of ethnoreligious conflicts are different from the dynamics of other ethnic conflicts. Political and cultural discrimination is higher against ethnoreligious minorities. (Fox, 1997) Ethnoreligious conflicts are more likely to involve issues of self-determination. (Fox, 1997) Also, while democracy influences the extent of discrimination against ethnoreligious minorities, it does not seem to be a relevant factor for other ethnic minorities. (Fox, 2000b) In studies based on different data, it was found that religious diversity increase the extent of violence. Rummel (1997) found that the more religious minorities are present in a state, the greater the extent of ethnic violence and Reynal-Querol (2002) found that religious fragmentation and polarization increase the extent of ethnic conflict.

Third, religious discrimination and the grievances formed over this discrimination influence ethnic conflict. Religious discrimination causes grievances to be formed over the issue. The presence of religious grievances will increase the violence of ethnic conflicts which involve issues of separatism. However, the relationship between religious grievances and protest is the opposite of what one would expect. That is, the more upset an ethnic minority gets over religious discrimination, the less it engages in protest. This holds true even when controlling for factors such as other types of grievances, religious legitimacy, democracy, repression, and mobilization! There is no explanation that can be tested by the available data which explains this result. One potential explanation is that, perhaps, religion is something so important that it is beyond protest and only violent responses are considered appropriate. Also, another form of religious grievance, active religious grievances, are positively correlated with protest. Unlike the previously discussed variable which measures complaints over religious discrimination, this variable measures active demands for more rights which are unconnected to discrimination. (Fox, 2000c; Fox and Squires, 2001)

Fourth, when religious issues are important in a conflict, this changes the dynamics of that conflict in a number of ways. Discrimination is higher. Grievances over political issues are higher. Rebellion is more likely if self-determination is also an issue in the conflict. (Fox, 1997; 2000b) Interestingly, religious issues tend to be more relevant when the conflict involves Muslims and does not involve Christians. (Fox, 2000a)

Fifth, religious institutions have a dual influence on ethnic conflict. The key for determining whether they will support or inhibit organized protest is whether religion is an important element of the conflict. When it is, religious institutions facilitate protest, and when it is not, they inhibit it. They also support rebellion, but only when self-determination is an element of the conflict. This is consistent with the findings described above showing that self-determination is more important than religious issues as a cause of rebellion. (Fox, 1999a)

Sixth, religious legitimacy can facilitate the formation of grievances held by minority groups. However, the type of grievances facilitated differ depending on the circumstances. Religious legitimacy always facilitates grievances over religious issues but only sometimes facilitates grievances over other issues. When religion is not an important element in a conflict, religious legitimacy facilitates the formation of grievances over nonreligious issues including political, economic, and cultural grievances. However, when religion is an important element in a conflict, religious legitimacy inhibits the formation of these types of nonreligious grievances. One interpretation for this is that religious elites try and remain relevant to their constituents and lend religious legitimacy to the complaints of these constituents unless the religion itself is at stake, in which case, they try to focus their constituents on the religious issues. (Fox, 1999b)

Seventh, while the discussion thus far has mostly focused on the behavior of minority groups, religion also influences the behavior of majority groups. Majority groups engage in more political and cultural discrimination against minority groups when religion variables are high. These include whether religion is an important element of the conflict, whether the minority expresses grievances over religious issues, and religious legitimacy. (Fox, 2000b)

Eighth, regime type influences the extent of discrimination against ethnoreligious minorities. As one would expect, autocracies discriminate more than do democracies. This includes political and cultural discrimination as well as repression. However, semi-democracies, those governments which fall somewhere between democracies and autocracies, discriminate even less. (Fox, 2000b)

Ninth, religion influences the extent of intervention in ethnic conflicts. Conflicts between groups of different religions attract intervention more often. (Fox, 2001e; Khosla, 1999) Also, states who intervene in ethnic conflicts are overwhelmingly religiously similar to the minorities on whose behalf they intervene. While this is true of Christian states, the relationship is strongest for Muslim groups. (Fox, 2001e)

Conclusions

In all, there is a considerable body of theory and comparative research positing that religion is an important influence on society, politics, and conflict. There is also significant quantitative evidence for a link between religion and conflict. However, most of these studies, whether they are theoretical, comparative, or quantitative, are limited. Most of them focus on only one aspect of religion's influence in a limited context. Also, they often focus only on one type of conflict.

Among the quantitative literature, the majority of articles have been written by me and suffer from these limitations. Most of the in-depth studies focus only on one specific correlation. For example, an article may focus on religious causes of discrimination against ethnic minorities (Fox, 2000b) or on religious motivations for international intervention (Fox, 2001e), among other topics. The only exception is perhaps my book *Ethnoreligious Conflict in the Late Twentieth Century*, which provides a full theoretical model and some basic testing of that model. Yet for nearly every statistical test in the book, an additional article was necessary to flesh out all of the details. Furthermore, all of these tests focus only on ethnic conflict, which is one among several types of conflict that exist in the world today and most of them only examine the first half of the 1990s.

Accordingly, the goal of this section of the book is to provide a larger study in which all of the quantitative analysis is in a single book. This will allow for a better examination of the data because it will allow a melding of what have in the past been separate analyses into a single larger one. This will allow for a more comprehensive examination of the interrelationship between the various aspects of the analysis.

It is important to emphasize that this study is not simply taking previous research and putting it together in one volume that reads more like an edited volume than an integrated book. Rather, this analysis improves upon previous ones in a number of ways. First, all analyses are performed anew for this book using updated data and the benefit of my experience from the previous round of analysis. Second, my previous analyses focused mostly on the early 1990s and none of them examined data that was not from the 1985 to 1998 period. This analysis examines trends over the time period of 1945 to 2001. This will allow, in addition to an examination of the correlation between religion and ethnic conflict, an examination of whether any of these correlations change over time. Finally, in addition to the MAR data on ethnic conflict, this study uses a second dataset, the State Failure (SF) dataset. As described in the previous chapter, this dataset includes data on all major domestic conflicts between 1948 and 2001. In addition to ethnic conflicts it also contains data on mass killings and revolutionary wars. Thus, it will allow an examination of whether the trends found in the MAR data are unique to ethnic conflict or even the MAR dataset itself.

Notes

1. For a survey of the literature on modernization, see, among others, Almond (1960), Apter (1965), Deutsch (1953), Foster-Carter (1985), Halpern (1964), Kautsky (1972), Randall and Theobald (1985), Rostow (1959), Donald Smith (1970, 1971, and 1974), and Sutton (1968). For a survey of the literature on secularization, see, among others, Beckford (1985), Cox (1965), Glasner (1977), David Martin (1978), and Wilson (1966 and 1976).
2. One notable exception is Hadden (1987b).
3. See *Sociology of Religion*, 60 (3), 1999.
4. The journals are *International Organization, International Studies Quarterly, World Politics*, and *International Security*.
5. These articles and books include Hoffman (1995), Juergensmeyer (1997; 2000), Kaplan (2002), Ranstorp (1996), Rapoport (1984; 1988), Rapoport and Alexander (1989), Weinberg and Eubank (1998), and Weinberg, Eubank, and Pedahzur, (2002). Other articles use religious terms in their titles but in reality claim the causes of the terror are something other than religion. See, for example, Ibrahim (2002), Schbley (2000), and Bron Taylor (1998). There are also numerous articles which focus on individual terrorist movements but this claim is made primarily in regard to theoretical articles examining the causes and motivation for terror.
6. For a more detailed description of functionalism, see Fox (2002a:6 5-68) and Geertz (1973: 201-279).
7. For other critiques of functionalism, see Beckford (1985), Chaves (1994: 7510, Coleman (1990: 336), and Robertson (1985: 356-367).
8. Barber (1998), Eisenstadt (2000: 616), Laustsen and Waever (2000: 705), Anthony Smith (2000: 791), and Tibi (2000: 844) similarly argue that Huntington's definition of civilizations is mostly based on religion.
9. For a further discussion of the primordial, instrumental and constructivist perspectives, see Comaroff and Stern (1995) and Connor (1972).
10. See, for example, Tarrow (1989), McArthy and Zald (1986), and McAdam (1982).
11. For a more detailed discussion of fundamentalism, see Marty and Appleby (1991; 1993; 1994), upon which this discussion of fundamentalism is based.

12. Rapoport (1984) describes three premodern terrorist movements: the Thugs in India, the Assassins, and the Zealots in ancient Israel.

13. One example of this is Israel. For studies on religion and politics in Israel, see Liebman and Don-Yehiya (1983) and Sandler (1996).

Chapter 3

Are Religious Conflicts Different?

The purpose of this chapter is to answer the seemingly simple question of whether religious conflicts are different from nonreligious conflicts. This question includes a number of questions. Are religious conflicts more common? Are they more violent? Who do members of specific religions fight? Is it members of their own religion or members of other religions and if it is the latter do they fight members of any particular religion? Do groups of different religions engage in different patterns of conflict with regard to all of the above questions? Are these patterns different for different types of conflict? Finally, do any of these patterns change over time?

The analysis in this chapter does not examine the issue of causality. Causality is examined in the Chapter 4. This chapter is intended to provide an accurate description of the nature of religious conflict. This exercise is necessary because of the continuing debate described in the previous chapter over whether religion is becoming an unimportant social factor. This debate makes it necessary to establish exactly what is happening before we can begin to explain why it is happening.

For the purposes of this chapter when examining ethnic conflict we examine simply whether those involved in the conflict belong to different religions. This applies to both the MAR and SF data. For the mass killings or revolutionary wars coded in the SF data, the conflict is considered religious if the two groups involved belong to different religions or the description of the conflict in the SF dataset describes the conflict as a religious one.

The analysis proceeds in several stages. The first stage examines whether interreligious conflicts are more common than intrareligious conflicts. The second examines whether interreligious conflicts are more violent than intrareligious conflicts. The third examines whether groups of any particular religions engage in more conflict or are more violent as compared to groups of other religions. The fourth examines the religion of the opponents which groups of particular religions fight. At each stage the MAR data is examined first, followed by the SF data.

Are Religious Conflicts More Common?

This section examines simply whether religious conflicts have been more common since 1945, both in general, and over time. The first aspect of this question that needs to be examined with the MAR data is whether there has been a change in the ratio of religiously differentiated ethnic minorities among politically active ethnic minorities over time. Effectively, the MAR coded this information during three periods of time: the Cold War period (1945-1989), the early 1990s (1990-1998), and 1999-2000. This is because for each major round of coding, the MAR project reassessed which groups were politically active and these time periods are those that were covered at each major update of the data.

The results, presented in Figure 3.1, demonstrate that the ratio of religiously differentiated ethnic minorities to nonreligiously differentiated ones is very stable over time. Those minorities who belong to different religions as the majority group range from 36.1 percent to 37.5 percent of all ethnic minorities. Those who belong to different denominations of the same religion as the majority group range from 9.3percent to 10.5 percent of all ethnic minorities. Finally, those who belong to the same religion and denomination as the majority group range from 51.9 percent to 54.6 percent of all ethnic minorities. Thus, ethnoreligious minorities have remained a minority of all politically active ethnic minorities between 1945 and 2000, though a significantly large one.

The second aspect of the MAR data relevant to this question is how many religiously differentiated groups rebel as compared to other ethnic groups. The results, presented in Figure 3.2, show that for the 1945-2000 period religiously differentiated groups rebelled less often than did other ethnic groups except for in the 1945-1949 period where thirteen religiously differentiated groups rebelled as compared to twelve other ethnic groups. However, both categories follow the same general pattern of a rise in the number of groups rebelling throughout this period. Also, the gap between the number of religious and nonreligious rebelling groups is less from the 1980s and 1990s than it is in the 1960s and 1970s.

However, an examination of the yearly levels of rebellion from 1985 to 2000, presented in Figure 3.3, tells a different story. During this period, rebellion by religiously differentiated minorities is more common in six of sixteen years. However, this is still consistent with less religiously differentiated minorities rebelling as they did rebel less in more years than not. Also, those years where more such minorities did rebel, the number of religiously differentiated groups rebelling was only slightly higher than that for other ethnic minorities. These results also show that for both categories of groups, the amount of rebellion peaked in the early 1990s then began to drop. Thus the overall pattern of ethnic conflict, whether it involves religiously differentiated minorities or not, is a steady rise from 1945 until the first

Figure 3.1: The Ratio of Religiously Distinct Ethnic Minorities

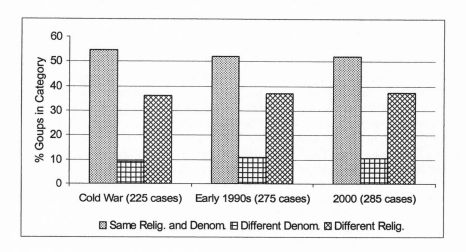

Figure 3.2: Number of Religious vs. Nonreligious Ethnic Minorities Rebelling, 1945-2000

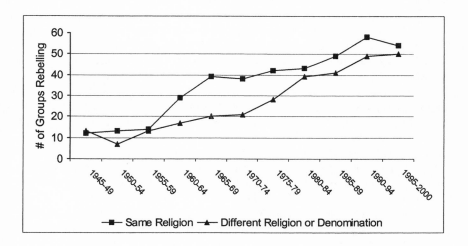

half of the 1990s, followed by a drop.

This discrepancy in the findings for the one-year and five-year codings does mean that there is a major contradiction in the data. Rather, this occurs because the time scale used in the MAR data influences the results. Within a given time period, any action that is considered rebellion which occurs causes that time period to be coded as positive for a given group. Thus, if a group were to rebel only for one year during the 1990 to 1994 period, say in 1992, it would be coded as positive only in 1992 for the yearly codings and for the 1990-1994 period for the five-year codings. Thus, for the 5-year codings it would be coded the same as a group which rebelled in each year during this period but differently on the yearly codings for 1990, 1991, 1993, and 1994. *This dynamic applies to all subsequent analyses in this book.*

Since, as previously demonstrated in Figure 3.1, politically active religiously differentiated minorities are less common than other ethnic minorities, it is important to assess the likelihood that a particular ethnic minority may rebel. That is, when examining only numbers of groups which rebel, we would expect more non-religious ethnic minorities to rebel more often, assuming all other things are equal, because they are more common than ethnoreligious minorities. The results, presented in Figure 3.4, show that for the 1945 to 1959 and 1980 to 2000 periods the likelihood that ethnoreligious minorities and other ethnic minorities are roughly equal, but from 1960 to 1979 nonreligious ethnic minorities are more likely to rebel. As presented in Figure 3.5, the yearly results demonstrate that from 1985 to 1989 and in 2000 ethnoreligious groups are more likely to rebel than nonreligious ethnic minorities, but from 1990 to 1999 both types of groups exhibit a similar likelihood to rebel. However, ethnoreligious minorities were never significantly more likely to rebel than other ethnic minorities and often were less likely to rebel.

An examination of 105 ethnoreligious minorities controlling for whether religion is a factor in the conflict[1] produces different results. The results for 1945 to 2000, presented in Figure 3.6, show no significant difference between conflicts for which religion is important and those for which it is not until the mid-1970s. From the mid-1970s, rebellion occurs more often in conflicts where religion is important. Interestingly, adding the likelihood of rebellion for nonreligious minorities to the figure (taken from Figure 3.4) shows that rebellion among these groups is as or more likely than conflicts among ethnoreligious minorities involved in conflicts where religion is important until the 1990s when rebellion among ethnoreligious minorities engaged in conflicts involving religious issues is slightly more likely. The yearly results for the 1985 to 2000 period, presented in Figure 3.7, for the most part, conform to this pattern.

In all, the results from the MAR data show that overall ethnoreligious minorities tend to be slightly less likely to rebel than nonreligious ethnic minorities. This is true even for cases where religion is a factor in a conflict, except in the 1990s where rebellion is slightly more likely in conflicts involving ethnoreligious minorities where religion is an issue in the conflict.

The examination of the SF dataset produces similar results. The results for the entire SF dataset, presented in Figure 3.8, show that from 1965 to 1990, religious

Figure 3.3: Number of Religious vs. Nonreligious Ethnic Minorities Rebelling, 1985-2000

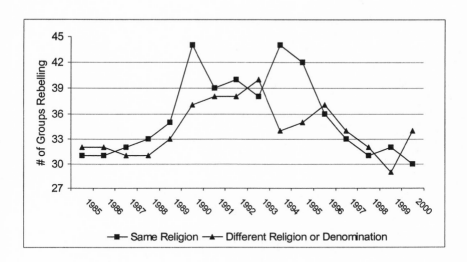

Figure 3.4: Percentage of Minorities Who Rebel, Controlling for Religion, 1945-2000

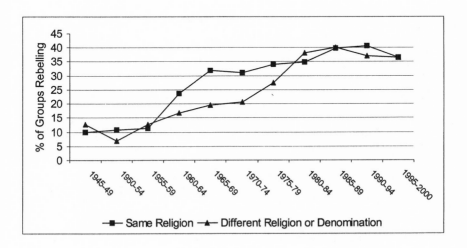

Figure 3.5: Percentage of Minorities Who Rebel, Controlling for Religion, 1985-2000

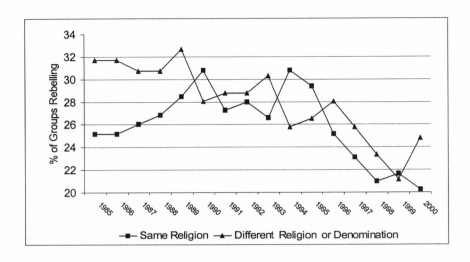

Figure 3.6: Percentage of 105 Ethnoreligious Minorities Who Rebel, Controlling for Importance of Religion, 1945 to 2000

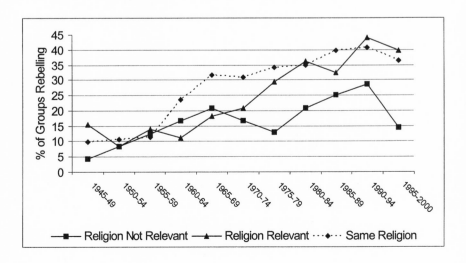

Figure 3.7: Percentage of 105 Ethnoreligious Minorities who Rebel, Controlling for Importance of Religion, 1985 to 2000

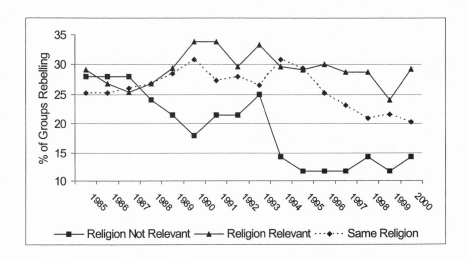

Figure 3.8: Number of Overall State Failures, Controlling for Religion, 1965-2001

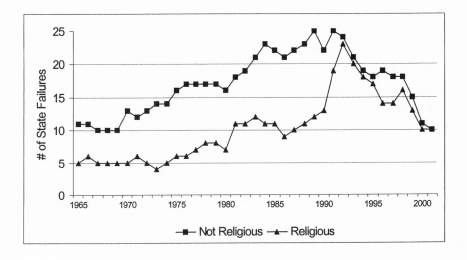

Figure 3.9: Number of Ethnic State Failures, Controlling for Religion, 1965-2001

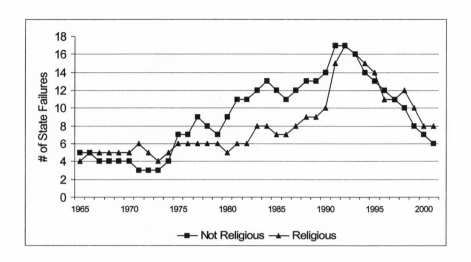

Figure 3.10: Number of Mass Killing State Failures, Controlling for Religion, 1965-2001

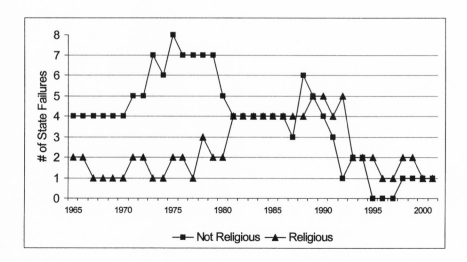

Figure 3.11: Number of Revolutionary War State Failures, Controlling for Religion, 1965-2001

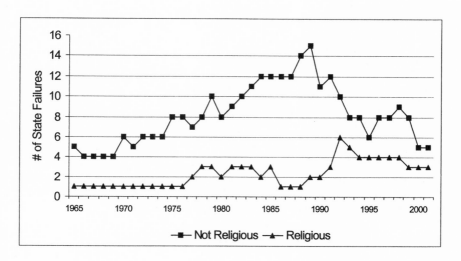

state failures were considerably less common than other state failures. In 1991 and 1992 religious state failures increased in proportion to other state failures. From 1992 to 2001 religious state failures were only slightly less common than non-religious ones. The results for ethnic state failures, presented in Figure 3.9, show a similar pattern, except religious state failures were as common or slightly more common than other state failures in all but two years in the 1992 to 2001 period. In addition, both of these figures show a pattern of a general rise in conflict until the early 1990s, followed by a drop.

The results for mass killings, presented in Figure 3.10, differ slightly. Religious mass killings are less common than other mass killings until 1981. From 1981 onward, they are as or more common than nonreligious mass killings. Mass killings hit a peak of ten in 1975, 1978, 1988, and 1989. By 2002 they drop to two a year.

The results for revolutionary wars, presented in Figure 3.11, differ from all of the other results for the SF dataset in that in no year were religious state failures even nearly as common as nonreligious state failures. However, in the early 1990s religious revolutionary wars did increase both absolutely and in proportion to non-religious revolutionary wars. Also, the overall number of revolutionary wars peaked at seventeen in 1989, followed by a drop.

In all, the answer to our question of whether religious conflicts are more common than other types of conflicts is "No." However, the extent to which this is true changes over time. The gap between religious and nonreligious conflict narrows considerably during the 1980s or early 1990s. The exact timing of when this gap narrows depends upon how conflict is measured. Furthermore, religious conflicts are less likely to be violent, except for ethnic conflicts in the late 1990s when an ethnoreligious minority is involved in a conflict that involves religious issues. Also, the overall level of conflict tends to steadily rise until the late 1980s or early 1990s, followed by a drop. That these patterns remain consistent across several types of conflict in two datasets gives us considerable confidence in these results.

Are Religious Conflicts More Violent?

This section examines whether religious conflicts are more violent than other conflicts. The results for all groups in the MAR dataset between 1945 and 2000, presented in Figure 3.12, show that from 1945 to 1959 and 1995 to 2000 the levels of violence by religious and nonreligious ethnic minorities were about the same, from 1960 to 1979, nonreligious ethnic minorities were more violent and from 1980 to 1994 ethnoreligious minorities were more violent. The yearly results from 1985 to 2000, presented in Figure 3.13, show that in all but two years during this period ethnoreligious minorities were more violent. However, none of the differences in either figure is statistically significant.

An examination of the mean levels of violence by only those groups which engaged in violence (that is, when eliminating groups which did not engage in violence from the analysis) brings different results. The analysis of 1945 to 2000, presented in Figure 3.14, shows that ethnoreligious minorities were more violent in all but three of eleven time periods, and in those three the mean level of violence of ethnoreligious minorities is only slightly less than the mean level of violence for other ethnic minorities. However, the yearly analysis from 1985 to 2000, presented in Figure 3.15, shows that from 1985 to 1995, ethnoreligious minorities were mostly more violent, but from 1996 onward nonreligious ethnic minorities were more violent. None of the results in either of these figures are statistically significant.

An examination of the mean levels of violence of 105 ethnoreligious minorities, controlling for whether religion is an element of the conflict,[2] does show that religion can make a difference. The analysis of the 1945 to 2000 period, presented in Figure 3.16, shows that ethnoreligious conflicts involving religious issues are consistently more violent than other ethnoreligious conflicts. Furthermore, these differences are statistically significant in 8 of the 11 periods analyzed. Adding the level of rebellion by nonreligious ethnic minorities to the figure (taken from Figure 3.12) shows that for most of this period, ethnoreligious conflicts involving religious issues were more violent than ethnic conflicts involving nonreligious minorities, though these differences are not statistically significant. The yearly analysis of 1985 to 2000, presented in Figure 3.17, produces similar results. Ethnoreligious conflicts which involve religious issues are consistently more violent than other ethnoreli-

Figure 3.12: Mean Levels of Rebellion by All Groups, Controlling for Religion, 1945-2000

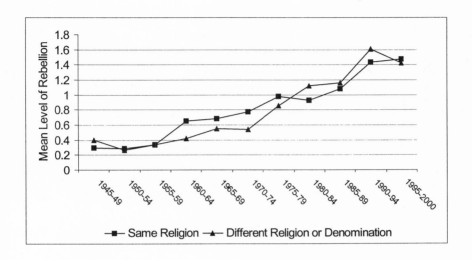

Figure 3.13: Mean Levels of Rebellion by All Groups, Controlling for Religion, 1985-2000

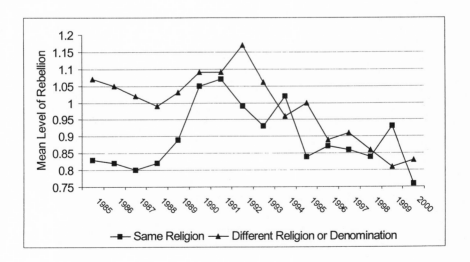

Figure 3.14: Mean Levels of Rebellion by Rebelling Groups, Controlling for Religion, 1945-2000

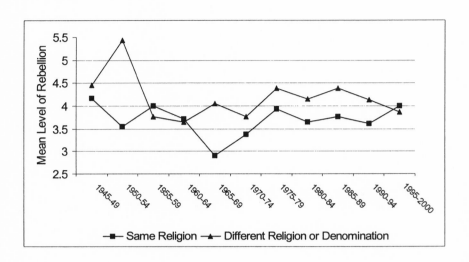

Figure 3.15: Mean Levels of Rebellion by Rebelling Groups, Controlling for Religion, 1985-2000

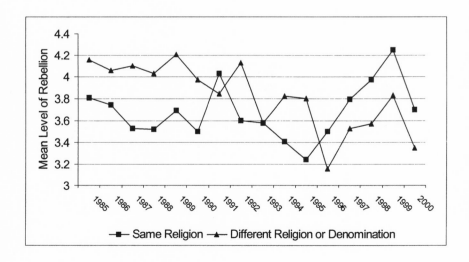

Figure 3.16: Mean Levels of Rebellion by 105 Ethnoreligious Minorities, Controlling for Importance of Religion, 1945-2000

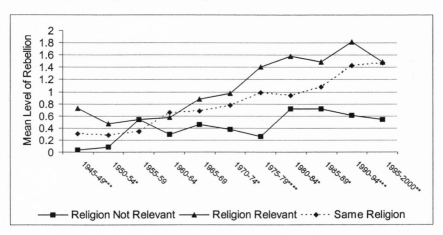

* = Significance (t-test) between Religion Not Relevant and Religion Relevant < .1
** = Significance (t-test) between Religion Not Relevant and Religion Relevant < .05
*** = Significance (t-test) between Religion Not Relevant and Religion Relevant < .01
**** = Significance (t-test) between Religion Not Relevant and Religion Relevant < .001

Figure 3.17: Mean Levels of Rebellion by 105 Ethnoreligious Minorities, Controlling for Importance of Religion, 1985-2000

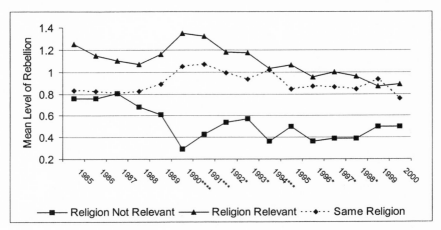

* = Significance (t-test) between Religion Not Relevant and Religion Relevant < .1
** = Significance (t-test) between Religion Not Relevant and Religion Relevant < .05
*** = Significance (t-test) between Religion Not Relevant and Religion Relevant < .01
**** = Significance (t-test) between Religion Not Relevant and Religion Relevant < .001

Figure 3.18: Magnitude of Ethnic State Failures, 1965-2001

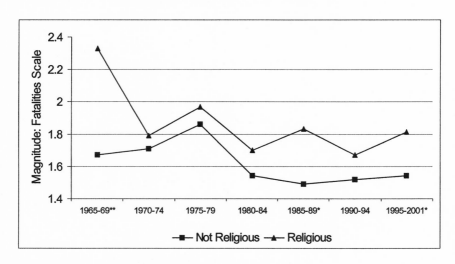

* = Significance (t-test) between Religious and Rot Religious < .1
** = Significance (t-test) between Religious and Not Religious < .05

Figure 3.19: Magnitude of Mass Killing State Failures, 1965-2001

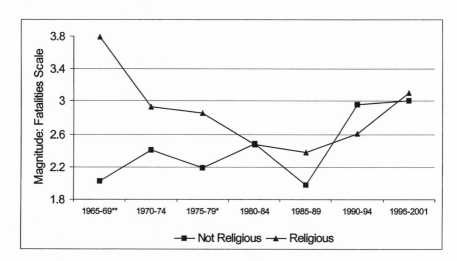

* = Significance (t-test) between Religious and Not Religious < .05
** = Significance (t-test) between Religious and Not Religious < .001

Figure 3.20: Magnitude of Revolutionary War State Failures, 1965 to 2001

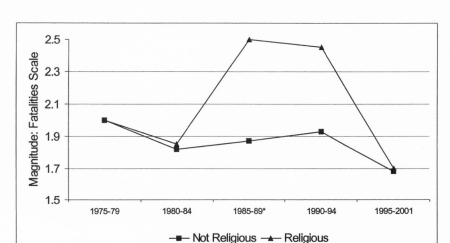

There is not a sufficient number of cases for the 1965 to 1974 period for comparison.
* = Significance (t-test) between Religious and Not Religious < .1

gious conflicts, with the differences being statistically significant in eight of the sixteen years analyzed. Also, for most of this period, ethnoreligious conflicts which involve religious issues are consistently more violent than ethnic conflicts involving non-religious minorities.

In all, the results from the analysis of the MAR data tend to support the contention that ethnoreligious conflicts are more violent. When examining the difference between ethnoreligious and nonethnoreligious conflicts, ethnoreligious conflicts were the more violent ones in most time periods, but these results are not statistically significant. However, conflicts involving ethnoreligious minorities where religion is an issue in the conflict tend to be more violent. The other side of this coin shows that ethnoreligious minorities involved in conflicts where religion is not an issue are the least violent of ethic minorities. Thus, the overall trend in the MAR data is that there is weak support for the contention that differences in religious identity alone make a conflict more violent and strong evidence that conflicts which involve religious issues are more violent.

The results from the SF dataset differ in that they tend to show that conflicts involving religious identity differences alone are more violent that other conflicts. The results for ethnic conflicts, presented in Figure 3.18, show that ethnoreligious conflicts are consistently more violent than other ethnic conflicts from 1965 to 2001, with these differences being statistically significant for three of seven periods. Religious mass killings, presented in Figure 3.19, involve more deaths than other mass killings in five of seven time periods, with these differences being statistically significant in two of these time periods. Religious revolutionary wars, presented in Figure 3.20, are as or more violent than other revolutionary wars in all five time periods for which meaningful comparison is possible, with these differences being statistically significant for one of these time periods.

In all, the answer to the question of whether religious conflicts are more violent is a qualified "Yes." The MAR data shows that they are more violent if the definition of religious conflicts is conflicts involving religious issues. However, if we simply look at conflicts between groups of different religions as compared to conflicts between groups of the same religion, there is at best weak evidence that religious conflicts are more violent. The SF data is more definitive in that it consistently shows religious conflicts to be more violent, even when comparing conflicts between groups of different religions to conflicts between groups of the same religion. Thus, there is considerable evidence that religious conflicts are more violent, but the answer varies depending upon the definition of religious conflict and which data is used to address the issue.

Do Groups of Different Religions Engage in Different Patterns of Conflict?

The question of whether groups of different religions engage in different patterns of conflict is not a simple one. A common stereotype involved with this question is the stereotype that Muslim groups are more violent. *It is important to emphasize that this stereotype is not endorsed here.* However, few would dispute that the stereotype exists and, accordingly, this analysis should help to provide evidence to either support or falsify this stereotype, at least with regard to domestic conflict. The arguments for and against this stereotype are discussed in more detail in the context of Samuel Huntington's predictions on the topic in Chapter 6.

The analysis is divided into two sections which parallel the two previous sections in this chapter. The first evaluates whether conflict is more common among groups of any particular religion. The second examines whether groups of any particular religion are more violent in comparison with groups of other religions.

It is important to note that, in this section, groups are divided into three categories: Christian, Muslim, and Other. While there are clearly major divisions within all of these religious groupings, especially the "Other" category, these more general categories have been selected so that each has a sufficient number of cases for meaningful statistical analysis. That is, this simplification of the categories is necessary in order to continue with the analysis because to do otherwise would put too few cases in any given category.

Also, unless otherwise noted, the analysis in this section of the MAR focuses on the behavior of the minority group. That is, only the religion of the minority group is taken into account. This is because the MAR data focuses on the behavior of minority groups. In contrast, the SF data focuses on two-sided conflicts. Accordingly, the analysis of the SF data includes both the minority and majority groups. That is, each year of conflict is coded twice, once for the minority group and once for the majority group.

Is Conflict More Common among Groups of Any Particular Religion?

The analysis of how many religious minorities rebel in the MAR data for 1945 to 2000, presented in Figure 3.21, has only one consistent result: that groups in the "Other" category consistently rebel less often than do Christian or Muslim ethnic groups. In six of the eleven time periods, Christian ethnic groups rebel more often than Muslim ethnic groups, though sometimes barely more often, Muslim ethnic groups rebel more often in three time periods, and Christian and Muslim ethnic groups rebel the same number of times in two time periods. The yearly analysis of 1985 to 2000, presented in Figure 3.22, also has ethnic groups in the "Other" category rebelling the least. Christian ethnic groups rebel more often than do Muslim ethnic groups until 1996, from 1996 to 1999 Muslim and Christian ethnic groups rebel about as often as each other, and in 2000 Muslim ethnic groups rebel more often. All of this shows a trend of Christian ethnic groups rebelling slightly more often until the late 1990s when Muslim ethnic groups seem to be beginning to rebel more often.

The above analysis has one drawback: it looks only at absolute numbers of rebelling groups and does not take population into account. Since there are more Christians in the world than there are Muslims, all other things being equal, we would expect Christian groups to rebel more often. That Muslim groups rebel nearly as often as Christian groups implies that, proportional to their population, Muslims may rebel more often.

According to Barrett et.al. (2001) Muslims constituted 15.0 percent of the world population in 1970, 18.3 percent in 1990, and 18.9 percent in 1995. Christians were 33.5 percent, 33.2 percent, and 33.1 percent, respectively. Using these population statistics it is possible to construct an analysis controlling for the population size of the world's religions. The number of groups rebelling in a particular category were divided by the proportion of the world's population that religion constituted (i.e., in the 1970-1974 period the number of rebelling Muslim groups was divided by .183 and the number of rebelling Christian groups by .335). The resulting number is the predicted number of rebellions if a particular religion constituted the entire world's population.

This analysis for the 1945 to 2000 period is presented in Figure 3.23. The results are much clearer, with Muslim ethnic groups consistently rebelling most often, "Other" ethnic groups consistently rebelling least often, and Christian ethnic groups rebelling more often than "other" ethnic groups but less often than Muslim ethnic groups. The results of the yearly analysis of 1985 to 2000, presented in

Figure 3.21: Number of Rebelling Groups, Controlling for Specific Religion, 1945-2000

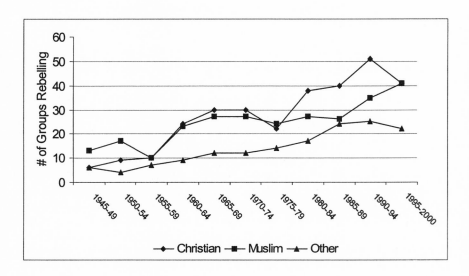

Figure 3.22: Number of Rebelling Groups, Controlling for Specific Religion, 1985-2000

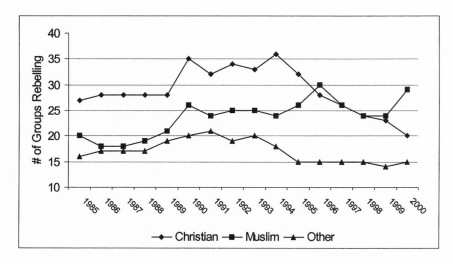

Figure 3.23: Predicted Number of Rebelling Groups, Controlling for Population Size and Specific Religion, 1945-2000

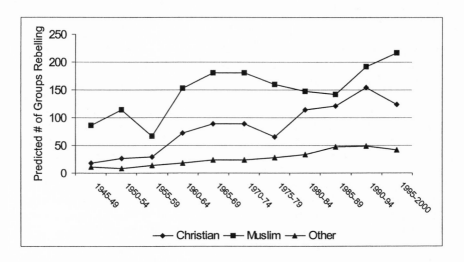

Figure 3.24: Predicted Number of Rebelling Groups, Controlling for Population Size and Specific Religion, 1985-2000

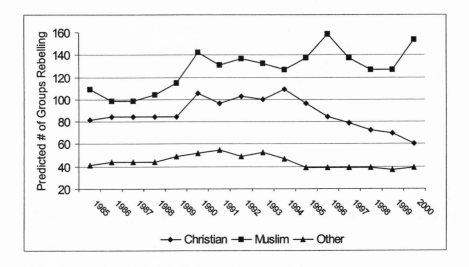

Figure 3.24, are similar. It is also interesting to note that according to both analyses the trend is that the amount of rebellion by Christian ethnic groups has been dropping since the mid-1990s, but Muslim ethnic groups have recently been rebelling more often.

The analysis of the SF data similarly shows that more Christian groups engage in violence, but when taking world population into account, Muslim groups are more likely to engage in violence. The analysis of all state failures, presented in Figures 3.25 and 3.26, shows that until 1994 Christian groups were involved in more state failures than groups of other religions but from 1995 to 2001 Muslim groups were involved in approximately the same amount of state failures as were Christian groups. When taking population size into account, Muslim groups were consistently the most likely to be involved in state failures. Whether looking at the absolute number of state failures or state failures proportional to population size, "Other" groups engaged in consistently the lowest amount of state failure.

The patterns for ethnic state failures, presented in Figures 3.27 and 3.28, are similar to those for all state failures. As this type of conflict is the most common in the SF dataset, this is not surprising. The patterns of conflict for mass killings, presented in Figures 3.29 and 3.30, are also similar to those for all state failures but exhibit some differences. When examining the absolute number of mass killings, Muslim group involvement becomes more common in the late 1980s and early 1990s, after which it is about as common as Christian involvement. The proportional analysis shows Muslims being more likely to be involved in conflict until 1995, when Christian involvement becomes as likely as Muslim involvement.

The pattern for revolutionary wars, presented in Figures 3.31 and 3.32, is different from the others. Christian groups are involved in more revolutionary wars than Muslims, but from 1995 the number of Muslim groups involved in revolutionary wars approaches the number of Christian groups. Even when taking population size into account, Christian groups are more likely to be involved in revolutionary wars than Muslim groups until the 1990s. From 1992 to 1999, Muslim groups are more likely to be involved. In 2000 and 2001 the likelihood that Muslim and Christian groups will be involved in revolutionary wars is roughly equal.

In all, the answer to the question of whether groups of any particular religion are more likely to engage in conflict is not a simple one. The only clear pattern is that no matter how you measure it, Muslim and Christian groups engage in more conflict than do groups of other religions. The question of whether Christian or Muslim groups engage in more conflict depends on how you measure conflict. If it is in the absolute amount of conflict, Christian groups engage in more conflict, but if conflict is measured in proportion to world population size, Muslim groups engage in more conflict. As it is arguable that the use of proportional measures is a more appropriate way to measure which religion more often engages in conflict, it is nevertheless possible to conclude that Muslim groups engage in more conflict than do Christian and "Other" groups.

However, even this relationship is not a simple one. It holds up best for ethnic conflict, but in other types of conflict it is not always true. Even when taking

Figure 3.25: Number of State Failures, Controlling for Specific Religion, 1965-2001

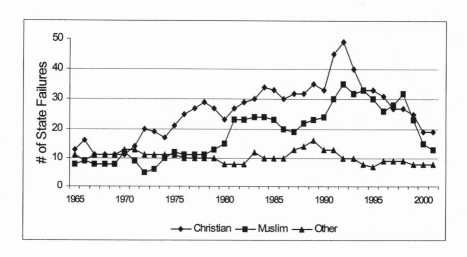

Figure 3.26: Number of State Failures, Controlling for Population Size and Specific Religion, 1965-2001

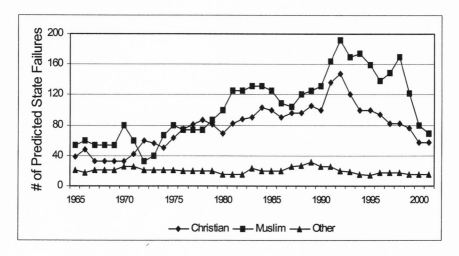

Figure 3.27: Number of Ethnic State Failures, Controlling for Specific Religion, 1965-2001

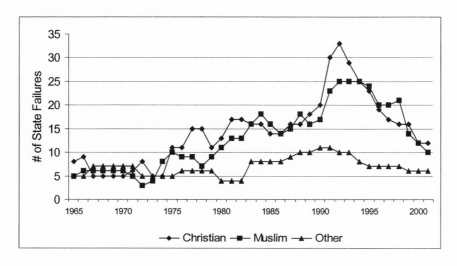

Figure 3.28: Number of Ethnic State Failures, Controlling for Population Size and Specific Religion, 1965-2001

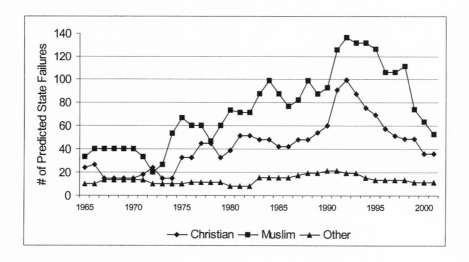

Figure 3.29: Number of Mass Killing State Failures, Controlling for Specific Religion, 1965-2001

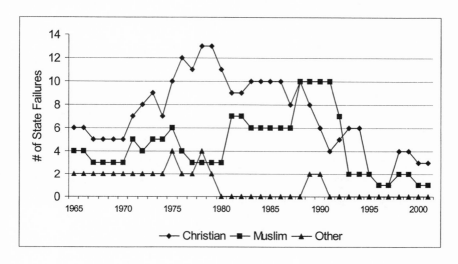

Figure 3.30: Number of Mass Killing State Failures, Controlling for Population Size and Specific Religion, 1965-2001

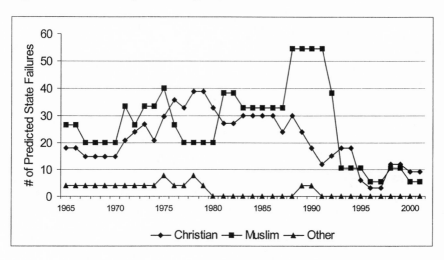

Figure 3.31: Number of Revolutionary War State Failures, Controlling for Specific Religion, 1965-2001

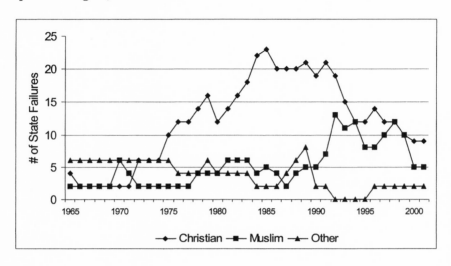

Figure 3.32: Number of Revolutionary War State Failures, Controlling for Population Size and Specific Religion, 1965-2001

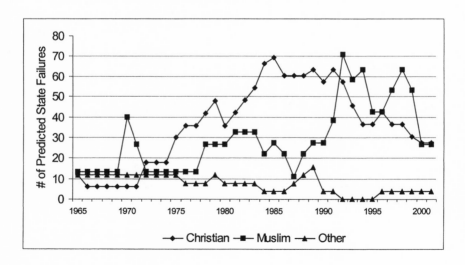

population size into account, Muslims only engaged in more revolutionary wars from 1992 to 1999. Also, on ten of the twelve figures analyzed in this section there can said to be a convergence in the level of conflict between Christian and Muslim groups by the end of the period analyzed here. Also, due to the low levels of conflict in the early parts of the period analyzed here, there is also a convergence in the early parts of seven of these figures. This begs the question of whether the relationships found here are consistent across a broader range of time or are more unique to a period of time beginning approximately in 1970 and ending in the mid-1990s. Only an analysis of conflict over a much broader period of time would fully answer this question. As the data for such an analysis are not available, this is not possible at this point in time.

Is Conflict More Violent among Groups of Any Particular Religion?

The analysis of which type of ethnic minority is more violent between 1945 and 2000 using the MAR dataset is presented in Figure 3.33. The results show that groups of no particular religion are consistently more violent than the others. However, Christian groups are generally less violent than Muslim or "Other" groups. This relationship is statistically significant in several time periods, especially from the mid-1980s onward. "Other" groups tend to be as or more violent than Muslim groups until the mid-1970s when Muslim groups start becoming the most violent. However, there is never any statistically significant difference between the levels of rebellion by Muslim and "Other" groups. The yearly analysis of 1985 to 2000, presented in Figure 3.34, confirms these trends. Christian groups consistently engage in the lowest levels of rebellion, with this relationship being statistically significant through much of the period. Except for 1986 to 1989, when Muslim groups are slightly less violent than "Other" groups, Muslims engage in higher levels of rebellion than do "Other" groups, though these differences never reach the level of statistical significance.

The results of the analysis of the SF dataset are less conclusive. For this analysis, the focus is on the minority groups for ethnic and revolutionary wars and on the majority groups for mass killings. This is because for these analysis, in order to separate out religion, it is necessary to focus on either the majority or minority group. As the level of violence in ethnic and revolutionary wars is largely determined by the rebelling group and the violence of mass killings is generally determined by the majority group, this is the most appropriate method of analysis in this instance.

The analysis of ethnic state failures, presented in Figure 3.35, does not show groups of any particular religion engaging in higher levels of violence. The results for mass killings, presented in Figure 3.36, show no consistent difference between Christian and Muslim groups. However, from 1965 to 1979, mass killings by "Other" groups are considerably more violent, with these differences having

Figure 3.33: Mean Levels of Rebellion Controlling for Specific Religion, 1945-2000

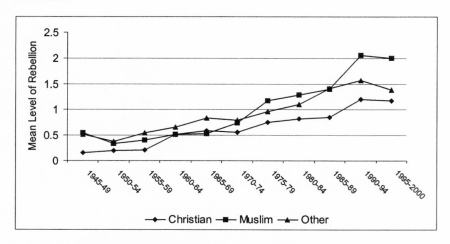

-Significance (t-test) between Christian and Muslim < .1 in 1985-89
-Significance (t-test) between Christian and Muslim < .05 in 1945-49, 1990-94, & 1995-2000
-Significance (t-test) between Christian and Other < .1 in 1985-89

Figure 3.34: Mean Levels of Rebellion Controlling for Specific Religion, 1985-2000

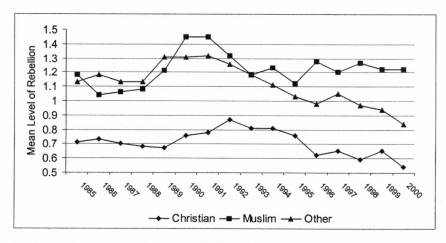

-Significance (t-test) between Christian and Muslim < .1 in 1989
-Significance (t-test) between Christian and Muslim < .05 in 1990, 1991, & 1996-2000
-Significance (t-test) between Christian and Other < .1 in 1990 & 1991
-Significance (t-test) between Christian and Other < .05 in 1989

Figure 3.35: Mean Ethnic State Failures Controlling for Specific Religion of Minority Group, 1965-2001

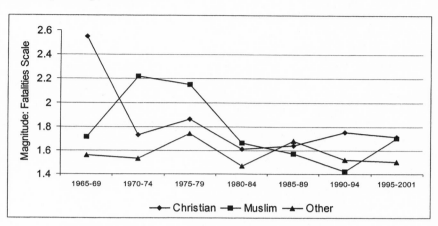

-Significance (t-test) between Christian and Muslim < .1 in 1990-94
-Significance (t-test) between Christian and Muslim < .05 in 1965-69
-Significance (t-test) between Christian and Other < .01 in 1965-69
-Significance (t-test) between Other and Muslim < .05 in 1970-74

Figure 3.36: Mean Mass Killing State Failures Controlling for Specific Religion of Majority Group, 1965-2001

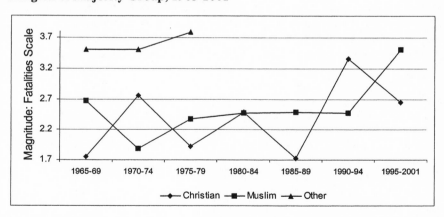

-Significance (t-test) between Christian and Muslim < .1 in 1970-74, 1990-94, & 1995-2001
-Significance (t-test) between Christian and Other < .05 in 1970-74
-Significance (t-test) between Christian and Other < .01 in 1965-69
-Significance (t-test) between Christian and Other < .001 in 1975-79
-Significance (t-test) between Other and Muslim < .1 in 1965-69
-Significance (t-test) between Other and Muslim < .05 in 1975-79
-Significance (t-test) between Other and Muslim < .001 in 1970-74

Figure 3.37: Mean Revolutionary War State Failures Controlling for Specific Religion of Minority Group, 1965-2001

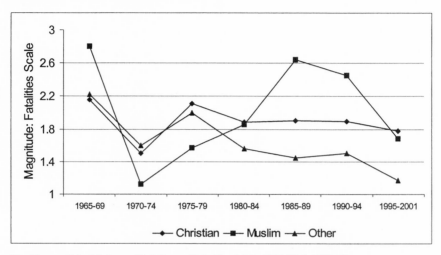

-Significance (t-test) between Christian and Muslim < .1 in 1985-99 & 1990-94
-Significance (t-test) between Christian and Muslim < .05 in 1965-69
-Significance (t-test) between Other and Muslim < .05 in 1985-89 & 1995-2001

statistical significance. There are too few of mass killings by "Other" groups after 1979 for analysis. The analysis of revolutionary wars, presented in Figure 3.37, also shows no consistent relationship. However, from the mid-1980s to the mid-1990s, Muslim groups were more violent, with these differences being statistically significant.

In all, there is no consistent answer to the question of whether any particular religion is more violent than other religions. However, some trends do emerge. There is considerable evidence that Christian groups are less violent than other groups and are certainly not the most violent. Also, there is evidence of a rise in the level of violence by Islamic groups in the 1990s that exists in all five figures in this section.

When combined with the results of the previous section on which type of group engages in violence more often, the answer to the more general question of whether different religions engage in different patterns of conflict becomes more confused. Christian groups are, perhaps, the least violent when looking at the average level of violence in conflicts. However, they engage in conflict more often than groups in the "Other" category, no matter how you measure it, and more often than Muslim groups in absolute terms but less often than Muslim groups when taking population size into account.

Muslim groups, when taking population size into account, engage in the most conflict. However, until the 1990s, their conflicts are not particularly violent. However, this rise in violence coincides with a drop in the level of conflict so it can be said that conflicts involving Muslims are becoming less common but more violent.

"Other" groups engage in the least conflict and except for mass killings these conflicts are not particularly violent.

All of this shows that the prevalent stereotype of the Islamic militant is supported by some aspects of the data but not by others. Muslim groups engage in the most conflict in most categories if you take population size into account. However, in absolute terms Christian groups engage in more conflict. Also, conflicts involving Muslims are not particularly violent, but the level of violence by Muslim groups seems to be on the rise. Thus, while this study certainly does not prove the stereotype of the violent of Muslim groups to be correct, neither can it falsify this stereotype.

Who Is Fighting Whom?

An important aspect of conflict in general and religious conflict specifically is who is fighting whom. That is, are conflicts between Christians and Muslims, for example, more common than conflicts between two Christian groups or two Muslim groups?

While this has implications for Samuel Huntington's (1993a; 1996a; 1996b) theory that intercivilizational conflict will be more common in the post-Cold War era, as his concept of civilizations is largely based on religion, this section does not directly address Huntington's theories. This is because while religion is a factor in his theory, religion and his concept of civilization are not exactly the same. A more detailed discussion and quantitative testing of his theory is presented in Chapters 6, 7, and 8.

Be that as it may, one relevant aspect of his theory is his prediction that Islam will be a particular threat to the West, especially in the post-Cold War era. If this is correct, we would expect a rise in conflicts between Muslim and Christian groups in the 1990s. He also discusses Islam's "bloody borders," predicting a general increase in conflict between Muslim and non-Muslim groups beginning in the 1990s. Of course, this aspect of his theory is controversial, with many disputing his predictions. A full discussion of this debate is presented in Chapter 6.

There are two types of analysis in this section. The first presents a straight cross tabulation of the conflicts using the categories of majority and minority groups. Thus, conflicts involving Muslim majorities vs. Christian minorities, for example, are considered separately from conflicts involving Christian majorities vs. Muslim minorities. In this type of analysis each conflict is counted once. The second type of analysis focuses on whom members of each religion are fighting regardless of whether the group is a majority or minority group. Thus, in the example described above, the Muslim majority vs. Christian minority and Christian majority vs. Muslim minority are considered together. This necessitates each conflict being considered twice, once for the majority group and once for the minority group. This means that when looking at conflicts involving Christians, for example, a conflict between two Christian groups would be considered twice, even though both conflicts would be placed in the same category. This methodology is necessary in order to get a better idea of exactly what type of opponents groups of a particular religion are fighting.

The most striking aspect of the analysis of the MAR data, presented in Tables 3.1 and 3.2, is that Christian, Muslim, and "Other" groups primarily fight members within their own category. That is, Christians primarily fight Christians, Muslims mostly fight Muslims, and "Other" groups primarily fight groups who are not Christians and Muslims. Furthermore, this pattern is consistent across time periods. This pattern is most pronounced for Christian groups who, about 75 percent of the time in all time periods, fight other Christian groups. Muslim and "other" groups fight other groups in their own category about half of the time.

There is some evidence that there has been an increase in conflict between Christian and Muslim groups in the post-Cold War era. During the Cold War, 14.2 percent of conflicts involving Christian groups are with Muslims and this increases to 16.5 percent in the early 1990s and 16.8 percent in 2000. During the Cold War 28.8 percent of conflicts involving Muslim groups are with Christian ones and this increases to 34.0 percent in the early 1990s and 33.3 percent in 2000.

However, this increase is by no means the dramatic one that Huntington's theory predicts and is within the range of change that one would expect when a major change in the international system, such as the end of the Cold War, occurs. States like the former USSR and Yugoslavia broke up making former minorities majorities in their own states. Similarly, former majorities, like ethnic Russians, became the new minorities in these states. This alone is enough to cause some change in the distribution of politically active ethnic minorities. In addition, the end of the superpower rivalry ended much of the sponsorship of rebel groups throughout the world. Thus, while the change in conflict is in the direction predicted by Huntington, it is too slight to fully support these predictions.

Furthermore, there is very little support for an increase in religious conflict in the post-Cold War era. As noted above, the majority of conflict is within religious groupings both during and after the Cold War era. The amount of conflict within religions in each category does not vary more than 1 percent for Christian and Muslim groups and actually drops for "other" groups. In all, the MAR data shows very little change over time in the distribution of ethnic conflict.

The results for the analysis of the entire SF dataset, presented in Tables 3.3 and 3.4, are similar. Due to the larger numbers of units of analysis in this analysis, it is possible to divide the "Other" category into Buddhists, Animists[3] and "Other." One striking difference between this and the MAR analysis is that Animist groups never fight other Animist groups. However, this is explained by the fact that there are few groups which rule states which follow Animist religions; thus, there is little potential

Table 3.1: Cross Tabulation of Conflicts between Religious Majority and Minority Groups in the MAR Dataset

Period	Minority Religion	Majority Religion		
		Christian	Muslim	Other
1945-1989	Christian	90	10	6
	Muslim	24	30	10
	Other	19	14	22
Early 1990s	Christian	114	23	5
	Muslim	27	38	9
	Other	20	13	26
2000	Christian	115	23	5
	Muslim	29	40	10
	Other	22	14	27
1945-2000	Christian	145	23	6
	Muslim	38	45	11
	Other	25	15	29

Table 3.2: Analysis of Opponents of Groups of Particular Religions in the MAR Dataset

Period	Minority Religion	Opponent					
		Christian		Muslim		Other	
		N	%	N	%	N	%
1945-1989	Christian	180	75.3%	34	14.2%	25	10.5%
	Muslim	34	28.8%	60	50.8%	24	20.3%
	Other	25	26.9%	24	25.8%	44	47.3%
Early 1990s	Christian	228	75.2%	50	16.5%	25	8.3%
	Muslim	50	34.0%	76	51.7%	21	14.3%
	Other	25	25.5%	21	21.4%	52	53.1%
2000	Christian	230	74.4%	52	16.8%	27	8.7%
	Muslim	52	33.3%	80	51.3%	24	15.4%
	Other	27	25.7%	24	22.9%	54	51.4%
1945-2000	Christian	290	75.9%	61	16.0%	31	8.1%
	Muslim	61	34.5%	90	50.8%	26	14.7%
	Other	31	27.0%	26	22.6%	58	50.4%

Table 3.3: Cross Tabulation of All State Failures Controlling for Religion

Period	Minority Religion	Majority Religion			
		Christian	Islam	Buddhist	Other
1945-1989	Christian	281	52	0	3
	Islam	39	144	0	5
	Buddhist	0	0	65	24
	Animist	0	25	19	0
	Other	0	14	15	13
1990-2001	Christian	152	44	0	0
	Islam	33	102	0	33
	Buddhist	0	0	12	2
	Animist	0	5	0	0
	Other	0	2	12	10
1945-2001	Christian	433	96	0	3
	Islam	72	246	0	38
	Buddhist	0	0	77	26
	Animist	0	30	19	0
	Other	0	16	27	23

Table 3.4: Analysis of Opponents of Groups of Particular Religions among All State Failures

Period	Religion	Opponent									
		Christian		Islam		Buddhist		Animist		Other	
		N	%	N	%	N	%	N	%	N	%
1945-1989	Christian	562	85.7%	91	13.9%	0	0.0%	0	0.0%	3	0.5%
	Islam	91	21.5%	288	68.1%	0	0.0%	25	5.9%	19	4.5%
	Buddhist	0	0.0%	0	0.0%	130	69.1%	19	10.1%	39	20.7%
	Animist	0	0.0%	25	56.8%	19	43.2%	0	0.0%	0	0.0%
	Other	3	3.4%	19	21.8%	39	44.8%	0	0.0%	26	29.9%
1990-2001	Christian	304	79.8%	77	20.2%	0	0.0%	0	0.0%	0	0.0%
	Islam	77	24.0%	204	63.6%	0	0.0%	5	1.6%	35	10.9%
	Buddhist	0	0.0%	0	0.0%	24	63.2%	0	0.0%	14	36.8%
	Animist	0	0.0%	5	100.0%	0	0.0%	0	0.0%	0	0.0%
	Other	0	0.0%	35	50.7%	14	20.3%	0	0.0%	20	29.0%
1945-2001	Christian	866	83.5%	168	16.2%	0	0.0%	0	0.0%	3	0.3%
	Islam	168	22.6%	492	66.1%	0	0.0%	30	4.0%	54	7.3%
	Buddhist	0	0.0%	0	0.0%	154	68.2%	19	8.4%	53	23.4%
	Animist	0	0.0%	30	61.2%	19	38.8%	0	0.0%	0	0.0%
	Other	3	1.9%	54	34.6%	53	34.0%	0	0.0%	46	29.5%

for conflicts in which both sides are Animists.

As was the case with the MAR data, the SF data shows that Christian and Muslim groups fight mostly members of their own religion. In fact this trend is even stronger in the SF data where overall 83.5 percent of conflicts involving Christian groups and 66.1 percent of conflicts involving Muslim groups are intrareligious, as opposed to 74.9 percent and 50.8 percent respectively in the MAR data. Buddhist groups also primarily fight Buddhist groups. Interestingly, this pattern weakens in the post-Cold War era with the amount of intra-religious conflict involving Christian, Muslim, and Buddhist groups all dropping between about 4.5 percent and 5.9 percent. However, even in the post-Cold War era, a large majority of conflicts for groups of all three religions remain intrareligious.

Also, similarly to the MAR results, the amount of conflict between Christian and Muslim groups increases slightly. Until 1989 13.9 percent of conflicts involving Christian groups are with Muslim groups, which increases to 20.2 percent in 1990 to 2001. Similarly, until 1989 21.5 percent of conflict involving Muslim groups is with Christian groups, increasing to 24.0 percent in the 1990 to 2001 period. While this rise does not seem substantial from the Islamic perspective, from the Christian perspective this is an increase of almost 69 percent in the proportion of all conflict which is with Muslim groups. Also, nearly all conflicts involving Christians which are not with other Christian groups are with Muslim groups. Thus, from this perspective Muslim groups are the only interreligious challenge to Christian groups and this challenge has increased with the end of the Cold War. Nevertheless, it should be recalled that intrareligious conflict remains far more common than interreligious conflict even in the post Cold War era.

An interesting finding from this analysis is that the majority of conflicts involving Animist groups are with Muslim groups. Since all Animist groups are minority groups, this implies that it is primarily Muslim states that are intolerant of what the Abrahamic tradition considers pagan religions. As there are numerous Animist minorities in Christian states (the MAR dataset lists thirteen) this seems to be particularly true of Muslim states.

Groups in the "Other" category also primarily fight groups of different religions. During the Cold War era, they fight mostly Buddhist groups and from 1990 onward they fight mostly Muslim groups.

The analysis of ethnic conflicts in the SF dataset, presented in Tables 3.5 and 3.6, follows nearly the same patterns as the analysis of the entire dataset. However, intrareligious conflict among Muslim and Christian groups, while still a majority of the conflicts involving these groups is markedly less common. While, as will be recalled, in the analysis of the entire SF dataset, 83.5 percent of conflicts involving Christian groups and 66.1 percent of conflicts involving Muslim groups are intrareligious, 72.6 percent and 53.1 percent, respectively, are intrareligious among ethnic conflicts in the SF dataset. These numbers are similar to the results from the MAR dataset where 74.9 percent and 50.8 percent of conflicts respectively are intrareligious. Thus, while ethnic conflicts among Christians and Muslims are most likely to be intrareligious, this is less true of ethnic conflicts than other types of

Table 3.5: Cross Tabulation of Ethnic State Failures Controlling for Religion

Period	Minority Religion	Majority Religion			
		Christian	Islam	Buddhist	Other
1945-1989	Christian	116	50	0	3
	Islam	36	71	0	5
	Buddhist	0	0	29	4
	Animist	0	25	19	0
	Other	0	14	7	12
1990-2001	Christian	92	43	0	0
	Islam	25	64	0	33
	Buddhist	0	0	12	0
	Animist	0	5	0	0
	Other	0	2	12	4
1945-2001	Christian	208	93	0	3
	Islam	61	135	0	38
	Buddhist	0	0	41	4
	Animist	0	30	19	0
	Other	0	16	19	16

Table 3.6: Analysis of Opponents of Groups of Particular Religions among Ethnic State Failures

Period	Religion	Opponent									
		Christian		Islam		Buddhist		Animist		Other	
		N	%	N	%	N	%	N	%	N	%
1945-1989	Christian	232	72.3%	86	26.8%	0	0.0%	0	0.0%	3	0.9%
	Islam	86	31.6%	142	52.2%	0	0.0%	25	9.2%	19	7.0%
	Buddhist	0	0.0%	0	0.0%	58	65.9%	19	21.6%	11	12.5%
	Animist	0	0.0%	25	56.8%	19	43.2%	0	0.0%	0	0.0%
	Other	3	5.3%	19	33.3%	11	19.3%	0	0.0%	24	42.1%
1990-2001	Christian	184	73.0%	68	27.0%	0	0.0%	0	0.0%	0	0.0%
	Islam	68	28.8%	128	54.2%	0	0.0%	5	2.1%	35	14.8%
	Buddhist	0	0.0%	0	0.0%	24	66.7%	0	0.0%	12	33.3%
	Animist	0	0.0%	5	100.0%	0	0.0%	0	0.0%	0	0.0%
	Other	0	0.0%	35	63.6%	12	21.8%	0	0.0%	8	14.5%
1945-2001	Christian	416	72.6%	154	26.9%	0	0.0%	0	0.0%	3	0.5%
	Islam	154	30.3%	270	53.1%	0	0.0%	30	5.9%	54	10.6%
	Buddhist	0	0.0%	0	0.0%	82	66.1%	19	15.3%	23	18.6%
	Animist	0	0.0%	30	61.2%	19	38.8%	0	0.0%	0	0.0%
	Other	3	2.7%	54	48.2%	23	20.5%	0	0.0%	32	28.6%

Table 3.7: Cross Tabulation of Mass Killing State Failures Controlling for Religion

Period	Minority Religion	Majority Religion		
		Christian	Islam	Non-Christian/Islam
1945-1989	Christian	93	47	0
	Islam	0	46	0
	Non-Christian/Islam	0	0	19
1990-2001	Christian	12	15	0
	Islam	6	10	0
	Non-Christian/Islam	0	0	1
1945-2001	Christian	105	62	0
	Islam	6	56	0
	Non-Christian/Islam	0	0	20

Table 3.8: Analysis of Opponents of Groups of Particular Religions among Mass Killing State Failures

Period	Religion	Opponent					
		Christian		Islam		Non-Christian/Islam	
		N	%	N	%	N	%
1945-1989	Christian	186	79.8%	47	30.2%	0	0.0%
	Islam	47	33.8%	92	66.2%	0	0.0%
	Non-Christian/Islam	0	0.0%	0	0.0%	38	100.0%
1990-2001	Christian	24	43.6%	21	56.4%	0	0.0%
	Islam	21	48.8%	20	51.2%	0	0.0%
	Non-Christian/Islam	0	0.0%	0	0.0%	2	100.0%
1945-2001	Christian	210	75.5%	68	24.5%	0	0.0%
	Islam	68	37.8%	112	62.2%	0	0.0%
	Non-Christian/Islam	0	0.0%	0	0.0%	40	0.0%

conflicts.

Also, among ethnic conflicts in the SF dataset, there is little increase in the extent of Christian vs. Muslim conflicts. Such conflicts are 26.8 percent of those involving Christian groups during the Cold War era and 27.0 percent of conflicts from 1990 onward. They drop from 31.6 percent of ethnic conflicts involving Muslims during the Cold War era to 28.8 percent after it. Also the extent of intra-religious ethnic conflict among Christian, Islamic, and Buddhist groups actually increases with the end of the Cold War from 72.3 percent, 52.2 percent, and 65.9 percent for Christian, Muslim, and Buddhist groups respectively to 73.0 percent, 54.2 percent, and 66.7 percent respectively. Thus there is little support for any of Huntington's predictions in this section of the data.

The analysis of mass killing state failures, presented in Tables 3.7 and 3.8, shows very different results. Due to the smaller number of cases in this category it is only possible to analyze the categories of Christian, Muslim, and "Other." One major difference is that while, overall, most mass killings are intrareligious, this is considerably less true of the post-Cold War era. All mass killings by "Other" groups are against other groups in the "Other" category. However, While 79.8 percent of mass killings involving Christians involve other Christian groups until 1989, from 1990 onward this number drops to 43.6 percent. The number of mass killings which involve two Muslim groups also drops, but less dramatically, from 66.2 percent during the Cold War to 51.2 percent after it.

Furthermore, all of this drop in intrareligious mass killings is replaced by inter-religious mass killings between Christians and Muslims. These numbers increase from 30.2 percent of mass killings involving Christians and 33.8 percent involving Muslims to 56.4 percent and 48.8 percent respectively. These mass killings are mostly Muslim groups killing Christians. Of sixty-eight cases of mass killings, only six involve Christians killing Muslims. Thus, in this respect, Islam is a considerable threat to Christianity. However, it is not a new threat as about 1.34 such events occurred yearly during the Cold War era and 1.25 a year after it. Thus, there has actually been a slight decrease in Muslims mass killing Christians in the post-Cold War era. Consequently, the drop in cases of Christian vs. Muslim mass killings is due to the fact that Christians commit this crime against other Christians less after the Cold War rather than Muslims committing it against Christians more.

The results for revolutionary war state failures, presented in Tables 3.9 and 3.10, show that revolutionary wars are almost exclusively intrareligious. In no category does the percentage of interreligious conflicts rise any higher than 5.7 percent. While there is a slight decrease in intrareligious revolutionary wars involv-ing Christian and Muslim groups, even in the post-Cold War era intrareligious conflict is 96.3 percent of revolutionary wars involving Christian groups and 94.3 percent involving Muslim groups. In both time periods conflicts involving groups within the "Other" category are with other groups in the same category.

Overall, several trends become clear when analyzing all of the data in this section. First, most conflict is intrareligious. The extent to which this is true varies depending on the time period and type of conflict analyzed, but this relationship nevertheless remains consistent. Second, while there is a slight increase in Christian vs. Muslim conflict with the end of the Cold War, it is by no means a dramatic one. Third, the majority of conflicts involving Christian and Muslim groups which are not intrareligious tend to be Christian vs. Muslim conflicts. In fact, there are no examples among nonethnic conflicts of Christian or Muslim groups fighting groups which are not Christian or Muslim and among ethnic conflicts, these types of conflicts are less common than Christian vs. Muslim conflicts.

Thus, Huntington's argument that Islam will be a challenge to Christianity is partially correct in that Muslim groups are the most common non-Christian oppo-nents for Christian groups. However, there is little change over time in this type of conflict, so it is not new to the post-Cold War era. Also, Huntington's predictions

Table 3.9: Cross Tabulation of Revolutionary War State Failures Controlling for Religion

Period	Minority Religion	Majority Religion		
		Christian	Islam	Non-Christian/Islam
1945-1989	Christian	165	1	0
	Islam	3	63	0
	Non-Christian/Islam	0	0	74
1990-2001	Christian	79	0	0
	Islam	6	50	0
	Non-Christian/Islam	0	0	8
1945-2001	Christian	244	1	0
	Islam	9	113	0
	Non-Christian/Islam	0	0	82

Table 3.10: Analysis of Opponents of Groups of Particular Religions Among Revolutionary War State Failures

Period	Religion	Opponent					
		Christian		Islam		Non-Christian/Islam	
		N	%	N	%	N	%
1945-1989	Christian	330	98.8%	4	1.2%	0	0.0%
	Islam	4	3.1%	126	96.9%	0	0.0%
	Non-Christian/Islam	0	0.0%	0	0.0%	148	100.0%
1990-2001	Christian	154	96.3%	6	3.7%	0	0.0%
	Islam	6	5.7%	100	94.3%	0	0.0%
	Non-Christian/Islam	0	0.0%	0	0.0%	16	100.0%
1945-2001	Christian	488	98.0%	10	2.0%	0	0.0%
	Islam	10	4.2%	226	95.8%	0	0.0%
	Non-Christian/Islam	0	0.0%	0	0.0%	164	100.0%

of a dramatic increase in interreligious conflict did not occur, at least as of 2001, among domestic conflicts.

Conclusions

It is clear from this analysis that despite arguments to the contrary religious conflict exists. While some aspects of this religious conflict have remained consistent over time, others have changed. The trends in religious conflict that emerge from this analysis are as follows. First, religious conflict was present throughout the entire

1945 to 2001 period analyzed here, but it was, in general, less common than nonreligious conflict.

Second, there was a rise in the extent of religious conflict in proportion to nonreligious conflict that began at some time between the mid-1970s and the early 1990s, depending on what specific type of conflict is being measured. By the late 1990s, the level of religious conflict approached that of nonreligious conflict and, on some measures, slightly exceeded it. Other than this, religious conflict tended to rise and fall roughly in proportion to nonreligious conflict.

Third, when looking only at who is fighting whom, it becomes clear that the majority of conflict is intrareligious, especially for Muslim and Christian groups. However, it should be noted that there are many intrareligious conflicts that involve religious aspects.

Fourth, the most common type of religious conflict is ethnoreligious conflict, but this is not surprising as ethnic conflict is the most common type of conflict of those analyzed here.

Fifth, ethnoreligious minorities were slightly less likely to rebel than other ethnic minorities unless religion was an issue in the conflict. If religion was an issue in the conflict, beginning in the 1970s, the likelihood of ethnoreligious rebelling increased to the point that by the late 1990s they were more likely to rebel than any other category of ethnic minority.

Sixth, when controlling for population size, Muslims were generally more likely than average to rebel and Christian groups less likely. However, as there are more Christians in the world than Muslims, there were more conflicts involving Christians. There are also some exceptions to this more general rule. Be that as it may, both Christians and Muslims engaged in more conflict than non-Christian and non-Muslim groups using either measurement.

Seventh, while groups of no particular religion are consistently more violent than others, Christian groups tend to be less violent.

Eighth, there is considerable evidence for a rise in conflict involving Muslims during the 1990s.

Ninth, there was a slight rise in Muslim vs. Christian conflict during the 1990s.

When these more specific trends are examined as a whole, two larger trends emerge. First, there has been a general rise in religious conflict during the second half of the twentieth century. Ethnic conflicts where religion is an important issue have consistently become increasingly violent in comparison to other ethnic conflicts since the 1970s. Also, the extent of religious conflict, in proportion to other types of conflict, began increasing in the 1980s or early 1990s depending on how it is measured. This suggests that those who theorize that the process of modernization is creating a resurgence of religion are correct.

Second, conflicts involving Muslim groups started becoming increasingly more common and violent during the 1990s. While it is tempting to say that Muslims are responsible for this trend of an increase in the extent of religious conflict, it is not clear that this is the case as, throughout the period covered in this study, the proportion of conflicts involving Muslim groups which are interreligious remains about the same. However, among intrareligious conflicts involving Muslim groups, the proportion of those conflicts which are religious in nature is increasing. Between 1965 and 1979 seven of fifty nine (11.9 percent) of intra-Muslim conflict years were religious conflicts. From 1980 to 1989, forty of ninety-one (44.0 percent) were religious conflicts. From 1990 to 2001 fifty-five of 124 (44.4 percent) were religious conflicts. The vast majority of these intra-Muslim conflicts from 1980 to 2001 involved militant Islamic fundamentalists vs. more secular Muslims. Thus, while there has been an increase in Islamic militancy, this militancy seems to be a greater threat to more secular Muslims than it is to non-Muslims.

Be that as it may, it is important to reiterate that while this chapter does provide a more detailed picture of the extent of religious conflict between 1945 and 2001, it does not provide the complete picture. This is because this chapter documents what occurred but does not examine why it occurred. In other words, the issue of causality is not addressed. This issue is dealt with in the next chapter.

Notes

1. For the purposes of this analysis, religion is considered relevant if the variable for religious relevance is coded as marginally relevant or higher.
2. For the purposes of this analysis, religion is considered relevant if the variable for religious relevance is coded as marginally relevant or higher.
3. Animists are polytheistic tribal religions generally followed by indigenous groups.

Chapter 4

Religious Causes of Ethnic Conflict

While the previous chapter examined the question of what is the nature of religious conflict, this one delves into the question of how does religion influence conflict with a specific focus on ethnic conflict. That is, we ask how, if at all, does religion cause, exert influence upon, or otherwise shape ethnic conflict? This question includes a number of more specific questions. When and how, if at all, does religion cause ethnic conflict? When and how does it influence ethnic conflicts caused by other factors? Is the fact that the two groups involved belong to different religions enough to influence the conflict or must the conflict involve religious issues for it to be affected? What, if any, are the roles of religious legitimacy and institutions in influencing ethnic conflict?

This focus on ethnic conflict is due to the fact that the MAR dataset, which contains data on ethnic conflict, has enough depth to ask this type of question while the SF dataset, which contains data on all types of civil wars, does not. As noted in Chapter 1, the MAR dataset contains data on 337 ethnic minorities, all of which are analyzed here. However, portions of this study focus on a subset of 105 ethnoreligious minorities for which more specific data on religion has been collected. Also, all of these religion variables as well as many other variables in the MAR dataset were collected only since 1990 or even for more limited time periods. Thus, many of the analyses requiring these variables are limited to the 1990s or other more limited time periods. Finally, it should be noted that this chapter, as does the previous one, focuses on violent conflict.

Religion and Separatism

Previous studies using the MAR dataset have found that separatism is one of the strongest causes of ethnic rebellion. (Gurr, 1993a; 1993b; 2000) In fact, no other

71

single variable is a better predictor of rebellion. Despite this, there are few theoretical or quantitative studies that address the combined impact of religion and separatism on conflict. The few that do combine the two either tend to lump religion in the
same category as ethnicity or tend to be discussions of a third topic that is influenced by both religion and separatism. For instance, Ferguson and Mansbach (2000:
89) argue that in the past people were more willing to give their lives in order to
defend the state but today ethnicity and religion have stronger claims. Similarly,
Kaufmann (1996: 137) discusses the necessity of separating warring religious and
ethnic groups in order to control conflicts. This lack of studies which deal more
actively with the combination of separatism and religion is surprising considering
the extensive coverage of both of these factors individually.

That separatism and other forms of the desire for self-determination are causes
of violence is rarely, if ever, disputed in the literature. Self-determination is an
ideology that is considered both a justification and cause for violence, including
terrorism and open rebellion. (Byman, 1998: 162; David, 1997: 572; Goldstone, et
al., 1991: 332; Hoffman, 1995: 272; and Schultz, 1995: 80) States usually consider
separatist demands "highly threatening because they challenge nationalist ideologies
held by most dominant groups and imply the breakup of the state." (Gurr, 1993a:
294) Consequently, states are rarely willing to give in to separatist demands and
tend to respond to separatists militarily. (Gurr and Harff, 1994: 118)

Even when a group successfully meets its separatist goals, the violence often
continues. This is because when separatists finally create their new state, there are
often new border disputes that replace domestic war with international war. There
is also often a need to relocate populations, fighting within the seceding group over
who will rule, and the fact that one group's success encourages groups elsewhere
to demand self-determination. Furthermore, partition rarely resolves the ethnic
hatred that existed before it. (Kaufmann, 1996: 169-174; Kumar, 1997: 25-32) In
fact, the violence associated with separatism both before and after partition is one
of the reasons that Lijphart (1990: 493-494) recommends power sharing over
partition as a solution to ethnic violence. However, in the long term, partition can
reduce the level of violence.(Kaufmann, 1998: 121)

The issues of separatism and self-determination have become increasingly
important over the past century. Some consider this a natural outgrowth of the
acceptance of the concept of the nation-state. (Fuller, 1995: 151) The doctrine of
self-determination did not appear until around World War I and that "in its pristine
form, the doctrine [of self-determination] makes ethnicity the ultimate measure of
political legitimacy, by holding that any self-differentiating people, simply because
it is a people, has the right, should it so desire, to rule itself." (Connor, 1972: 331)
In fact, some argue that the concept of self-determination has replaced the law of
conquest as the defining principle of sovereignty. (Wilmer, 1993) In other words,
the right of sovereign states to use force to achieve their foreign policy goals has
deteriorated in favor of the use of force for self-defense and humanitarian intervention, preferably sanctioned by an international body. Conversely, the use of force
in order to gain self-determination is becoming increasingly legitimate (Borntrager,

1999: 70) and separating warring populations rather than preserving multiethnic societies is gaining international support. (Kaufmann, 1998: 120) Thus, not only is separatism associated with violence, but this violence is also becoming more common and increasingly acceptable in the eyes of the international community.

Based on this, many consider self-determination and separatism to be threats to the current international order. They can undermine multiethnic societies (Carment and James, 1997b: 260) as well as the concept of the monolithic state. (Green, 2000: 73) This is because "all the durable states in the modern world established and consolidated rule over their national territories by the successful use of force: by revolution; by suppressing rebellions and secessions; by forcibly subordinating and integrating." (Gurr, 1988: 47) Even those that argue that these factors do not threaten the state itself agree that secession is often violent and can drastically change the international order.[1]

In any case, it is clear that secession is a major cause of violence that is becoming increasingly important on the international agenda. Furthermore, as documented in the previous chapters, religion is also an important element of domestic conflict. Thus, an analysis of the combined influence of separatism and religion on ethnic conflict is warranted.

An analysis of the impact of separatism alone on ethnic rebellion, presented in Figures 4.1 and 4.2, clearly demonstrates that separatism impacts upon ethnic rebellion. Separatist conflicts are consistently more violent than nonseparatist conflicts, with this difference being statistically significant from 1960 to 2000. Though, the gap between separatist and nonseparatist conflicts narrows toward the year 2000.

Factoring religion into the equation shows that religion impacts on this relationship. The results for 1945 to 2000, presented in Figure 4.3, show that for much of the period there is little difference between religious and nonreligious conflict. In fact, until the 1960s there was little difference between any of the categories in the figure, though this was likely due to the generally low levels of ethnic conflict during the 1940s and 1950s. However, beginning in the first half of the 1980s this begins to change. From the 1980 to 1984 period onward, religious-separatist conflict is more violent than other separatist conflicts, with this relationship increasing in strength through time until it reaches the level of statistical significance in the 1995 to 2000 period. Also, beginning in the 1990s, nonseparatist religious conflict becomes increasingly less violent than other nonseparatist conflicts. This relationship also reaches the level of statistical significance in the 1995 to 2000 period.

The yearly results for 1985 to 2000, presented in Figure 4.4, show the same dynamic. In addition, they show that by the late 1990s there is little difference in the level of rebellion by separatist and non-separatist conflict nonreligious ethnic minorities. This phenomenon began with a simultaneous drop in rebellion by non-religious separatist minorities and a rise in rebellion by nonreligious nonseparatist minorities in 1996.

Thus, between 1980 and 2000 there was a dramatic change in the dynamics of ethnic conflict. Until 1980, separatism was the main determinant of which conflicts

Chapter 4

Figure 4.1: Mean Levels of Rebellion Controlling for Separatism, 1945-2000

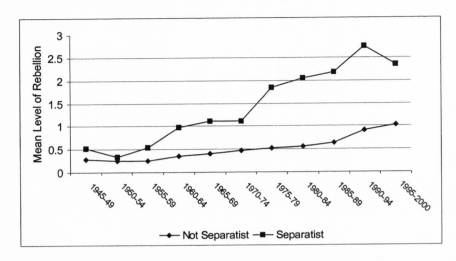

-Significance (t-test) between Not Separatist and Separatist < .01 in 1960-1974
-Significance (t-test) between Not Separatist and Separatist < .001 in 1975-2000

Figure 4.2: Mean Levels of Rebellion Controlling for Separatism, 1985-2000

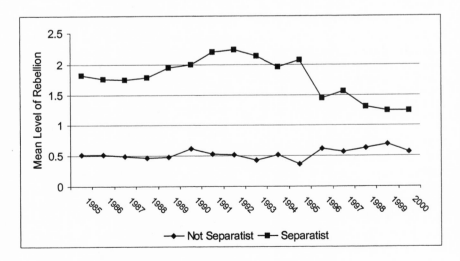

-Significance (t-test) between Not Separatist and Separatist < .05 in 1999
-Significance (t-test) between Not Separatist and Separatist < .01 in 1998 & 2000
-Significance (t-test) between Not Separatist and Separatist < .001 in 1985-1997

Figure 4.3: Mean Levels of Rebellion Controlling for Religion and Separatism, 1945-2000

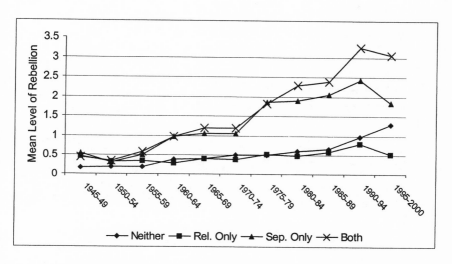

-Significance (t-test) between Neither and Rel. Only < .01 in 1995-2000
-Significance (t-test) between Neither and Sep. Only < .1 in 1945-49 & 1970-74
-Significance (t-test) between Neither and Sep. Only < .05 in 1960-69
-Significance (t-test) between Neither and Sep. Only < .001 in 1975-94
-Significance (t-test) between Neither and Both < .1 in 1970-74
-Significance (t-test) between Neither and Both < .05 in 1965-69
-Significance (t-test) between Neither and Both < .01 in 1975-79
-Significance (t-test) between Neither and Both < .001 in 1980-2000
-Significance (t-test) between Rel. Only and Sep. Only < .05 in 1960-74
-Significance (t-test) between Rel. Only and Sep. Only < .001 in 1975-2000
-Significance (t-test) between Rel. Only and Both < .1 in 1965-79
-Significance (t-test) between Rel. Only and Both < .01 in 1980-84
-Significance (t-test) between Rel. Only and Both < .001 in 1985-2000
-Significance (t-test) between Sep. Only and Both < .05 in 1995-2000

were likely to be violent. Starting in 1980, a combination of separatism and religion determined which conflicts would be violent. By 2000, it was still a combination of separatism and religion, but separatism only influenced ethnoreligious conflicts and not other ethnic conflicts. Thus, since 1980, religion has been steadily becoming a more important influence on ethnic conflict and the impact of separatism has been declining.

This rise in the importance of religion since the early 1980s is consistent with the theories described in Chapter 2 that modernization is causing a resurgence or revitalization of religion. It also confirms the results from Chapter 3 which similarly indicate that this is the case. More importantly, it shows that while religious factors

Figure 4.4: Mean Levels of Rebellion Controlling for Religion and Separatism, 1985-2000

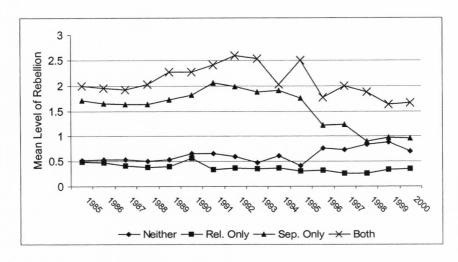

-Significance (t-test) between Neither and Rel. Only < .1 in 1991 & 1996
-Significance (t-test) between Neither and Rel. Only < .05 in 1997 & 1999
-Significance (t-test) between Neither and Rel. Only < .01 in 1998
-Significance (t-test) between Neither and Sep. Only < .01 in 1985-88
-Significance (t-test) between Neither and Sep. Only < .001 in 1989-95
-Significance (t-test) between Neither and Both < .05 in 1996, 1998, & 2000
-Significance (t-test) between Neither and Both < .01 in 1985-87, 1994, & 1997
-Significance (t-test) between Neither and Both < .001 in 1988-93 & 1995
-Significance (t-test) between Rel. Only and Sep. Only < .05 in 1998-2000
-Significance (t-test) between Rel. Only and Sep. Only < .01 in 1985-86 & 1996
-Significance (t-test) between Rel. Only and Sep. Only < .001 in 1987-1995 & 1997
-Significance (t-test) between Rel. Only and Both < .01 in 1985-87 & 1999-2000
-Significance (t-test) between Rel. Only and Both < .001 in 1988-98
-Significance (t-test) between Sep. Only and Both < .05 in 1998

can influence ethnic conflict, they do not always do so. Until 1980, there were no real differences in the levels of violence of religious and nonreligious conflict, after which religious conflicts became increasingly different. By 2000, the conflicts most likely to be violent were all religious conflicts.

However, religion is likely not the primary cause of ethnic conflict. This is because those ethnoreligious conflicts which do not involve separatism are consistently the least violent of all conflicts. Only when separatism is added to religion does it become a cause of ethnic conflict. Furthermore, nonreligious separatist conflicts, for most of the period analyzed here, are more violent than other nonreligious conflicts. In short, religion without separatism equals no conflict, separatism without religion equals conflict, and separatism plus religion equals more conflict (since 1980). This implies that separatism is a basic cause of conflict and, since 1980, religion has been an exacerbating factor. That the strength of this intensification of separatist conflict by religion has been increasing since 1980 does not change the fact that it is an exacerbating factor rather than a basic cause.

Nonreligious Causes of Conflict

While the analysis in the previous section produces some important results, it is necessary to remember that separatism, while likely a major, if not the major, cause of ethnic conflict, is not the only cause and is surely not the only influential factor. Rather, it is only one among many potential influences on ethnic conflict. Accordingly, in this section we examine the influence of multiple potential causes of ethnic conflict, other than religious causes. The religious causes are examined later.

The Variables

A number of factors are believed to cause or influence the course of ethnic conflicts. Below is a list of the factors examined here along with a short description of the reasons they are believed to cause ethnic conflict. In short, this list is taken from those variables that Gurr (1993a; 1993b, 2000) found to be important influences on ethnic conflict. A full description of the variables used here can be found in Appendix B.

As a general note, many of the variables used here were collected for various time periods. Some are general variables which change little over time. Others were collected for five-year periods, for two-year periods, or yearly. In the tests performed here the variable that is closest to the time period of the dependent variable but is not subsequent to the dependent variable is used. That is, if we are examining rebellion in 1993, for example, all independent variables in the regression would either include 1993 in their time span or have been coded previous to 1993.

Separatism: As discussed above, separatism is one of the basic causes of ethnic conflict. In this part of the study two variables are used to measure separatism. The first is the same as used in the previous section which measures whether or not a group is actively separatist. The second, *autonomy grievances*, is a more dynamic variable which measures in more detail the strength of a group's desire for autonomy. This variable was measured twice in the 1990s, once for 1990 to 1994 and once for 1995 to 1999.

Grievances: According to Gurr (1993a; 1993b) a fundamental element of ethnic conflict is ethnic grievances which are basically the public expression of complaints over various issues by ethnic minorities. The reasoning is that ethnic conflict does not occur without a political motive. This concept has it roots in relative deprivation theory, also developed by Gurr (1970), among others.[2] This body of theory posits that people rebel when they feel deprived relative to some point of comparison. This point of comparison can be another group, what they had in the past, what they believe they deserve, or some other standard by which they can measure their situation. While the theory originally applied primarily to economic issues, it has been expanded to include other political and social issues. Accordingly, three grievance variables are used here in addition to the autonomy grievances variable described above. First, *cultural grievances* measures complaints over cultural issues including the promotion of group culture, language issues, protection from attacks by other groups, and other cultural issues. While the original variable in the MAR dataset also included religious issues, this is excluded from the version used here because we account for this later in the analysis with more detailed variables. Second, *economic grievances* measures complaints over economic issues including access to public funds, land, jobs and resources, economic opportunities, and working conditions. Third, *political grievances* measures complaints over political issues including communal rights, participation in decision making, civil rights, and changes in public policy. All of these variables are measured twice, once for 1990 to 1994 and once for 1995 to 1999.

Cultural differences: This variable measures whether the cultures of the two groups involved in the conflict are different. It is posited by many that the more culturally different two groups, the more likely they are to conflict with each other. The measure is based on differences in ethnicity, nationality, language, historical origin, social customs, and area of residence. Like cultural grievances, religion is excluded from this variable because it is accounted for separately later in this analysis. The variable is coded once for the entire time period covered by the MAR dataset.

Regime type (polity): The setting in which an ethnic conflict occurs is important. This is because democratic governments behave differently from autocratic ones. For example, autocratic governments are less likely to have avenues available for minorities to express and address their grievances through legal channels than are democratic governments. The variable used here to measure this phenomenon is taken by the MAR dataset from the Polity dataset. It measures competitiveness of political participation, regulation of political participation, competitiveness of executive recruitment, openness of executive recruitment, and constraints on the chief executive.[3] This variable is measured for three years in the MAR data, 1990, 1995, and 2000.

Repression: The extent of government repression of political activities influences conflict in two ways. First, at sufficient levels, it restricts the group's ability to engage in conflict. Second, it can antagonize a minority and actually increase the extent of conflict. The variable used here measures twenty-three types of government activities, including: small-scale arrests of group members; large-scale arrests of group members; the arrest of group leaders; show trials of group leaders; torture of group members; execution of group members; execution of group leaders; reprisal killings of civilians; killings by death squads; property confiscated or destroyed; restrictions on movement; forced resettlement; interdiction of food supplies; ethnic cleansing; systematic domestic spying; states of emergency; saturation of police/military; limited use of force against protestors; unrestrained use of force against protestors; military campaigns against armed rebels; military targets and destroys rebel areas; military massacres of suspected rebel supporters; and other government repression. It is important to note that this variable is not specific to a single minority and, rather, measures government behavior against the entire population. This variable is measured yearly from 1996 to 2000 and, accordingly, is not included in tests involving rebellion before 1996.

International military support: International intervention is an important influence on ethnic conflict. In fact, few rebellions are successful without at least some outside support. The variable used here measures funds for military supplies, direct grants of military equipment, military training, provision of military advisors, rescue missions, cross-border raids, peacekeeping, cross-border sanctuaries, and in-country combat units. It is measured for the 1990 to 1991, 1992 to 1993 and 1994 to 1995 periods.

The spread of conflict across borders: The spread of conflict across borders is a modern phenomenon that is unique to neither ethnic nor religious conflicts. Gurr (1993a, 1993b, 2000) divides the spread of conflict across borders into two processes, *contagion* and *diffusion*. Contagion is when a conflict spreads through a region. Diffusion is the demonstration effect that antiregime activity can have for ethnic kindred living elsewhere, whether they live in bordering states or on the other side of the world. Each of these processes is included in our study. They are both measured for two time periods, 1985 to 1989 and 1990 to 1995.[4]

Mobilization: This final type of variable measures the influence of political organizing on conflict. That organized groups are better able to pursue collective objectives is not seriously challenged in the literature.[5] Two variables are used here to measure mobilization for rebellion. The first measures the number of militant organizations. The second measures the scope of support for militant organizations. Both variables are measured for the 1990 to 1995 period. For tests involving rebellion from 1996 onward, a variable measuring the change in support for militant organizations since 1995 is included.

The Analysis

All analyses in this section are performed three times, once for all 285 groups in the analysis, once for the 107 religious minorities, and once for the 178 other minorities in the analysis. This is in order to determine whether the patterns of conflict differ between religious and nonreligious minorities. For the purposes of the analyses performed in this chapter, religious minorities are those who belong to a different religion than the majority group in their state.

Two types of analyses are performed here. The first is bivariate correlation analysis which is designed to see which of the variables have an individual impact on rebellion. The second is multiple regression analysis which is designed to measure the combined impact of these variables on rebellion. In the multiple regression analyses, those variables which did not have a statistically significant impact on rebellion were removed from the analysis. In general this did not significantly reduce the extent to which the analyses were able to explain rebellion. This strength is measured by its Adjusted R^2 which is expressed as a decimal between 0 and 1 and measures the proportion of the variance in rebellion which the regression explains. Thus, this methodology allows us to focus on those variables which impact upon rebellion and eliminate those that do not.

All tests here examine rebellion in 1990, 1993, 1996, and 2000. While the rebellion variable was collected yearly for 1985 to 2000 and for every five-year period form 1945 to 2000, the analysis is limited to the 1990s because nearly all of the independent variables were not collected before 1990. Also, these four years are considered sufficient to examine whether the causes of rebellion change over time during the 1990 to 2000 period.

The correlation analysis between causes of rebellion and rebellion for all minorities, presented in Table 4.1, shows that most of the independent variables influence the extent of rebellion in the manner we expected. Separatism and autonomy grievances both cause more rebellion. Interestingly, the simpler variable of the two, separatism, which measures only whether or not a group is actively separatist is more strongly correlated with rebellion than the more dynamic autonomy grievances variable which measures the extent of desire for autonomy. This implies that it is more important whether or not a group is separatist than the extent to which the group is separatist.

Two of the mobilization variables, as expected, are strongly positively correlated with rebellion. However, the variable for change in time over support for militant group organizations is negatively correlated with rebellion. This implies that rebellion is more likely when group support for militant organizations is stable over time. The polity score shows that, as expected, rebellion is more common in autocratic regimes. Also, as expected, international intervention and the spread of conflict across borders contribute to rebellion.

The only result which is counter to expectations is that the cultural, economic, and political grievance variables as well as the cultural differences variable are not significantly correlated with rebellion except for weak correlation between political grievances and rebellion in 2000. This implies that the only relevant direct motivation for rebellion is separatism. Other political, economic, and cultural factors do not seem to play a role.

The results of the separate analyses for religious and nonreligious minorities, presented in Tables 4.2 and 4.3, are similar to the general results but are different in a few ways. First, the influence of separatism is considerably stronger for religious minorities. In fact, for nonreligious minorities the correlations are not significant for 1996 and 2000 at all. This is consistent with the findings presented earlier in this chapter that by the late 1990s separatism only influenced ethnic conflict

Table 4.1: Correlations between Potential Causes for Rebellion and Rebellion by All Minorities

Independent Variables	Correlated with Rebellion in			
	1990	1993	1996	2000
Separatism	.326****	.421****	.218****	.178***
Autonomy Grievances	.160***	.286****	.109*	.126**
Cultural Grievances	-.034	.048	-.070	-.095
Economic Grievances	.032	.054	-.048	.012
Political Grievances	.020	.087	.093	.107*
Cultural Differences	.029	.048	.027	-.067
Polity Score	-.198***	-.151**	-.100	-.146**
Repression	–	–	.466****	.686****
Int. Military Support	.381****	.511****	.503****	.397****
Contagion of Reb. 1980s	.325****	.165***	.246****	.218****
Contagion of Reb. 1990-95	–	.238****	.315****	.281****
Diffusion of Reb. 1980s	.125**	.102*	.089	.070
Diffusion of Reb. 1990-95	–	.266****	.214****	.139**
# of Militant Orgs. 1990-95	.518****	.553****	.471****	.496****
Support, Mil. Orgs. 1990-95	.570****	.671****	.490****	.511****
ΔMil. Org. to Year of Corr.	–	–	-.173***	-.135**

* = Significance < .1, ** = Significance < .05, *** = Significance < .01, **** = Significance < .001

Table 4.2: Correlations between Potential Causes for Rebellion and Rebellion by Religious Minorities

Independent Variables	Correlated with Rebellion in			
	1990	1993	1996	2000
Separatism	.379****	.504****	.405****	.352****
Autonomy Grievances	.173*	.356****	.242**	.292***
Cultural Grievances	-.061	.066	-.066	-.062
Economic Grievances	-.056	-.018	.010	.037
Political Grievances	.017	.143	.060	.116
Cultural Differences	-.020	.045	-.093	-.036
Polity Score	-.179	-.097	-.056	-.001
Repression	–	–	.507****	.680****
Int. Military Support	.295***	.453****	.521****	.451****
Contagion of Reb. 1980s	.268***	-.002	.110	.085
Contagion of Reb. 1990-95	–	.121	.197**	.173*
Diffusion of Reb. 1980s	.189*	.028	.086	.008
Diffusion of Reb. 1990-95	–	.229**	.129	.151
# of Militant Orgs. 1990-95	.437****	.493****	.485****	.461****
Support, Mil. Orgs. 1990-95	.507****	.653****	.543****	.491****
ΔMil. Org. to Year of Corr.	–	–	-.460****	.018

* = Significance < .1, ** = Significance < .05, *** = Significance < .01, **** = Significance < .001

Table 4.3: Correlations between Potential Causes for Rebellion and Rebellion by Nonreligious Minorities

Independent Variables	Correlated with Rebellion in			
	1990	1993	1996	2000
Separatism	.287****	.359****	.111	.069
Autonomy Grievances	.145*	.224***	.092	.058
Cultural Grievances	-.023	.028	-.070	-.117
Economic Grievances	.074	.085	-.074	.001
Political Grievances	.038	.052	.110	.102
Cultural Differences	.055	.035	.025	-.100
Polity Score	-.208***	-.177**	-.128*	-.228***
Repression	–	–	.466****	.708****
Int. Military Support	.436****	.554****	.496****	.369****
Contagion of Reb. 1980s	.366****	.289****	.347****	.310****
Contagion of Reb. 1990-95	–	.312****	.400****	.350****
Diffusion of Reb. 1980s	.064	.152**	.098	.114
Diffusion of Reb. 1990-95	–	.290****	.281****	.202***
# of Militant Orgs. 1990-95	.582****	.598****	.469****	.524****
Support, Mil. Orgs. 1990-95	.612****	.684****	.464****	.524****
ΔMil. Org. to Year of Corr.	–	–	-.021	-.221***

* = Significance < .1, ** = Significance < .05, *** = Significance < .01, **** = Significance < .001

Table 4.4: Correlations Between Potential Causes for Rebellion and Mobilization

Independent Variables	# of Militant Orgs. 1990-95			Support, Mil. Orgs. 1990-95		
	All Min.	Rel. Min.	Other Min.	All Min.	Rel. Min.	Other Min.
Separatism	.301****	.351****	.262****	.320****	.385****	.278****
Autonomy Grievances	.242****	.272***	.210***	.215****	.225**	.207***
Cultural Grievances	-.027	-.142	.041	-.002	-.086	.044
Economic Grievances	.143**	.049	.191**	.089	-.029	.146*
Political Grievances	.097	.076	.106	.088	.074	.094
Cultural Differences	-.002	-.059	.025	-.008	-.027	-.002
Polity Score	-.117*	-.003	-.178**	-.192***	-.134	-.220***
Int. Military Support	.515****	.279***	.673****	.483****	.176*	.649****
Contag. of Reb. 1980s	.325****	.281***	.356****	.423****	.162	.298****
Contag. of Reb. 1990-95	.336****	.339****	.328****	.278****	.239**	.304****
Diff. of Reb. 1980s	.205****	.018	.361****	.127**	-.028	.245****
Diff. of Reb. 1990-95	.223****	.054	.379****	.227****	.136	.383****

* = Significance < .1, ** = Significance < .05, *** = Significance < .01, **** = Significance < .001

Table 4.5: Multiple Regression for General Causes of Rebellion for All Minorities

Independent Variables	Regressions for Rebellion in			
	1990	1993	1996	2000
Separatism	.167****	.178****	(.021)	(.043)
Autonomy Grievances	(-.009)	(.055)	(.015)	(.062)
Cultural Grievances	(.000)	(.011)	(-.027)	-.106**
Economic Grievances	(-.004)	(.012)	-.107**	(-.030)
Political Grievances	(-.023)	(.014)	(.079)	(-.001)
Cultural Differences	(.050)	(.030)	(.053)	(-.040)
Polity	(-.036)	(-.027)	(.079)	(.061)
Repression	–	–	.311****	.578****
Int. Military Support	.115**	.221****	.294****	.142***
Contagion of Reb. 1980s	.197****	(.015)	(-.019)	-.161**
Contagion of Reb. 1990s	–	(.055)	.122**	.149**
Diffusion of Reb. 1980s	(-.005)	(.006)	-.100*	(-.026)
Diffusion of Reb. 1990s	–	(.059)	.138**	(.027)
# of Militant Orgs. 1990-95	(.104)	(.033)	(.072)	.178****
Support, Mil. Orgs. 1990-95	.403****	.479****	.156***	(.070)
ΔMil. Org. to Year of Regr.	–	–	(-.052)	(-.013)
df	284	284	284	284
Adjusted R²	.376	.513	.410	.545

* = Significance < .1, ** = Significance < .05, *** = Significance < .01, **** = Significance < .001
All values in table are beta values. Means are substituted for missing data. Values in parentheses were excluded from the regression due to the fact they proved to be insignificant. The values in the parentheses are what the beta of the variable would have been if it were included in the regression.

when it was combined with religion.

Second, regime type is only important for nonreligious minorities. Finally, while the spread of conflict across borders is correlated with both types of conflicts, it is more strongly correlated with rebellion by nonreligious minorities. These three trends imply that religious minorities are more influenced by factors internal to the group like their desire for separatism and that nonreligious groups are more influenced by external factors like the nature of the state in which they live and violence by groups outside their state.

One potential explanation for why many of the factors which are predicted to influence rebellion do not is because while they do not directly influence rebellion, they do influence mobilization for rebellion. That is, they cause people to organize and, as already shown, these organizations contribute to rebellion. This possibility is examined in Table 4.4 which correlates the predicted causes of rebellion with the mobilization variables. Interestingly, the causes of militant mobilization are very similar to the direct causes of rebellion. Except for a slight influence by economic grievances, the nonautonomy grievance variables as well as cultural differences do

Table 4.6: Multiple Regression for General Causes of Rebellion for Religious Minorities

Independent Variables	Regressions For Rebellion in			
	1990	1993	1996	2000
Separatism	.202**	.247****	(.111)	(.081)
Autonomy Grievances	(-.012)	(.087)	(.029)	.166***
Cultural Grievances	(.016)	(.097)	(.029)	-.119*
Economic Grievances	(-.055)	(.005)	(.055)	(.018)
Political Grievances	(-.076)	(.091)	(-.010)	(.004)
Cultural Differences	(.026)	(.031)	(.035)	(-.058)
Polity	(-.099)	(-.045)	(-.005)	(.054)
Repression	–	–	.418****	.609***
Int. Military Support	.148*	.242****	.274****	.256***
Contagion of Reb. 1980s	.174**	(-.053)	(-.042)	-.244**
Contagion of Reb 1990-95	–	(-.004)	(-.031)	.259**
Diffusion of Reb. 1980s	.154*	(-.051)	(.064)	(-.019)
Diffusion of Reb. 1990-5	–	.136**	.136**	(-.008)
# of Militant Orgs. 1990-95	(.032)	(.012)	.157**	(.119)
Support, Mil. Orgs. 1990-95	.361***	.462****	(.076)	(.058)
ΔMil. Org to Year of Reg	–	–	-.326***	.153**
df	106	106	106	106
Adjusted R²	.334	.524	.566	.575

* = Significance < .1, ** = Significance < .05, *** = Significance < .01, **** = Significance < .001
All values in table are beta values. Means are substituted for missing data. Values in parentheses were excluded from the regression due to the fact they proved to be insignificant. The values in the parentheses are what the beta of the variable would have been if it were included in the regression. Religious conflicts are those where the two groups belong to different religions.

not influence ethnic rebellion. Separatism is a stronger influence on religious minorities. Regime type only influences nonreligious minorities. Also, the spread of conflict across borders is stronger for nonreligious minorities.

The multivariate regression analysis for the most part provides similar results to the correlation analysis. The analysis of all groups, presented in Table 4.5, shows separatism to be significant in 1990 and 1993 but not in 1996 and 2000. Repression and international military support are consistently influential. At least one of the spread of conflict across borders is significant in each time period. Mobilization is significant for every regression except the one for 2000. However, regime type is not at all significant. Also, the nonautonomy grievance variables are sometimes significant but have a weak negative influence on rebellion.

The results of the separate regressions for religious and nonreligious minorities, presented in Tables 4.6 and 4.7, are also similar to the correlation analysis. Separatism is more important for religious minorities. The spread of conflict across borders is stronger for the nonreligious minorities. However, while as before, regime type

Table 4.7: Multiple Regression for General Causes of Rebellion for Nonreligious Minorities

Independent Variables	Regressions For Rebellion in			
	1990	1993	1996	2000
Separatism	.101*	.196****	(-.093)	(-.052)
Autonomy Grievances	(-.020)	(.014)	(-.052)	(-.009)
Cultural Grievances	(.021)	(-.013)	(-.046)	(-066)
Economic Grievances	(.028)	(.004)	-.285***	-.136***
Political Grievances	(.015)	(-.010)	.152**	(-.001)
Cultural Differences	(.072)	(.019)	.110*	(-.035)
Polity	(-.005)	(.024)	(.095)	-.143**
Repression	–	–	.302****	.609****
Int. Military Support	(.019)	.204***	.237***	(.029)
Contagion of Reb. 1980s	.215****	(.000)	(.068)	(-.059)
Contagion of Reb. 1990s	–	.106*	.208***	.114*
Diffusion of Reb. 1980s	-.190***	(-.027)	-.187***	(-.045)
Diffusion of Reb. 1990s	–	(.003)	.168**	(.003)
# of Militant Orgs. 1990s	.268***	(.032)	.136*	.160**
Support, Mil. Orgs. 1990s	.354****	.466****	(.055)	.150*
ΔMil. Org. to Year of Regr.	–	–	(.036)	(-.064)
df	177	177	177	177
Adjusted R²	.450	.523	.439	.585

* = Significance < .1, ** = Significance < .05, *** = Significance < .01, **** = Significance < .001
All values in table are beta values. Means are substituted for missing data. Values in parentheses were excluded from the regression due to the fact they proved to be insignificant. The values in the parentheses are what the beta of the variable would have been if it were included in the regression.

is not significant for religious, it is also not important for nonreligious minorities except in 2000.

There is also an interesting dynamic where some of the variables for the spread of conflict across borders have a negative influence on rebellion and others have a positive influence. In most cases where this occurs, in this and subsequent analyses, the dynamic has a variable for the spread of conflict in the 1980s being negative and one for the 1990s being positive. This means that the relevant influence is the change in the level of conflict in other states over time. Thus, if conflict in other states rose between the 1980s and 1990s, rebellion increases, and if conflict in other states dropped, so does rebellion in the state being analyzed.

In all, this section of the analysis establishes two important facts. First, nonreligious causes of conflict are important. Second, the dynamics of religious conflicts and nonreligious conflicts are not exactly the same.

Religious Identity and Conflict

The next logical step is to include religious identity in the analysis. Three religious identity variables are added. The first measures whether the conflict is between groups of different religions or not. The second two look at the combined impact of religion and separatism on rebellion. These two variables are included because of the finding earlier in this chapter that starting from the 1980s it is the combination of religion and separatism which produces the most violent conflicts. The first of these two variables multiplies the separatism variable with the religion variable using the following formula:

$$(\text{Religious Identity} + 1) * \text{Separatism}$$

We use this specific formulation because while separatism without religion causes conflict, religion without separatism does not. Thus, if separatism is at zero, it does not matter how high the religious identity coding is because there is likely to be little or no conflict. But if the religious identity coding is at zero, separatism may still cause some conflict. Thus, we add one to the religious identity variable so that if separatism is above zero, it will not be multiplied by zero. The same formulation is used with the autonomy grievances variable combined with the religious identity variable for the same reason to create the third religious identity variable.

The results of the analysis, presented in Table 4.8, confirm that the combination of religion and separatism is an important influence on ethnic rebellion. In all four regressions at least one of the combined religious identity and separatism variables are significant. These regressions also show the increasing importance of the combination of religion and separatism over time. In the regression for 1990, one of the combined religious identity and separatism variables is the only religion or separatism variable to be significant. In 1993, a combined variable and a separatism variable are both significant. This indicates that while the combined impact of separatism and religious identity are important, so is separatism on a separate basis.

In the 1996 and 2000 regressions, the combined religious identity and separatism variable remain important, but the dynamics of the individual variables for religion and separatism change. The religion variable is negative in both of these regressions. This, along with the fact that the combined religious identity and separatism variable is positive, means that when religion and not separatism is a factor, there is less violence, but when the two are combined there is more violence. The separatism variable is significant and negative for the 1996 regression only. This indicates a similar dynamic where separatism alone is not enough to cause rebellion, but the combination of religious identity and separatism is enough. These results are wholly consistent with the analysis earlier in this chapter which focused only on religious identity and separatism, without controlling for other factors.

It is important to note that the religion and separatism variables, whether in combination or individually, are not the only or even the strongest influences on

Table 4.8: Multiple Regression for Causes of Rebellion for All Minorities, Including Religious Identity Variables

Independent Variables	Regressions for Rebellion in			
	1990	1993	1996	2000
Different Religions	(-.029)	(.011)	-.166***	-.092**
Separatism	(.070)	.191****	-.237*	(.019)
Separatism * Diff. Religion	.170***	(.121)	.291**	(.027)
Autonomy Grievances	(-.005)	(-.122)	(.018)	(.094)
Aut. Griev. * Diff. Relig.	(-.013)	.085*	(.033)	.087*
Cultural Grievances	(.001)	(.005)	(.023)	-.112***
Economic Grievances	(-.008)	(-.033)	-.140***	(.034)
Political Grievances	(-.026)	(.006)	.086*	(-.012)
Cultural Differences	(.049)	(.017)	(.058)	(-.039)
Polity	(.031)	(-.045)	(.074)	(.049)
Repression	–	–	.298****	.577****
Int. Military Support	.115**	.219****	.282****	.141***
Contagion of Reb. 1980s	.198****	(.024)	(-.063)	-.165**
Contagion of Reb. 1990s	–	(.062)	.144***	.174**
Diffusion of Reb. 1980s	(-.011)	(-.002)	(-.088)	(-.016)
Diffusion of Reb. 1990s	–	(.049)	.092*	(.023)
# of Militant Orgs. 1990s	(.098)	(.019)	(.050)	.160***
Support, Mil. Orgs. 1990s	.403****	.475****	.143**	(.059)
ΔMil. Org. to Year of Regr.	–	–	(-.056)	(-.010)
df	284	284	284	284
Adjusted R²	.377	.517	.421	.552

* = Significance < .1, ** = Significance < .05, *** = Significance < .01, **** = Significance < .001
All values in table are beta values. Means are substituted for missing data. Values in parentheses were excluded from the regression due to the fact they proved to be insignificant. The values in the parentheses are what the beta of the variable would have been if it were included in the regression. Religious conflicts are those where the two groups belong to different religions.

rebellion. Factors like international intervention, the spread of conflict across borders, repression, and mobilization also play a role. Thus, while this analysis shows that religious identity is an influence on ethnic rebellion, it is not the strongest influence. It only causes more rebellion when combined with separatism, but when it is present alone, actually causes less rebellion. Also, other factors tend to be as or more important.

Another aspect of religious identity that needs to be addressed is the specific religion of the minority group. That is, are some religious minorities more violent than others? As in the previous chapter we divide religious minorities into three religious groupings, Christians, Muslims, and Others. Again, while the diversity within Christianity and Islam, not to mention the "Other" category is acknowledged, these larger groupings are necessary in order to have enough cases in each category for statistical analysis. Also, when using multiple regression analysis, as we do here,

Table 4.9: Multiple Regression for Causes of Rebellion for All Minorities, Including Religious Identity and Specific Religion Variables

Independent Variables	Regressions for Rebellion in			
	1990	1993	1996	2000
Different Religions	(-.029)	(-.048)	-.166***	-.092**
Minority Christian	(-.023)	-.095*	(-.070)	(-.021)
Minority Muslim	(-.027)	-.131**	(.016)	(.002)
Separatism	(.070)	(.080)	-.237*	(.019)
Separatism * Diff. Religion	.170***	.115****	.291**	(.027)
Autonomy Grievances	(-.005)	(.057)	(.018)	(.094)
Aut. Griev. * Diff. Relig.	(-.013)	(-.058)	(.033)	.087*
Cultural Grievances	(.001)	(-.006)	(.023)	-.112***
Economic Grievances	(-.008)	(-.032)	-.140***	(.034)
Political Grievances	(-.026)	(-.001)	.086*	(-.012)
Cultural Differences	(.049)	(.017)	(.058)	(-.039)
Polity	(.031)	(-.025)	(.074)	(.049)
Repression	–	–	.298****	.577****
Int. Military Support	.155**	.217****	.282****	.141***
Contagion of Reb. 1980s	.198****	(.016)	(-.063)	-.165**
Contagion of Reb. 1990s	–	(.047)	.144***	.174**
Diffusion of Reb. 1980s	(-.011)	(-.042)	(-.088)	(-.016)
Diffusion of Reb. 1990s	–	.072*	.092*	(.023)
# of Militant Orgs. 1990s	(.098)	(.038)	(.050)	.160***
Support, Mil. Orgs. 1990s	.403****	.466****	.143**	(.059)
ΔMil. Org. to Year of Regr.	–	–	(-.056)	(-.010)
df	284	284	284	284
Adjusted R²	.377	.525	.421	.552

* = Significance < .1, ** = Significance < .05, *** = Significance < .01, **** = Significance < .001
All values in table are beta values. Means are substituted for missing data. Values in parentheses were excluded from the regression due to the fact they proved to be insignificant. The values in the parentheses are what the beta of the variable would have been if it were included in the regression. Religious conflicts are those where the two groups belong to different religions.

there is no need to include a variable for all three religions. If two of them are included, the third is accounted for by the other two. That is, if a group is neither Christian nor Muslim, for example, it must be in the "Other" category. In fact, if variables for all three were included in the regression, the statistical software would remove one of them automatically.

The analysis which includes the variables for specific religions, presented in Table 4.9, shows that in three of the four regressions the variables are not significant. In 1993, the one year in which they are significant, the variables for both Christian and Muslim minorities are negative, meaning that in this year only the minorities in the "Other" category are the most violent. However, these results are weak and apply only to one of four years tested. Accordingly, the overall trend is that the specific religion of a minority has little influence on the level of rebellion in which it engages. This result is both consistent and inconsistent with the bivariate analysis of the MAR dataset in the previous chapter. The bivariate analysis showed that during the 1990s while Christian minorities tended to be less violent, Muslim minorities tended to be more violent. However, the overall results were generally confused and no uniform trend of any particular religion being more violent emerged. Thus, while some of the specifics of the analysis presented here are inconsistent with the analysis in the previous chapter, the general conclusions are similar.

Religious Causes of Ethnic Rebellion

The analysis presented above looks at the influence of religious identity on ethic rebellion. However, doing this only takes into account whether the two groups involved in a conflict belong to different religions. It does not deal with whether the conflict involves religious factors. That is, just because Muslims are fighting Christians, for example, does not mean that the issues in the conflict have anything to do with religion. Accordingly, this section deals with religious issues and other religious factors and their influence on ethnic rebellion in a subset of 105 conflicts from the MAR dataset.

All of these conflicts involve religious minorities which belong to different religions or different denominations of the same religion as the majority group in their state. They were selected from an earlier verison of the MAR dataset which contained 267 religious minorities and include all groups which met any of the following criteria: (1) the groups belong to different religions; (2) the groups belong to different branches of Islam; or (3) both groups are Christian but one is Catholic and the other Protestant.

As the data was collected for the 1990 to 1995 period, it is inappropriate to extend it too far away from that period. However, as there is little change in the codings from that period, it is fair to extend the codings five years on either end, thus allowing comparisons for the 1990 to 2000 period. It can be extended past 1995 because most of the relevant groups which were active in 1995 continued to be active until 2000. However, before 1990 many of the relevant groups, especially those in the former Soviet bloc, were not active, so extending the analysis to before 1990 is not appropriate.

The following analysis analyzes four aspects of religion: religious grievances, religious demands, religious legitimacy, and religious institutions. Religious grievances are complaints expressed over religious discrimination. Religious demands are demands for additional rights or privileges for a minority's religion. Religious legitimacy is measured here by whether or not the state has an official religion. Religious institutions are measured here as the extent to which religious institutions are formal ones.

Figure 4.5: The Influence of Religious Grievances on Rebellion, 1990-2000

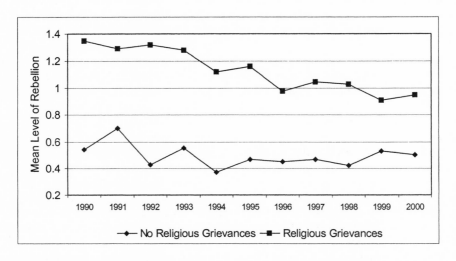

Religious grievances are considered to be present when the religious grievances variable > 1
-Significance (t-test) between Rel. Grievances and No Rel. Grievances < .1 in 1995-97
-Significance (t-test) between Rel. Grievances and No Rel. Grievances < .05 in 1990, 1993, & 1994
-Significance (t-test) between Rel. Grievances and No Rel. Grievances < .01 in 1992

The influence of all of these factors on rebellion are assessed independently and in combination with separatism. This is because of the dynamic discovered earlier in this chapter where religious identity and separatism have more influence on rebellion in combination than they do individually. Thus, we try to assess whether this is also true for the impact of religious factors and separatism on ethnic rebellion.

Religious Grievances

The same reasons one would expect other types of grievances to influence ethnic conflict, which are discussed earlier in this chapter, also apply to religious grievances. In short, groups that feel their religious freedoms are being restricted should be more likely to rebel against the government that is seen to be restricting those freedoms.

The variable for religious grievances is based on several types of more specific religious grievances, which include: nonspecific religious grievances; grievances over the right to observe religious festivals, holidays and/or other forms of public observance; grievances over the right to build, repair and/or maintain places of worship; grievances over the imposition of religious laws of other group; grievances

Figure 4.6: The Influence of Religious Grievances and Separatism on Rebellion, 1990-2000

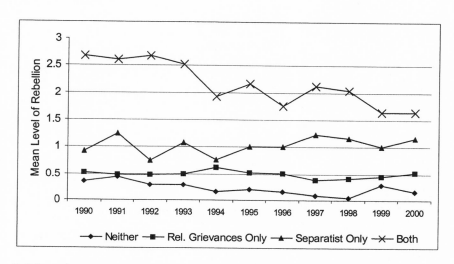

Religious grievances are considered to be present when the religious grievances variable > 1
-Significance (t-test) between Neither and Rel. Griev. Only < .1 in 1997
-Significance (t-test) between Neither and Rel. Griev. Only < .05 in 1998
-Significance (t-test) between Neither and Separatist Only < .1 in 1993 & 1995
-Significance (t-test) between Neither and Separatist Only < .05 in 1996 & 2000
-Significance (t-test) between Neither and Separatist Only < .01 in 1997 & 1998
-Significance (t-test) between Neither and Both < .05 in 1999
-Significance (t-test) between Neither and Both < .01 in 1994-98 & 2000
-Significance (t-test) between Neither and Both < .001 in 1990-93
-Significance (t-test) between Rel. Griev. Only and Both < .05 in 1994, 1996, & 1998-2000
-Significance (t-test) between Rel. Griev. Only and Both < .01 in 1995 & 1997
-Significance (t-test) between Rel. Griev. Only and Both < .05 in 1990-93
-Significance (t-test) Separatist Only and Both < .1 in 1991, 1993, & 1994
-Significance (t-test) Separatist Only and Both < .05 in 1990 & 1992

over the right to maintain formal religious organizations; grievances over the right to maintain religious schools and/or teach religion; and grievances over the right to ordain and/or have access to clergy. Each of these variables is coded on a scale of 0 to 3 based on the strength of the grievances. For more details see Appendix A.

For the purposes of this analysis religious grievances are considered to be present when religious grievances are coded as greater than 1 in order for there to be a sufficient number of groups in each category for meaningful comparison. Also, this filters out very low level grievances which a preliminary analysis shows do not significantly influence ethnic rebellion.

Figure 4.7: Combined Influence of Religious Identity and Religious Grievances on Rebellion, 1990-2000

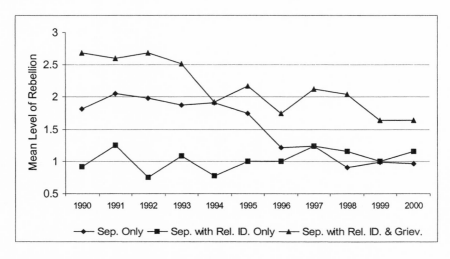

Religious grievances are considered to be present when the religious grievances variable > 1

The analysis of the impact of religious grievances on ethnic rebellion, presented in Figure 4.5, shows that religious grievances are associated with higher levels of rebellion and that this relationship has statistical significance for seven of the eleven years covered in the analysis. However, the relationship gets slightly weaker in the late 1990s.

The analysis of the combined impact of religious grievances and separatism, presented in Figure 4.6, shows a significant combined effect. Those minorities which are separatist and express religious grievances engage in the highest levels of rebellion. They are followed by groups which are separatist only, groups which are not separatist but express religious grievances, and finally by groups which are not separatist and do not express religious grievances. Thus, religious grievances and separatism add to each other's impact. That is, they both have an independent influence and the two influences can be added to reach higher levels of rebellion. But, at least for the first half of the 1990s, this relationship was more than just adding the two influences. Rather, the levels of rebellion by those groups which are both separatist and express religious grievances were much higher than one would expect if this were the case. In some years the level of rebellion by separatist groups who expressed religious grievances was about three times as high as groups which were separatist but did not express religious grievances.

When comparing these results to the results for separatist groups who belong to the same religion as the majority group in their state, presented in Figure 4.7, we get further evidence of the combined impact of religious grievances and separatism.

Same-religion separatist groups engage in less violence than do ethnoreligious minorities who are separatist and express religious grievances. Interestingly, ethnoreligious minorities who express no religious grievances engage in less ethnic rebellion than same-religion separatist groups. However, by the late 1990s the levels of rebellion by these two types of groups are nearly identical. This bolsters the trend documented earlier that by the year 2000, the most violent conflicts are those that combine religion and separatism.

Thus, in all, we see a profound impact of religious grievances on ethnic rebellion. The presence of religious grievances results in higher levels of rebellion. While this trend weakens by the late 1990s, another one emerges. Specifically, by the late 1990s it is especially the combination of religious grievances and separatism which produces the most violent conflicts.

Religious Demands

Religious demands are different from religious grievances in that they represent demands for more religious rights which are in no way connected to religious discrimination whereas religious grievances are precisely complaints caused by religious discrimination. Nevertheless, these religious demands provide a potential motive for ethnic rebellion because, like religious grievances, they represent a demand that the state is not meeting.

The analysis of the impact of religious demands on ethnic rebellion, presented in Figure 4.8, shows that until 1998 groups expressing religious demands engaged is higher levels of rebellion than groups who did not. However, for none of these years is the relationship statistically significant. The results are similar for the combined impact of religious demands and separatism, presented in Figure 4.9. The combined impact of religious demands and separatism is stronger than the individual impact of separatism until 1998, when whether a group expresses religious demands makes little difference in the levels of rebellion among separatist minorities.

Also, as presented in Figure 4.10, the level of rebellion by nonreligious separatist minorities is similar throughout the 1990 to 2000 period to the level of rebellion by separatist religious minorities who do not express religious demands. Thus, in this case, it is purely religious issues which add to the level of rebellion, not religious identity.

Religious Legitimacy

Religious legitimacy is posited to influence ethnic rebellion because religion has the ability to legitimize most political activities, including violence. Few dispute that this is the case. We measure religious legitimacy through the surrogate variable

Figure 4.8: The Influence of Religious Demands on Rebellion, 1990-2000

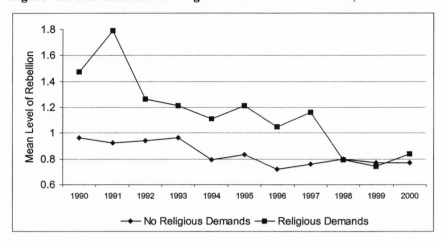

Figure 4.9: The Influence of Religious Demands and Separatism on Rebellion, 1990-2000

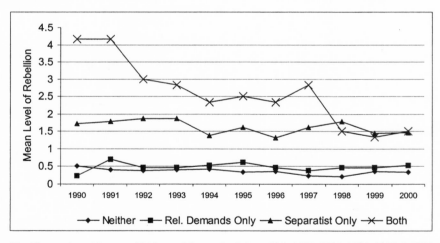

-Significance (t-test) between Neither and Separatist Only < .05 in 1990, 1994, 1996, 1999, & 2000
-Significance (t-test) between Neither and Separatist Only < .01 in 1991-93, 1995, 1997, & 1998
-Significance (t-test) between Neither and Both < .1 in 1992, 1993, & 1997
-Significance (t-test) between Neither and Both < .05 in 1990 & 1991
-Significance (t-test) between Rel. Griev. Only and Sep. Only < .1 in 1992, 1993, 1996, & 2000
-Significance (t-test) between Rel. Griev. Only and Sep. Only < .05 in 1990 & 1997-98
-Significance (t-test) between Rel. Griev. Only and Both < .1 in 1992, 1993 & 1997
-Significance (t-test) between Rel. Griev. Only and Both < .05 in 1990 & 1991
-Significance (t-test) Separatist Only and Both < .1 in 1990 & 1991

Figure 4.10: Combined Influence of Religious Identity and Religious Demands on Rebellion, 1990-2000

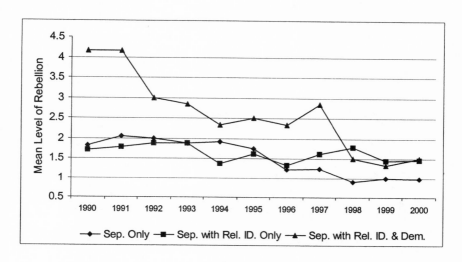

Figure 4.11: The Influence of Religious Legitimacy on Rebellion, 1990-2000

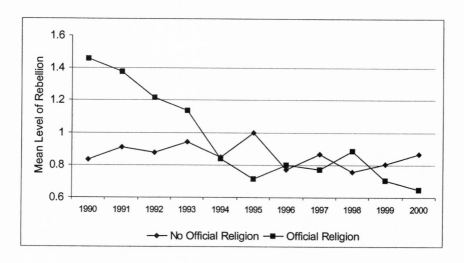

Figure 4.12: The Influence of Religious Legitimacy and Separatism on Rebellion, 1990-2000

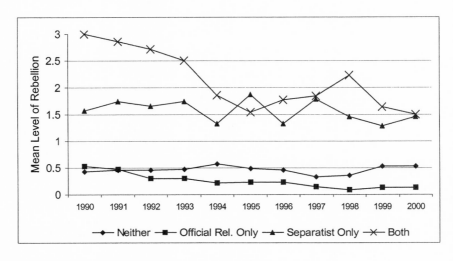

-Significance (t-test) between Neither and Rel. Legit. Only < .1 in 2000
-Significance (t-test) between Neither and Separatist Only < .1 in 1996 & 2000
-Significance (t-test) between Neither and Separatist Only < .05 in 1990-93, 1995, 1997 & 1998
-Significance (t-test) between Neither and Both < .1 in 1992, 1994, & 1996-98
-Significance (t-test) between Neither and Both < .05 in 1993
-Significance (t-test) between Neither and Both < .01 in 1990 & 1991
-Significance (t-test) between Rel. Legit. Only and Sep. Only < .1 in 1990
-Significance (t-test) between Rel. Legit. Only and Sep. Only < .05 in 1991, 1992, 1996, & 1999
-Sig. (t-test) between Rel. Legit. Only and Sep. Only < .01 in 1993, 1995, 1997, 1998, & 2000
-Significance (t-test) between Rel. Legit. Only and Both < .1 in 1996, 1999, & 2000
-Significance (t-test) between Rel. Legit. Only and Both < .05 in 1992-94, 1997, & 1998
-Significance (t-test) between Rel. Legit. Only and Both < .01 in 1990 & 1991

of whether or not a state has an official religion. We consider this to be an indirect indicator of whether the use of religion in political discourse is considered legitimate. Previous studies have found this to be an accurate indicator. (Fox, 1999b)

The analysis of the impact of religious legitimacy on ethnic rebellion, including the analysis of its combined impact with separatism and religious identity, presented in Figures 4.11, 4.12, and 4.13, all show the same result. This result is that until the mid-1990s conflicts in states which have official religion and are separatist were more violent. From the mid-1990s onward, religious legitimacy had little impact.

Religious legitimacy also influences the grievance formation process. That is, whether or not religion is legitimate influences the extent to which minorities complain about various types of discrimination. The link between religious legitimacy and grievances over religious issues is presented in Figure 4.14. As one would

Figure 4.13: Combined Influence of Religious Identity and Religious Legitimacy on Rebellion, 1990-2000

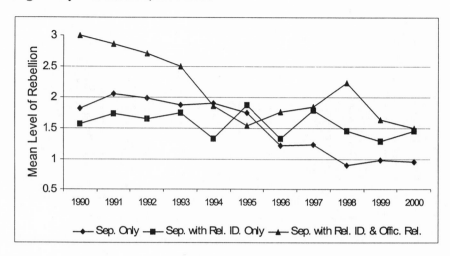

Figure 4.14: The Influence of Religious Legitimacy on Religious Grievances

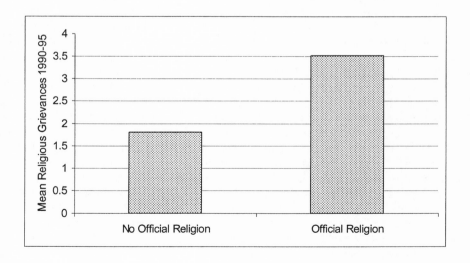

Figure 4.15: The Influence of Religious Legitimacy and Religious Grievances on Nonreligious Grievances

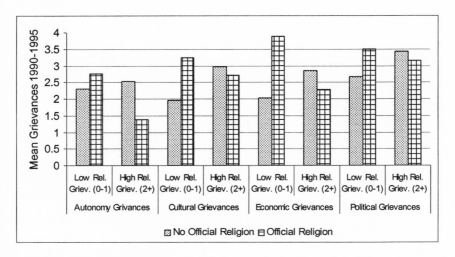

expect, when religion is legitimate in a state, religious grievances are higher. Thus, religious legitimacy facilitates the formation or grievances over religious issues.

The relationship between religious legitimacy and other types of grievances, presented in Figure 4.15, is more complicated. This is because it is related to whether religious grievances are expressed in the conflict. When religious grievances are not expressed, religious legitimacy facilitates the formation of all four types of nonreligious grievances which include grievances over autonomy, political, economic, and cultural issues. However, when religious grievances are expressed, religious legitimacy inhibits the formation of these types of nonreligious grievances.

One interpretation for this phenomenon provides some insight into the role of religious elites in mobilization. Religious elites have an interest in involving their religious institutions in mass movements in order to keep those institutions relevant. That is, if religious institutions are seen as part of a movement that is seeking the best interests of the group, this increases the importance of those institutions within the group. Thus, it is in those institutions' interests to facilitate group opinion over political, economic, cultural, and autonomy issues. However, if religious grievances are expressed by the group, this means that the religion itself is perceived to be at risk. In this case other issues become less important to religious elites than the preservation of the religion itself. Thus, religious elites inhibit the formation of grievances over nonreligious issues in order to bring focus to the religious issues at stake in the conflict.

Figure 4.16: The Influence of Religious Institutions on Rebellion, 1990-2000

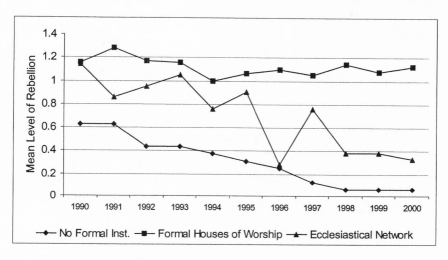

-Significance (t-test) between Formal and No Formal < .1 in 1993 & 1994
-Significance (t-test) between Formal and No Formal < .05 in 1992, 1995, & 1996
-Significance (t-test) between Formal and No Formal < .001 in 1997-2000
-Significance (t-test) between Formal and Ecclesiastical < .1 in 1999
-Significance (t-test) between Formal and No Formal < .05 in 1998 & 2000
-Significance (t-test) between Formal and No Formal < .01 in 1996

Religious Institutions

The direct analysis of religious institutions also shows that they can have a dual role in ethnic conflict. As presented in Figure 4.16, groups with no formal religious institutions (though they may have an official clergy) engage in the lowest levels of ethnic rebellion. However, it is not the groups with the most organized religious institutions–those with large-scale formal ecclesiastical networks–who rebel the most, but rather those with formal houses of worship that do not have many formal ties to each other.

This indicates that there are crosscutting pressures with regard to religious institutions and ethnic rebellion. On one hand, the presence of religious institutions seems to facilitate ethnic rebellion. This is logical in that it is generally accepted that any institution that organizes groups of people can be used to facilitate mobilization for political activities including rebellion. However, if that institution is tied into a large-scale formal network, this facilitation of political activity seems to be mitigated. This implies that religious institutions can also inhibit conflict.

One explanation for why religious institutions behave this way is based on crosscutting pressures within religious hierarchies. Many religious leaders,

Figure 4.17: The Influence of Religious Institutions and Separatism on Rebellion, 1990-2000

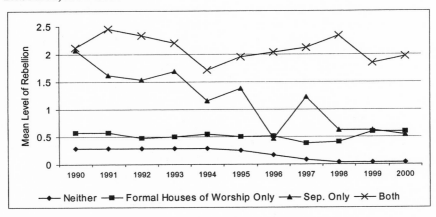

-Significance (t-test) between Neither and Formal Only < .1 in 1997
-Significance (t-test) between Neither and Formal Only < .05 in 1998-2000
-Significance (t-test) between Neither and Separatist Only < .1 in 1991 & 1993
-Significance (t-test) between Neither and Separatist Only < .05 in 1990
-Significance (t-test) between Neither and Both < .01 in 1990, 1993-95, & 1999
-Significance (t-test) between Neither and Both < .001 in 1991,1992, 1996-98, & 2000
-Significance (t-test) between Formal and Sep. Only < .1 in 1990 & 1993
-Significance (t-test) between Rel. Legit. Only and Both < .05 in 1990, 1994, 1995, 1999, & 2000
-Significance (t-test) between Rel. Legit. Only and Both < .01 in 1991-93 & 1996-98
-Significance (t-test) between Separatist Only and Both < .1 in 1999
-Significance (t-test) between Separatist Only and Both < .05 in 1998 & 2000
-Significance (t-test) between Separatist Only and Both < .01 in 1996

Figure 4.18: Combined Influence of Religious Identity and Religious Institutions on Rebellion, 1990-2000

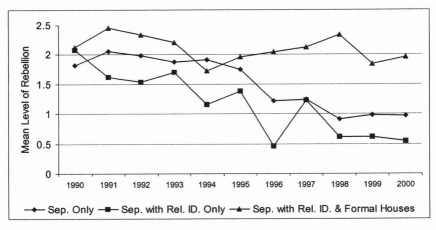

especially those closer to the people, often sympathize with their causes and want to help. Others may sympathize but feel that violence is not the proper way to address the issue. Others may even side with the government, especially if they derive benefits from government support. In a system where formal houses of worship are not organized into a larger network, the leaders of each individual house of worship can make this policy decision for themselves. Thus, in any given conflict where this type of house of worship is present, it is likely that at least some of them will side with the rebels and give them aid.

In cases where there is a formal ecclesiastical network, this decision is made at the top of the hierarchy and even if some of the more grassroots leaders oppose the decision the hierarchy can generally exert enough control to prohibit or at least limit the use of religious institutions in mobilization. It is also more likely that such hierarchies will wish to do so, as often these hierarchies are international ones which are more removed from domestic considerations. Given their unified status, they are also more likely to have political clout and have developed a mutually beneficial relationship with the state. Such arrangements generally involve state political and monetary support for religious institutions in return for those institutions' political support of the state.

Given this, in the analysis of the combined role of religious institutions and separatism on ethnic rebellion, we focus on whether or not the religious institutions associated with the minority involved in the conflict are unaffiliated houses of worship. The results, presented in Figure 4.17, show that the combined impact of separatism and religious institutions produces the highest levels of rebellion. Furthermore, this dynamic increases in strength over time. By 1998, separatism alone does not significantly increase the level of rebellion. The analysis of the combined impact of religious institutions and religious identity, presented in Figure 4.18, shows that this applies also to religious identity.

Multivariate Analysis of Religious Causes of Ethnic Conflict

While all of the above analyses are important, it is essential to evaluate whether these trends remain significant when accounting for the other causes of ethnic conflict discussed earlier in this chapter. Each of these factors is considered individually and in combination with separatism.

The results, presented in Table 4.10, confirm that religious factors influence ethnic conflict. The exact variables which influence the conflict change from year to year, but this is not surprising, as all of the religious variables are strongly associated with each other.

However, there are some interesting trends which should be discussed. First, when religious variables are significant, it is generally in combination with separatism. Based on the results presented earlier in this chapter, this is not surprising.

Second, in 1993 the only significant religion variable, the combination of

Table 4.10: Multiple Regression for Religious Causes of Rebellion

Independent Variables	Regressions for Rebellion in			
	1990	1993	1996	2000
Religious Grievances	(-.124)	(.002)	(-.075)	(-.047)
Religious Demands	(-.032)	(-.038)	(-.096)	(-.065)
Religious Legitimacy	(-.069)	(.047)	(-.014)	-.104*
Formal Houses of Worship	(.072)	(-.029)	(-.098)	(.011)
Separatism	(.041)	.438****	-.198***	(-.028)
Separatism * Relig. Griev.	.281****	(.088)	(-.033)	(-.010)
Separatism * Relig. Demands	(.063)	-.341****	(-.140)	-.344****
Separatism * Relig. Legit.	(.124)	(.116)	(-.004)	(.016)
Separatism * Formal Houses	(.013)	(.002)	.664****	.446****
Autonomy Grievances	(.004)	(.033)	(-.001)	(.076)
Cultural Grievances	(.015)	(.062)	-.127**	-.174***
Economic Grievances	(.045)	(.049)	.108*	.144**
Political Grievances	(-.014)	(.077)	(-.025)	(-.012)
Cultural Differences	(.109)	(.015)	(.063)	(-.005)
Polity	(.016)	(-.002)	(.058)	(.080)
Repression	–	–	.210***	.376****
Int. Military Support	.162**	.427****	.387****	.418****
Contagion of Reb. 1980s	.160**	(.007)	(-.043)	(.003)
Contagion of Reb. 1990s	–	(.048)	(-.038)	(.049)
Diffusion of Reb. 1980s	(.086)	(.029)	(.059)	(.000)
Diffusion of Reb. 1990s	–	.142**	(.070)	(.053)
# of Militant Orgs. 1990s	(-.049)	(.005)	(-.028)	(.037)
Support, Mil. Orgs. 1990s	.463****	.467****	.208***	.184**
ΔMil. Org. to Year of Regr.	–	–	-.250****	.106*
df	102	102	102	102
Adjusted R²	.517	.618	.674	.691

* = Significance < .1, ** = Significance < .05, *** = Significance < .01, **** = Significance < .001
All values in table are beta values. Means are substituted for missing data. Values in parentheses were excluded from the regression due to the fact they proved to be insignificant. The values in the parentheses are what the beta of the variable would have been if it were included in the regression.

separatism and religious demands, had a negative impact. It also had a negative impact in 2000. This is not wholly surprising, as of the religion variables this one had the weakest positive influence on rebellion in the analysis of the individual factors. As will be seen in the next chapter, one explanation for this phenomenon is that when this type of demand is expressed, it is usually in a state which is willing to accommodate a minority's demands if they are expressed through legitimate channels, thus making rebellion unnecessary.

Third, while in 1990 it is the combination of religious grievances and separatism which causes rebellion, in 1996 and 2000 it is the combination of religious institutions and separatism. This is also not wholly surprising, as in the analysis of the influence of individual religious factors on ethnic rebellion the influence of religious grievances declined over the 1990s but the influence of religious institutions increased over the same period.

Finally, other nonreligious factors also influenced the extent of rebellion, but there are some differences between this analysis and the previous one which accounted only for religious identity. The influence of repression, international military support, and mobilization remain strong in these regressions. However, the influence of the spread of conflict across borders is very limited. Conflicts are less likely if they involve economic issues. Also, conflict is more likely if the group has few cultural differences other than religion. That is, if religion is the only difference between the groups, religious issues are more likely to cause rebellion.

The Overall Influence of Religion on Ethnic Rebellion

The overall analysis of the role of religious factors in causing ethnic rebellion reveals that religious factors do play a role. However, the specific factors which play a role change over time. Nevertheless, this finding is important in that it shows that ethnic conflict between groups belonging to different religions cannot be understood unless taking religion into account.

However, it is also important to remember that religion is by no means the only cause of ethnic rebellion. Its influence is generally present only when combined with separatism, and a number of other factors also play a role. Thus, religion is unlikely a basic cause of ethnic rebellion and is rather an important intervening variable which can seriously exacerbate a conflict.

These results also shed light on the role of religious identity in ethnic rebellion. They show that while differences in identity may play a small role in facilitating ethnic conflict, much of the difference between ethnoreligious conflicts and other ethnic conflicts can be explained by the impact of religious factors other than identity. That is, the difference between conflicts which involve religious identity and those which do not is that religious factors, including legitimacy, institutions, demands, and grievances, do not come into play when there are no differences in religious identity between the two groups involved in the conflict. Thus, they only have the potential to exacerbate conflicts which do involve differences in religious identity.

This means that the analysis which shows that religious identity began to impact ethnic rebellion in 1980 and that this impact has steadily increased overtime must be reinterpreted. By implication, this result shows that religious factors were not important before 1980 and from 1980 have become increasingly important. This involves a deeper connection between religion and nationalism than implied by only a connection between separatism and identity. This is because this connection is not with identity issues but with the religion in question itself.

Thus, the entire picture produced by the analysis in this chapter of the causes of ethnic rebellion indicates that there is a growing influence of religion on ethnic nationalism which is responsible for the most violent ethnic conflicts of our era. Furthermore, this trend is new, as it did not exist before 1980. Thus, the role of religion in ethnic rebellion is not only an important one, but it is also becoming increasingly more important.

Religious Causes of Discrimination

Most previous cross-sectional quantitative studies of ethnic conflict in general and ethnoreligious conflict specifically focus on the behavior of minority groups. That is, the major research question thus far has been why minorities rebel or engage in other oppositional activities. This is illustrated by the fact that the major project which has gathered data on ethnic conflict, and one of the sources for data in this study, is titled the "Minorities at Risk" project and the studies based on this project have titles like "Why Minorities Rebel" and "Peoples Versus States." (Gurr, 1993a, 1993b, 2000)

However, the question of what motivates the behavior of the majority group has received, at best, secondary attention. That is, the focus of most quantitative research on ethnic and ethnoreligious conflict thus far has focused on the behavior of minority groups at the expense of examining the behavior of majority groups. This tendency in the literature is a gap which should be addressed, because it takes two parties to make a conflict and the dynamics of a conflict cannot be fully understood without an understanding of the behavior of both sides.

It is clear that it takes two to fight and that the extent to which ethnic minorities fight is measured by factors like mobilization, rebellion, and protest. The other side of the fight is generally a state government. The form of state government participation in ethnic conflict evaluated here is discrimination and repression. These actions are conscious policy decisions by governments to somehow restrict or repress ethnic minorities.

Four types of discrimination are included in this study. The first is cultural discrimination which includes the following: general restrictions on religious practices; restrictions on the use of the minority's language; restrictions on the use of the minority's language as a language of instruction in schools; restrictions on ceremonies; restrictions on appearance, including dress; restrictions on family life; and restrictions on cultural organizations. The second is political discrimination which includes the following: restrictions on freedom of expression; restrictions on freedom of movement; restrictions on organizing; restrictions on voting rights; restrictions on the ability to serve in the police, military, or civil service; and restrictions on the ability to be elected to higher offices. The third is economic discrimination which measures the extent to which the government has policies to restrict or improve the group's economic status. The final variable is repression which is described earlier in this chapter among the control variables for the regressions predicting the extent of ethnic rebellion.

These variables were codes for the 1990 to 2000 period only, except repression which was coded only from 1996 to 2000. Also, the cultural and political discrimination variables were coded biyearly until the end of 1995. That is, the years 1990 and 1991, 1992 and 1993, and 1994 and 1995 were coded jointly for these two variables. For purposes of using standardized figures, the data presentation below treats these two variables as if they were coded yearly for this period.

The focus of this section is on the religious causes of discrimination. We ask two questions. First, do religious minorities suffer from more discrimination than do other ethnic minorities? Second, do religious factors influence the extent of discrimination against ethnoreligious minorities?

Religious Identity and Discrimination

In this part of the analysis we examine whether religious minorities experience more discrimination than do other minorities. This is done by comparing the mean level of discrimination against each type of minority for the four types of discrimination examined here. The analysis for cultural discrimination, presented in Figure 4.19, shows that ethnoreligious minorities clearly suffered from higher levels of cultural discrimination than did other ethnic minorities, with this relationship having statistical significance throughout the 1990 to 2000 period. However, the gap in the levels of cultural discrimination narrows over the period analyzed.

The analysis for economic discrimination, presented in Figure 4.20, shows that governments discriminated more against religious minorities for the 1990 to 1995 and 1999 to 2000 periods, but these differences have no statistical significance. From 1996 to 1998 the levels of economic discrimination against ethnoreligious and other ethnic minorities were about equal.

The analysis for political discrimination, presented in Figure 4.21, shows that ethnoreligious minorities consistently suffer from higher levels of political discrimination than do other ethnic minorities. However, this gap is statistically significant only for 1990 and 1991. Also, the gap in political discrimination narrows considerably by the year 2000.

The analysis for repression, presented in Figure 4.22, shows that ethnoreligious minorities suffer from higher levels of repression than do other ethnic minorities. This relationship is statistically significant for the 1996 to 1998 period but not for 1999 and 2000. Also, the gap in repression narrows by 2000.

Overall, discrimination against ethnoreligious minorities is consistently higher than it is against other ethnic minorities. The only exception is economic discrimination in 1996 to 1998. While the gap in discrimination between ethnoreligious and other ethnic minorities is not always statistically significant, that it exists in thirty-five of thirty-eight of the years of discrimination and repression covered by these variables and is statistically significant for sixteen of them provides strong evidence for a clear pattern of higher discrimination against ethnoreligious minorities.

Figure 4.19: Cultural Discrimination against Religious and Nonreligious Minorities, 1990-2000

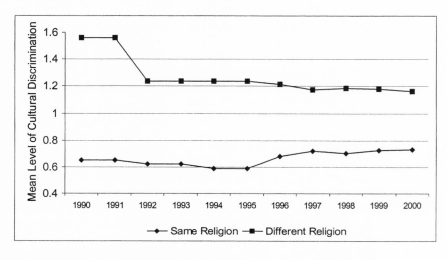

-Significance (t-test) between Same and Different Religion < .05 in 1997 & 2000
-Significance (t-test) between Same and Different Religion < .01 in 1996, 1998, & 1999
-Significance (t-test) between Same and Different Religion < .001 in 1990-95

Figure 4.20: Economic Discrimination against Religious and Nonreligious Minorities, 1990-2000

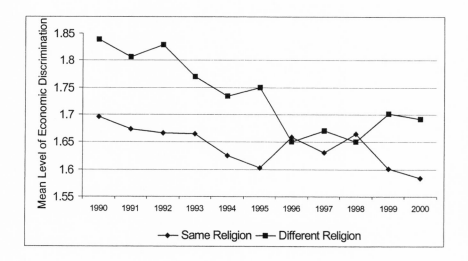

Figure 4.21: Political Discrimination against Religious and Nonreligious Minorities, 1990-2000

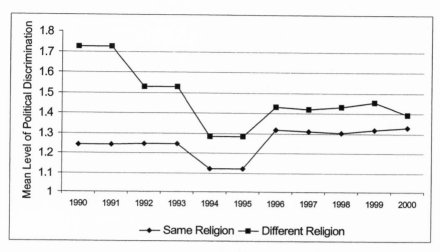

-Significance (t-test) between Same and Different Religion < .05 in 1990 & 1991

Figure 4.22: Repression against Religious and Nonreligious Minorities, 1996-2000

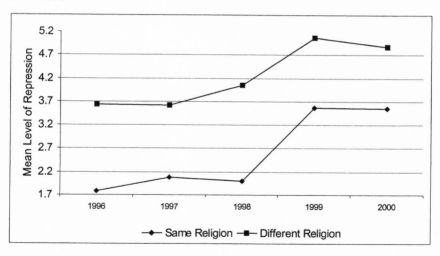

-Significance (t-test) between Same and Different Religion < .05 in 1997
-Significance (t-test) between Same and Different Religion < .01 in 1996
-Significance (t-test) between Same and Different Religion < .001 in 1998

Another fairly consistent pattern is that this gap was larger in 1990 than it was in 2000. In fact this is true of all four variables examined here. This is likely due to the general drop in levels of ethnic conflict that are clear from the earlier analyses of ethnic rebellion. That is, as minorities engage in conflict less, so do majority groups.

Religious Causes of Discrimination

While the previous analysis shows that ethnoreligious minorities are subject to higher levels of discrimination than are other ethnic minorities, it still needs to be determined whether or not this is due to religious causes. Accordingly, the following analysis examines the impact of religious grievances, religious legitimacy, and religious demands on the extent of discrimination against ethnoreligious minorities. Each of these variables provides a good indicator of whether religion influences the conflict. The presence of religious grievances and demands shows that the minority includes religious issues in their dispute with the majority group. The presence of religious legitimacy, which is measured by whether the state has an official religion, shows that religion is an important aspect of the state's political system.

While the primary analysis presented here involves only our subset of 105 ethnoreligious minorities, the results are compared to those for nonreligious ethnic minorities. This is in order to establish whether there is a difference in the extent of discrimination against ethnoreligious minorities in cases where religion is not important and against nonreligious ethnic minorities. If there is no difference, then this means that it is religious issues which cause the increase in discrimination against ethnoreligious minorities. If ethnoreligious minorities in cases where religion is not important experience more discrimination than do non-religious ethnic minorities, this indicates that religious identity also plays a role. As the mean levels of discrimination against nonreligious ethnic minorities were taken from the previous analysis, no tests of statistical significance between the results for this group and the other categories analyzed here were performed.

Religious Grievances

The analysis of the influence of religious grievances[6] on cultural discrimination, presented in Figure 4.23, shows that minorities expressing religious grievances experience significantly higher levels of discrimination than those groups that do not express religious grievances. This result is statistically significant and consistent throughout the 1990 to 2000 period analyzed here. Also, there is little difference in the levels of discrimination against groups which express low religious grievances and against nonreligious ethnic minorities.

Figure 4.23: The Influence of Religious Grievances on Cultural Discrimination, 1990-2000

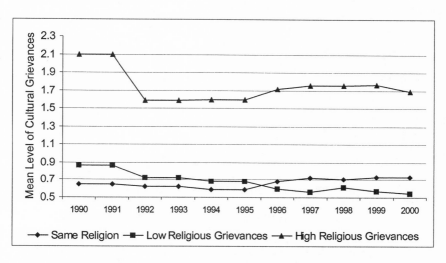

-Significance (t-test) between Low and High Rel. Grievances < .01 in 1992-95
-Significance (t-test) between Low and High Rel. Grievances < .001 in 1990, 1991, & 1996-2000

Figure 4.24: The Influence of Religious Grievances on Economic Discrimination, 1990-2000

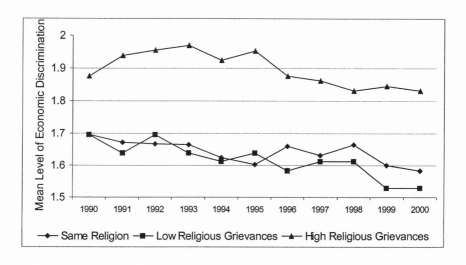

Figure 4.25: The Influence of Religious Grievances on Political Discrimination, 1990-2000

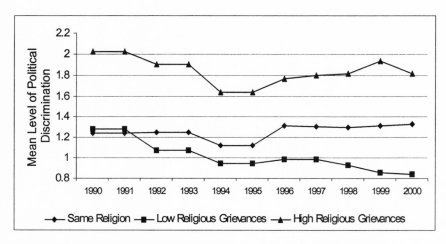

-Significance (t-test) between Low and High Rel. Grievances < .1 in 1990, 1991, 1994, & 1995
-Significance (t-test) between Low and High Rel. Grievances < .05 in 1992, 1993, & 1996-98
-Significance (t-test) between Low and High Rel. Grievances < .01 in 1999 & 2000

Figure 4.26: The Influence of Religious Grievances on Repression, 1996-2000

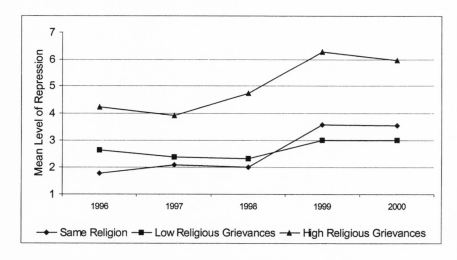

-Significance (t-test) between Low and High Rel. Grievances < .1 in 1996 & 1997
-Significance (t-test) between Low and High Rel. Grievances < .05 in 1999 & 2000
-Significance (t-test) between Low and High Rel. Grievances < .01 in 1998

Figure 4.27: The Influence of Religious Legitimacy on Cultural Discrimination, 1990-2000

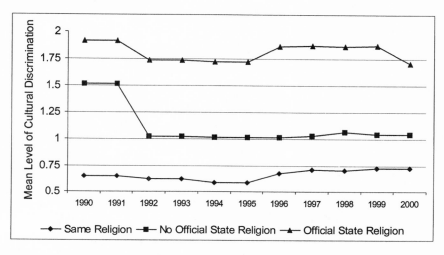

-Significance (t-test) between Official and No Official Rel. < .1 in 1990-95 & 2000
-Significance (t-test) between Official and No Official Rel. < .05 in 1996-99

Figure 4.28: The Influence of Religious Legitimacy on Economic Discrimination, 1990-2000

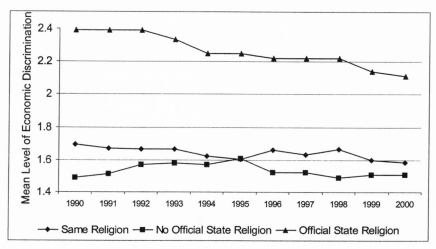

-Significance (t-test) between Official and No Official Rel. < .1 in 1990-93
-Significance (t-test) between Official and No Official Rel. < .05 in 1994-2000

Figure 4.29: The Influence of Religious Legitimacy on Political Discrimination, 1990-2000

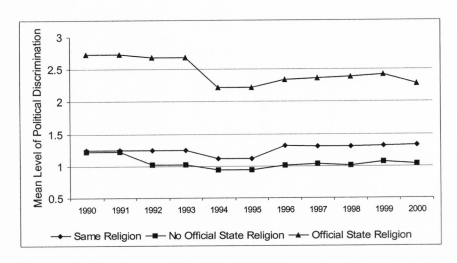

-Significance (t-test) between Official and No Official Rel. < .05 in 2000
-Significance (t-test) between Official and No Official Rel. < .01 in 1990, 1991, & 1994-99
-Significance (t-test) between Official and No Official Rel. < .001 in 1992 & 1993

Figure 4.30: The Influence of Religious Legitimacy on Repression, 1996-2000

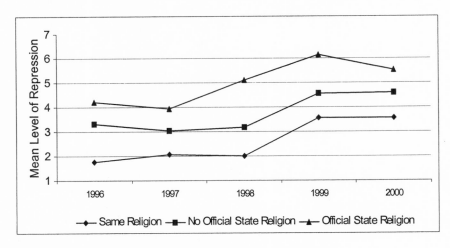

-Significance (t-test) between Official and No Official Rel. < .1 in 1998

The influence of religious grievances on economic discrimination, presented in Figure 4.24, produces similar results. Those groups expressing religious grievances consistently experience more discrimination. However, none of these differences is statistically significant. Also, as is the case with cultural discrimination, there is little difference in the levels of economic discrimination against groups which express low religious grievances and against nonreligious ethnic minorities.

The results for the influence of religious grievances on political discrimination, presented in Figure 4.25, are also similar. Those groups expressing religious grievances consistently experience more political discrimination than those groups which do not. These results are statistically significant for the entire 1990 to 2000 period. However, while there is little difference in the levels of political discrimination against ethnoreligious groups which express low religious grievances and against nonreligious ethnic minorities during the early 1990s, this is not true for the entire period. By 2000, ethnoreligious groups which express low religious grievances suffer from substantially more political discrimination than do nonreligious minorities.

The results for repression, presented in Figure 4.26, also show that ethnoreligious minorities who express religious grievances suffer from the highest levels of repression. These results are significant for the entire 1996 to 2000 period which is analyzed here for this variable. As is the case with most of the other discrimination variables, there is little difference in the levels of repression against groups which express low religious grievances and against nonreligious ethnic minorities.

In all, this shows that if the importance of religious issues in a conflict are measured by a minority expressing high religious grievances, it is religious issues and not religious identity which are the cause of higher levels of discrimination against ethnoreligious minorities. For most of these variables, those groups which expressed high religious grievances experienced the most discrimination and there was little difference in the levels of discrimination against nonreligious ethnic minorities and ethnoreligious minorities who expressed low levels of religious grievances. The one exception to this is for political discrimination in the late 1990s and 2000, where religious identity seems to also play a role.

Religious Legitimacy

The analysis of the influence of religious legitimacy on cultural discrimination, presented in Figure 4.27, shows that religious legitimacy does have an influence. Ethnoreligious minorities in states which have an official religion experience more cultural discrimination than do ethnoreligious minorities living in other states. This relationship is statistically significant for the entire 1990 to 2000 period examined here. Also, even ethnoreligious minorities in states which have no official religion experience more discrimination than do nonreligious ethnic minorities.

As presented in Figure 4.28, religious legitimacy also influences the levels of economic discrimination. Ethnoreligious minorities in states which have official religions suffer from more economic discrimination than do ethnoreligious minorities living in other states with this relationship being statistically significant for the entire 1990 to 2000 period analyzed here. Also, there is little difference between the levels of discrimination against ethnoreligious minorities living in states without official religions and all nonreligious ethnic minorities.

The analysis of the influence of religious legitimacy on political discrimination, presented in Figure 4.29, produces nearly the same results. Ethnoreligious minorities in states which have official religions suffer from more political discrimination than do ethnoreligious minorities living in other states with this relationship being statistically significant for the entire 1990 to 2000 period analyzed here. Also, there is little difference between the levels of political discrimination against ethnoreligious minorities living in states without official religions and all nonreligious ethnic minorities.

The analysis for repression, presented in Figure 4.30, also shows that religious legitimacy has an influence. Ethnoreligious minorities in states which have official religions suffer from more repression than do ethnoreligious minorities living in other states with this relationship being statistically significant for 1998 only. Also, ethnoreligious minorities in states which have no official religion experience more repression than do nonreligious ethnic minorities.

In all, the analysis shows that all forms of discrimination are higher against ethnoreligious minorities living in states with official religions than against ethnoreligious minorities living in other states. However, on two of four types of discrimination religious identity seems to play a role as even ethnoreligious minorities living in states with no official religion suffer from more cultural discrimination and repression than do nonreligious minorities.

Religious Demands

The analysis of the influence of religious demands on cultural discrimination, presented in Figure 4.31, shows that it has an impact. Ethnoreligious minorities who express religious demand suffer from more cultural discrimination than do ethnoreligious minorities who do not with this relationship being statistically significant for the entire 1990 to 2000 period analyzed here. However, both categories of ethnoreligious minorities suffer from more discrimination than do nonreligious ethnic minorities. It should be noted that the gap between ethnoreligious minorities who express religious demands and those that do not is greater than the gap between ethnoreligious minorities who do not express religious demands and nonreligious ethnic minorities.

The analysis of economic discrimination, presented in Figure 4.32, shows that religious demands have an influence. Ethnoreligious minorities who express religious demand suffer from more economic discrimination than do ethnoreligious minorities who do not with this relationship being statistically significant for seven of the eleven years analyzed here. Also, there is little difference between the levels

Figure 4.31: The Influence of Religious Demands on Cultural Discrimination, 1990-2000

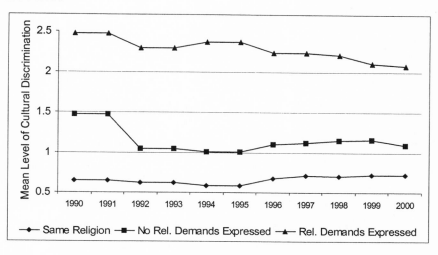

-Significance (t-test) between Rel. Demands and None < .1 in 1990, 1991, 1994, 1995, & 1999
-Significance (t-test) between Rel. Demands and None < .05 in 1992, 1993, 1996-98, & 2000

Figure 4.32: The Influence of Religious Demands on Economic Discrimination, 1990-2000

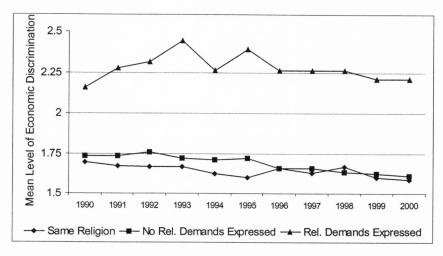

-Significance (t-test) between Rel. Demands and None < .1 in 1995-2000
-Significance (t-test) between Rel. Demands and None < .05 in 1993

Figure 4.33: The Influence of Religious Demands on Political Discrimination, 1990-2000

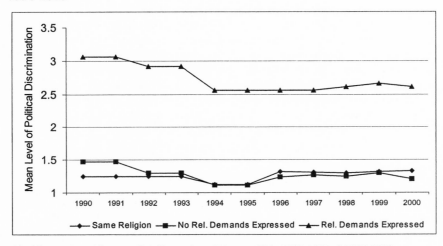

-Significance (t-test) between Rel. Demands and None < .05 in 1990, 1991, & 1994-2000
-Significance (t-test) between Rel. Demands and None < .01 in 1992 & 1993

Figure 4.34: The Influence of Religious Demands on Repression, 1996-2000

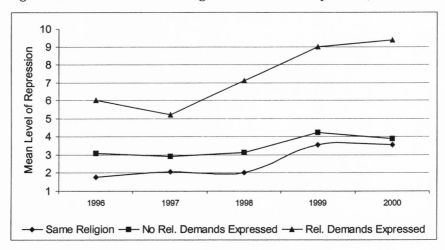

-Significance (t-test) between Rel. Demands and None < .1 in 1996 & 1999
-Significance (t-test) between Rel. Demands and None < .05 in 1998 & 2000

of economic discrimination against ethnoreligious minorities who express no religious demands and all nonreligious ethnic minorities.

The results for political discrimination, presented in Figure 4.33, are similar. Ethnoreligious minorities who express religious demands suffer from more political discrimination than do ethnoreligious minorities who do not. This relationship is statistically significant for the entire 1990 to 2000 period analyzed here. Also, there is little difference between the levels of political discrimination against ethnoreligious minorities who express no religious demands and all nonreligious ethnic minorities.

The results for repression, presented in Figure 4.34, show that religious demands also increase the levels of repression against ethnoreligious minorities. Ethnoreligious minorities who express religious demand suffer from more repression than do ethnoreligious minorities who do not. This relationship is statistically significant for all years analyzed here except 1997. Also, there is little difference between the levels of repression against ethnoreligious minorities who express no religious demands and all nonreligious ethnic minorities.

In all, the analysis for religious demands shows that it has a significant influence on all four types of discrimination and repression examined here. Furthermore, with the exception of cultural discrimination, this seems to be due to religious causes rather than religious identities. This is because on the other three variables there is little difference between the levels of repression against ethnoreligious minorities who express no religious demands and all nonreligious ethnic minorities. There is little difference between the levels of discrimination and repression against ethnoreligious minorities who express no religious demands and all nonreligious ethnic minorities.

As a whole, the examination of religious causes of discrimination shows that it is mostly religious issues and not religious identity which causes the increased levels of discrimination against ethnoreligious minorities. According to the criteria set earlier, if there is little difference in discrimination against ethnoreligious minorities in cases where religious issues are not important and against nonreligious minorities, we can conclude that it is religious issues and not religious identity which is causing the higher levels of discrimination.

As this is the case in eight of twelve tests performed here, it is fair to conclude that it is mostly religious issues which cause the disproportionately high levels of discrimination found by this study to be present against ethnoreligious minorities. However, in four of twelve cases ethnoreligious minorities for whom religious issues are not important suffer from higher levels of discrimination than do nonreligious ethnic minorities. This means that religious identity still plays a role in discrimination against ethnoreligious minorities, but a weaker one than do religious issues.

Religious Causes of International Intervention

Until now, we discussed the influence of religion on domestic actors in ethnic conflict. However, as shown in these analyses, international actors also play a role. In fact, international intervention is becoming more significant in world politics for two reasons. First, intervention has become easier than it was during the superpower rivalry during the Cold War. For example, if the United States wishes to intervene, it is no longer automatically opposed by the Soviets. Both interventions in Iraq, the intervention in Afghanistan, and the NATO intervention in Kosovo all would likely have been much harder, if not impossible, during the Cold War. Thus, the context within which intervention is considered has changed in that the decision to intervene is no longer tied up in Cold War calculations.

Second, this increasing ease of intervention implies that the nature of sovereignty is changing in the post-Cold War era. There are increasing limits to what states can do within their own borders because outside powers, especially when condoned by some international body, are considered justified in intervening under certain circumstances. These circumstances included humanitarian intervention (Cooper and Berdal, 1993; Carment and Rowlands, 1998) as well intervention in states that support terrorism. The latter type of justification for intervention has become even more important in the wake of the bombings of the World Trade Center and the Pentagon by Islamic terrorists on September 11, 2001.

The factors that influence intervention are by no means purely religious. One such factor is ethnic affinities. The emotional ties created by shared ethnic identity can create feelings of affinity and responsibility for oppressed kindred living elsewhere. A classic example of this is Israel's stated feeling of responsibility for the well being of Jewish diasporas throughout the world. Thus, the argument that "geostrategic interests of states can explain third-party intervention in ethnic strife . . . grossly underestimates the impact of identity-based linkages." (Carment and James, 1996: 421)

In fact, these ethnic affinities are so influential that they may be a cause of not just intervention, but also international war. Several studies have shown that the presence of an oppressed minority living in one state with ethnic affinities to the majority group in another state increases the level of conflict between those states. One well-documented manifestation of this phenomenon is the tensions between Pakistan and India over the mostly Islamic Kashmiri state of India. Even an influential ethnic minority living in a state can pressure that state to intervene on behalf of its kindred living elsewhere, especially if their support is necessary or even desirable for the politicians in power. The influence of the Jewish lobby on U.S. foreign policy could be seen as just one example of this phenomenon. (Carment and James, 2000; Davis and Moore, 1997; Davis, Jaggers, and Moore, 1997; and Vasquez, 1992)

It is arguable that religious affinities should similarly influence international intervention. That is, states should be more likely to intervene on behalf of minorities to whom they are religiously similar. Given this, religious affinities should make intervention more likely, if only as an important aspect of ethnic identity like any other. However, it is argued here that religion is not like other aspects of ethnic identity. Rather, it is one of the most influential aspects of ethnic identity as well as one of the most powerful influences on identity and behavior in general. The results of this study up to this point clearly demonstrate that this is the case.

However, it is also clear that ethnic and religious affinities are not the only factor that influences the decision to intervene. Nonethnic factors that have been linked to intervention by other studies include: the extent of internal disruption caused by the ethnic conflict; the extent to which the conflict spills over international borders, including through refugees and the extent to which the conflict inspires or is believed likely to inspire similar minorities elsewhere to oppose their government; a rational cost-benefit analysis by the interveners; the extent to which the ethnic conflict in question constitutes a threat to the core value of the intervener; the lower institutional constraints on the elites of the intervening state; the proximity of the intervener to the conflict; if the potential intervener is a regional or international power; if the conflict involves autonomy or secession; if the potential intervener has hegemonic ambitions; the extent to which the conflict is seen to threaten regional stability; "a sense of international responsibility, perhaps allied to some notion of world order or regional order"; "humanitarian concerns"; an interest in the parties and issues involved in the conflict; the character of international system; the size of the potential intervener; moral imperatives such as upholding human rights; transnational economic, military, educational, social, and political linkages; whether both the intervener and intervenee's governments are democracies; and the end of the Cold War. (Carment and James, 1996; 1998; 2000; Cooper and Berdal, 1993; Deihl, Reifschnieidr, and Hensel, 1996; Heraclides, 1990; Kegley, 1997; Khosla, 1999; Regan, 1996; 1998)

In the empirical analysis of this section we ask two questions. First, do religious conflicts attract more intervention? Second, is religion a factor in the intervention? For the purposes of these analyses we look at two types of intervention by foreign governments, political intervention and military intervention. Political intervention includes the following activities by a foreign state on behalf of a minority: ideological encouragement, providing nonmilitary financial support, providing access to external markets and communications, using peacekeeping units, and instituting a blockade. Military intervention includes the following activities by a foreign state on behalf of a minority: providing funds for military supplies, direct military equipment donations or sales, providing military training, the provision of military advisors, rescue missions, engaging in cross-border raids, providing cross-border sanctuaries, and sending in-country combat units.

The analysis of whether religious conflicts attract more intervention begins with the question of whether conflicts involving groups of different religions attract more intervention. This analysis, presented in Figure 4.35, shows that political interventions are about 50 percent more common in cases where the minorities are ethnoreligious minorities as compared to conflicts involving nonreligious ethnic

Figure 4.35: Intervention by Foreign Governments in Ethnic Conflicts Controlling for Religious Differences, 1990-1995

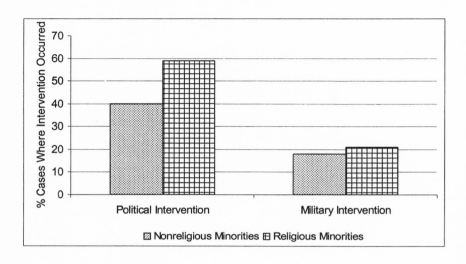

Figure 4.36: Intervention by Foreign Governments in Ethnic Conflicts Controlling for Religious Grievances, 1990-1995

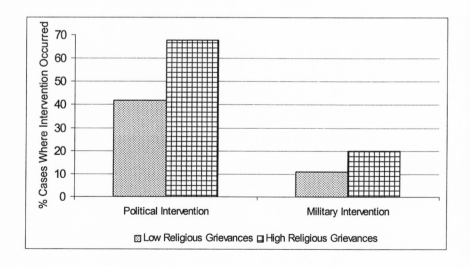

Figure 4.37: Intervention in Ethnic Conflicts Controlling for Religion of Minority Group

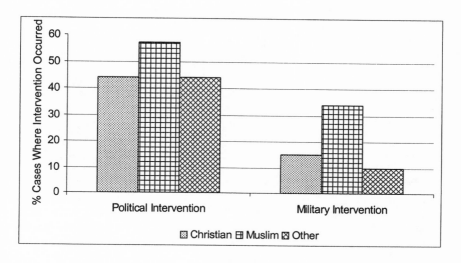

minorities. However, there is little difference in military intervention.

The second aspect of the analysis of whether religious conflicts attract more intervention, presented in Figure 4.36, examines whether among 105 ethnoreligious conflicts those conflicts which involve religious issues attract more intervention. For the purposes of this analysis ethnoreligious minorities who express high religious grievances[7] are considered to be involved in conflicts where religious issues are important. The analysis shows that both political and military intervention is more common in cases where religious issues are important. Political intervention is about 62 percent more common and military intervention is about 80 percent more common when religious issues are important.

The final aspect of whether religious conflicts attract more intervention is whether patterns of intervention differ according to religion. The analysis presented in Figure 4.37 examines whether Christian, Muslim, or other minorities attract more intervention. The analysis clearly shows that Muslim minorities attract more political and military intervention than do non-Muslim groups.

As noted above, religion is not the only factor that influences intervention. Accordingly, the following analysis evaluates the combined impact of religious and other factors on intervention in ethnic conflicts. Most of the control variables are the same as used in previous analyses in this chapter. Several of these variables are included because they measure whether the conflict is more intense on the theory that more intense conflicts are more likely to attract intervention. The direct intensity of the conflict is measured by the amount of rebellion and protest that occurred in the conflict between 1990 and 1994, the same time period for which intervention

Table 4.11: Binary Regression Predicting Whether an Ethnic Conflict Will Attract Intervention, Controlling for Religious Differences, 1990-1995

Variables	Intervention by Foreign Government 1990-1995	
	Political	Military
Religious Differences	(0.5752)	(0.0595)
Separatism	-1.8982**	(0.0595)
(Religious Differences + 1) * Separatism	1.0672**	(0.0014)
Minority is Christian	(0.2619)	(0.0017)
Minority is Islamic	(0.0683)	(1.0542)
Cultural Differences	(0.3957)	(0.0333)
Protest 1990-1995	0.1748*	(0.0698)
Rebellion 1990-1995	0.1368*	0.6732****
Contagion Protest 1980s	-1.4300****	(1.6154)
Contagion Protest 1990s	2.8499****	(0.6515)
Diffusion Protest 1980s	(1.0873)	0.3608***
Diffusion Protest 1990s	(0.9051)	(0.0470)
Contagion Rebellion 1980s	(0.8663)	(0.0101)
Contagion Rebellion 1990s	1.4980****	(0.0925)
Diffusion Rebellion 1980s	(0.1019)	(0.1228)
Diffusion Rebellion 1990s	(0.5241)	(0.0374)
N	262	262
% Correctly Predicted, Overall	68.32%	86.26%
Simulated R^2 (Nagelkerke)	.192	.446

* = Significance < .1, ** = Significance < .05, *** = Significance < .01, **** = Significance < .001
All values in table are real values. Values in parentheses were excluded from the regression due to the fact they proved to be insignificant. The values in the parentheses are what the value of the variable would have been if it were included in the regression.

is measured. Separatism and combined separatism and religion variables are used because these conflicts tend to be more violent. Several variables for the spread of conflict across borders are used because when conflicts spread across borders, they are more of an international issue and, thus, more likely to attract intervention. Finally, the analysis controls for the specific religion of the minority group. As the dependent variables in these analyses have only two possible values, an intervention occurred or it did not, binary regressions are used.

The analysis of the causes of intervention for all ethnic groups, presented in Table 4.11, shows that religious differences are important for political intervention but not military intervention. This is consistent with the analysis presented above. The analysis of the causes of intervention for ethnoreligious minorities, presented in Table 4.12, shows that religious variables are important for both political and military intervention. This is also consistent with the analysis presented above.

The next stage of the analysis examines whether religion influences states' decisions to intervene. That religious conflicts attract more intervention certainly

Table 4.12: Binary Regression Predicting Whether an Ethnoreligious Conflict Will Attract Intervention, Controlling for Religious Grievances, 1990-1995

Variables	Intervention by Foreign Government 1990-1995	
	Political	Military
Religious Grievances	0.3492**	(0.3253)
Separatism	(0.0308)	(0.0456)
(Religious Grievances + 1) * Separatism	(0.0118)	-0.8707*
Autonomy Grievances	(0.2979)	-0.4582
(Autonomy Grievances + 1) * Separatism	-0.1078***	0.2130**
Minority is Christian	(1.7944)	(0.9068)
Minority is Islamic	(0.8730)	(0.0153)
Cultural Differences	(0.0821)	(1.7353)
Protest 1990-1995	0.5615**	(0.0037)
Rebellion 1990-1995	0.3416**	0.8093****
Contagion Protest 1980s	(1.8747)	-4.5667***
Contagion Protest 1990s	-1.5130***	12.1120****
Diffusion Protest 1980s	(0.6441)	(0.2340)
Diffusion Protest 1990s	(0.4992)	(0.0428)
Contagion Rebellion 1980s	(0.9873)	1.3572*
Contagion Rebellion 1990s	1.6586**	(0.7653)
Diffusion Rebellion 1980s	(0.4004)	(0.1753)
Diffusion Rebellion 1990s	(1.7590)	(0.9875)
N	93	93
% Correctly Predicted, Overall	75.00%	91.67%
Simulated R^2 (Nagelkerke)	.398	.579

* = Significance < .1, ** = Significance < .05, *** = Significance < .01, **** = Significance < .001
All values in table are real values. Values in parentheses were excluded from the regression due to the fact they proved to be insignificant. The values in the parentheses are what the value of the variable would have been if it were included in the regression.

implies that this is the case, but it is only an implication. Accordingly, we examine whether states intervene more often on behalf of minorities who share the same religion as the majority group in the intervening state.

It is important to note that, while the MAR dataset does not contain the identities of the foreign governments which intervened in these conflicts, this information was collected by the MAR project. Accordingly, I obtained copies of the relevant part of the MAR code sheets in order to identify those foreign governments that intervened in ethnic conflicts. As many as four different interveners were coded for each minority. Also, many ethnic minorities experienced no interventions. Accordingly, the analyses based on the identities of the interveners use an intervener in a conflict as the basis of the analysis. This means that this part of the analysis looks only at those instances where interventions took place, and if a single conflict attracted more than one intervener it is included in the table once for each intervener.

Figure 4.38: Religious Affinities between Interveners and Intervenees, 1990-1995

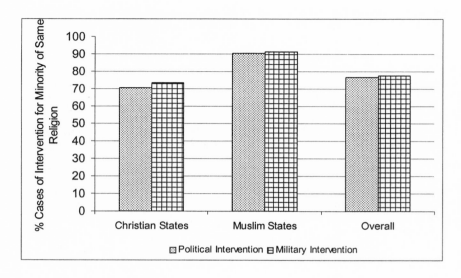

This part of the study is subject to an important limitation: that multivariate analysis is not feasible on this portion of the data. This is because when asking when and why a state intervenes, one is also asking when and why a state does not intervene. Unfortunately, it is only possible to code those interventions which did occur and not those which failed to occur. Thus, we only have data on those cases where intervention occurred. In order to execute a multivariate analysis we need a dependent variable with at least two possible values. Ideally, in order to ask why specific states intervene in specific conflicts, we would need one with two values: (1) that the state intervened and (2) that it did not. Since all of the interveners for which we have data fit into the first category, a multivariate analysis examining the characteristics of the intervener is not possible.

The analysis, presented in Figure 4.38, shows that in general states intervene most often on behalf of minorities religiously similar to them. It also shows that this trend is strongest for Muslim states. This helps to explain the earlier finding that Muslim minorities attract more intervention.

In all, the analysis shows that religious factors do influence whether intervention occurs. Both religious identity and religious issues influence political intervention and religious issues influence military intervention. It also shows that states prefer to intervene on behalf of minorities religiously similar to them. All of this combined provides considerable evidence that religion is a strong influence on international intervention.

Conclusions

In all, the results presented in this chapter clearly show that religion influences all aspects of ethnic conflict. It is among the causes of rebellion by ethnoreligious minorities. It strongly influences discrimination by ethnic majority groups who control state governments. It also influences international intervention in ethnic conflict. Thus, all three potential players in ethnic conflicts, majority groups, minority groups, and international actors, are influenced by religion. Furthermore, even the general dynamics of ethnoreligious conflicts differ from those of other ethnic conflicts.

A cursory analysis shows that religious identity– whether the conflict involves two groups who belong to different religions–influences the conflict. However, a deeper analysis shows that it is religious factors like religious grievances, religious demands, religious institutions, and religious legitimacy which account for most of religion's influence on ethnic conflict. Nevertheless, religious identity still plays a minor role, even if it is a much weaker one than is played by religious factors.

However, this influence is not by any means total or monolithic. In fact, religion is rarely the only cause or even the strongest cause of ethnic conflict. Other factors like separatism, international intervention, repression, mobilization, and the spread of conflict across borders influence ethnic conflict. In most of the multivariate analyses these factors proved to be more important determinants of ethnic conflict than did religion variables.

The extent to which this is true cannot be understated. For example, when religion influenced ethnic rebellion it only did so in combination with separatism. In fact, unless a minority was separatist, religious variables, if anything, were associated with lower levels of rebellion. However, when a group was separatist, religion often exacerbated the conflict. Thus, it can be concluded that rather than being a basic cause of ethnic conflict, religion is an important intervening variable.

Another important finding is that the impact of religion on ethnic conflict changed over time. For example, until 1980 religion had no impact on ethnic rebellion even in combination with separatism. But, since 1980 religion has been steadily becoming a more important influence on ethnic conflict and the impact of separatism has been declining. Beginning in 1980 the combination of religion and separatism created more violent conflicts than did separatism alone. This phenomenon increased in strength throughout the next twenty years. By 2000, only the combination of religion and separatism resulted in more violent conflicts. Separatism alone had little impact.

This particular result has wider importance and is perhaps the most important individual result presented in this chapter. This is because it documents a change in the nature of nationalism. Until 1980 nationalism, or at least the type of nationalism which caused violent domestic conflict, was a secular one. Around 1980 this began to change and the most violent nationalist conflicts involved religious nationalism. By 2000, secular nationalist conflicts became relatively calm and only religious nationalist conflicts were violent. Thus, the last two decades of the twentieth century saw a clear rise in religious nationalism and a fall in secular nationalism.

This rise in religious nationalism supports the arguments described in Chapter 2 that modernity is causing a resurgence or revitalization of religion. It also coincides with non-ethnic phenomena like the Iranian revolution and the rise of religious fundamentalism. This latter trend is cross-religious and includes the rise of the religious right in the United States, Hindu nationalism in India, Buddhist nationalism in Sri Lanka, and political Islam throughout the globe. Thus, it is likely part of a much larger pattern of the increasing importance of religion in world politics.

Notes

1. See, for example, Borntrager (1999: 72-73) and Young (1997: 47, 59).
2. See, for example, Davies (1962), Feierabend and Feierabend (1973), Lichbach (1989), Olson (1963), and Rule (1988).
3. For more details on the Polity dataset see Jaggers and Gurr (1995) and the Polity website at www.cidcm.umd.edu/inscr/.
4. Previous empirical studies including those of Ayres and Saideman (2000), Saideman and Ayres (2000), Gurr (2000: 232-236), Hill and Rothchild (1986), and Hill, Rothchild, and Cameron (1998) confirm that contagion and diffusion influence conflict.
5. For more details on mobilization theory see, among others, Chong (1991), Rule (1988), and Tilly (1978).
6. For the purposes of this section of the study, religious grievances are coded as high if the original variable is coded as 2 or higher.
7. See previous note.

Chapter 5

Religious Causes of Ethnic Protest

The previous two chapters examine the nexus between religion and violence. Yet not all disputes are violent ones. Accordingly, this chapter analyzes the link between religion and nonviolent conflict. More specifically, it deals with religious causes of nonviolent ethnic protest.

The theoretical reasons to believe that religion can influence mass protest are the same as those that posit a connection between religion and violence. In fact, the general causes of ethnic protest are also similar to the general causes of ethnic violence. It is simply the case that a number of factors, including regime type, opportunity, and group power, affect whether ethnic conflicts manifest themselves as violent conflict or nonviolent political organizing and activities. However, the specific dynamics can often differ. Thus, a separate examination of how religion influences ethnic protest is in order.

As is the case with the previous chapter, the analysis presented here is limited to the MAR dataset. This is because the SF dataset does not contain information on mass protest. Thus, the empirical analysis presented here focuses on the 337 ethnic minorities contained in the dataset with particular attention given to the subset of 105 ethnoreligious minorities for which more specific data on religion was collected. The analyses for this subset of 105 groups are limited to the 1990s onward for the same reasons as described in the previous chapter.

Given this, the operational definition of protest for this chapter is based on the definition used by the MAR project which is implicit in the way its protest variable is coded. Protest includes demonstrations attended by either a small or large number of people as well as verbal opposition and symbolic protest acts by ethnic group members. This definition intentionally focuses on the nonviolent facets of political contention between ethnic groups in a society.

This chapter proceeds in several stages. First, it examines whether protest among ethnoreligious minorities is more common or intense than protest by other ethnic minorities. Second, it examines whether specific minorities engage in different levels of protest. Third, it examines the combined impact of religion and separatism on protest. Fourth, it examines the causes of protest using multivariate methodology. Finally, it examines the impact of religious factors like religious discrimination, grievances, legitimacy, and institutions on ethnic protest.

Do Ethnoreligious Minorities Engage in More Protest?

This section examines the question of whether protest among ethnoreligious minorities is more common or intense than protest by other ethnic minorities since 1945. The first aspect of this question which is examined here is whether ethnoreligious minorities or other ethnic minorities are more likely to engage in protest. The results, presented in Figures 5.1 and 5.2, show that there is little difference between the two groups. The results for 1945 to 2000 show that which type of group is more likely to protest varies from year to year with the gap between them generally being small. The yearly results for 1985 to 2000 show that ethnoreligious minorities were more likely to protest between 1985 and 1995, following which their likelihood of protesting was nearly identical to those of nonreligious ethnic minorities. However, the gap between ethnoreligious minorities and other ethnic minorities during this period in the 1945 to 2000 analysis, while also showing that ethnoreligious minorities were more likely to protest, is no greater than in other periods. Also, in many parts of the 1945 to 2000 analysis nonreligious ethnic minorities are more likely to engage in protest. Thus, there results show no long-term difference in the propensity of ethnoreligious minorities and other ethnic minorities to protest.

The next question to be asked here is, among the sample of 105 religious minorities for which more detailed religion data is available, does whether religion is relevant to the conflict[1] influence the extent of protest? The answer, presented in Figures 5.3 and 5.4, is "No." Both in the 1945 to 2000 and 1995 to 2000 analyses, whether religion is relevant to the conflict makes little difference in the likelihood of protest by religious minorities.

The third aspect of whether ethnoreligious minorities protest more is whether their protests are more intense than those of other ethnic minorities. The analysis, presented in Figures 5.5 and 5.6, shows that the mean levels of protest by both types of groups are similar. In the few cases where there is a statistically significant difference between the two types of group, nonreligious ethnic minorities engage in higher levels of protest.

The final analysis of this section, presented in Figures 5.7 and 5.8, examines whether the relevance of religion to a conflict[2] influences the extent of protest by ethnoreligious minorities. The results show that there is no statistically significant difference between the two categories.

Figure 5.1: Percentage of Minorities Who Protest, Controlling for Religion, 1945-2000

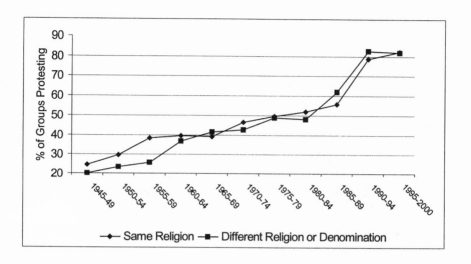

Figure 5.2: Percentage of Minorities Who Protest, Controlling for Religion, 1985-2000

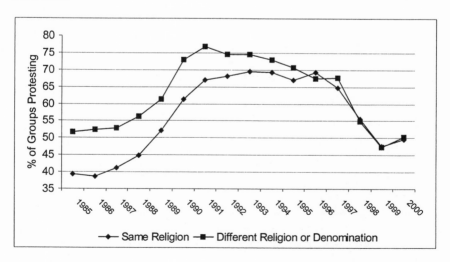

Figure 5.3: Percentage of Religious Minorities Who Protest, Controlling for Relevance of Religion, 1945-2000

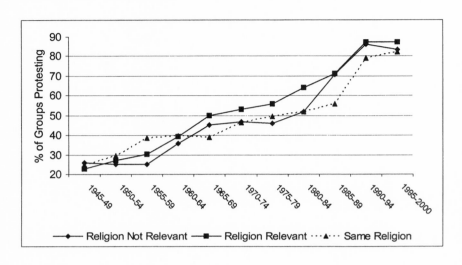

Figure 5.4: Percentage of Religious Minorities Who Protest, Controlling for Relevance of Religion, 1985-2000

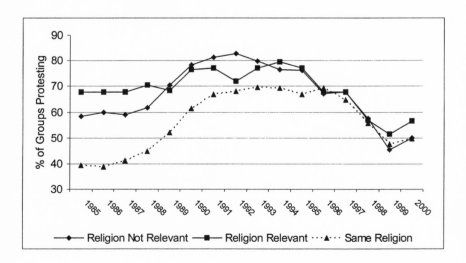

Figure 5.5: Mean Levels of Protest, Controlling for Religion, 1945-2000

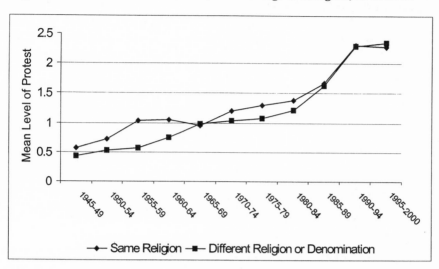

-Significance (t-test) between Same Relig. and Different Relig. and Denom. < .1 in 1960-64
-Significance (t-test) between Same Relig. and Different Relig. and Denom. < .01 in 1955-59

Figure 5.6: Mean Levels of Protest, Controlling for Religion, 1985-2000

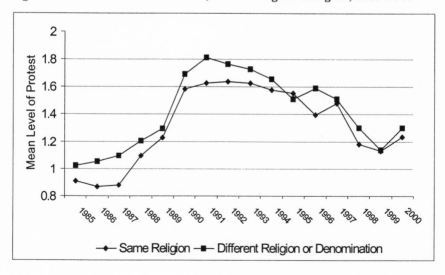

Figure 5.7: Mean Levels of Protest by Religious Minorities, Controlling for Relevance of Religion, 1945-2000

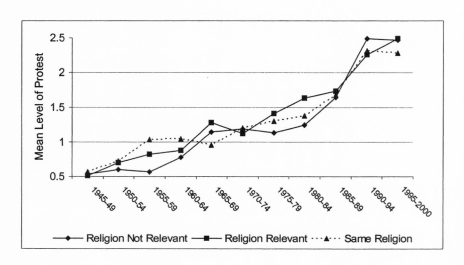

Figure 5.8: Mean Levels of Protest by Religious Minorities, Controlling for Relevance of Religion, 1985-2000

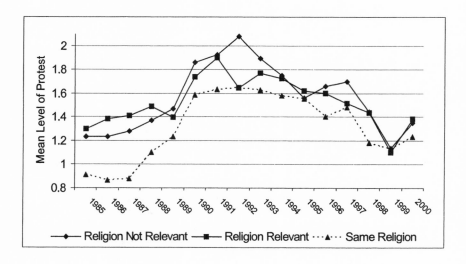

Protest by Minorities of Specific Religions

The question of whether minorities of specific religions engage in more protest is also an important one. As described in Chapter 2, there is some dispute over whether certain minorities engage in higher levels of conflict. As protest is a form of conflict, this dispute also applies to protest. As is the case with other analyses in this book focusing on specific religions, the categories examined are Christian groups, Muslim groups, and other groups. While this is not to deny the diversity among groups within these categories, it is necessary to use these more general categories in order to have enough cases for analysis within each category.

An examination of the absolute number of groups protesting within each category, presented in Figures 5.9 and 5.10, clearly show that Christian minorities engage in more protest than do Muslim or "Other" groups. In fact, about the same number of Muslim and "Other" groups engage in protest.

The above analysis has one drawback: it looks only at absolute numbers of protesting groups and does not take population into account. Since there are more Christians in the world than there are Muslims, all other things being equal, we would expect Christian groups to protest more often. According to Barrett et. Al (2001) Muslims constituted 15.0 percent of the world population in 1970, 18.3 percent in 1990, and 18.9 percent in 1995. Christians were 33.5 percent, 33.2 percent and 33.1 percent, respectively. Using these population statistics it is possible to construct an analysis controlling for the population size of the world's religions. The number of groups protesting in a particular category were divided by the proportion of the world's population that religion constituted (i.e., in the 1970 to 1974 period the number of protesting Muslim groups was divided by .183 and the number of protesting Christian groups by .335). The resulting number is the predicted number of protesting groups if a particular religion constituted the entire world's population.

The analysis controlling for population size, presented in Figures 5.11 and 5.12, gives us very different results. Muslim and Christian groups have similar levels of protest throughout the period analyzed here. "Other" groups, in contrast, consistently protest much less often. In the 1945 to 2000 analysis the level of protest by "Other" groups ranged between 25 percent and 31 percent of the level of protest by Muslim and Christian groups. In the 1985 to 2000 analysis the level of protest by "Other" groups ranged between 24 percent and 37 percent of the level of protest by Muslim and Christian groups. Thus, there seems to be a huge difference between the propensity of groups belonging to Abrahamic religions to protest as compared to groups belonging to other religions.

This result, however, is not confirmed by the analysis of the intensity of protest by groups of specific religions, presented in Figures 5.13 and 5.14. The results for the 1945 to 2000 analysis show almost no difference between the three types of groups. The results for 1985 to 2000 show Muslim groups engaging in more protest after 1990, but for most of this period this result is not statistically significant. Thus,

Figure 5.9: Number of Protesting Groups, Controlling for Specific Religion, 1945-2000

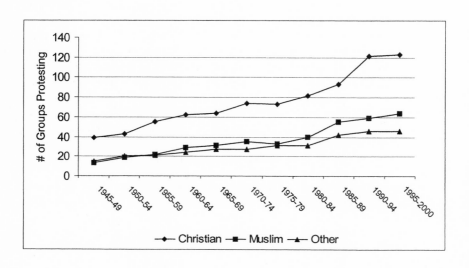

Figure 5.10: Number of Protesting Groups, Controlling for Specific Religion, 1985-2000

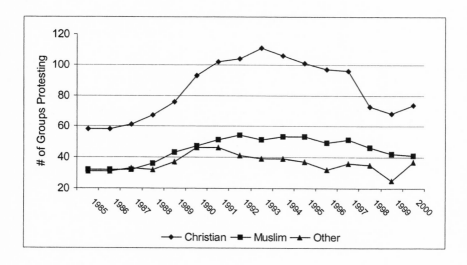

Figure 5.11: Predicted Number of Protesting Groups, Controlling for Population Size and Specific Religion, 1945-2000

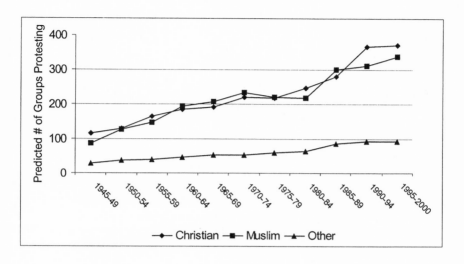

Figure 5.12: Predicted Number of Protesting Groups, Controlling for Population Size and Specific Religion, 1985-2000

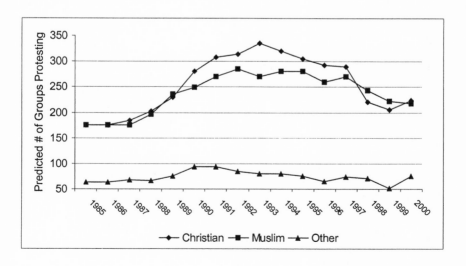

Figure 5.13: Mean Level of Protest, Controlling for Specific Religion, 1945-2000

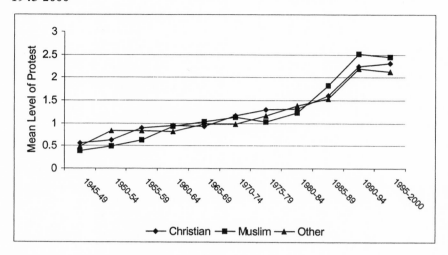

-Significance (t-test) between Muslim and Other. < .1 in 1950-54

Figure 5.14: Mean Level of Protest, Controlling for Specific Religion, 1985-2000

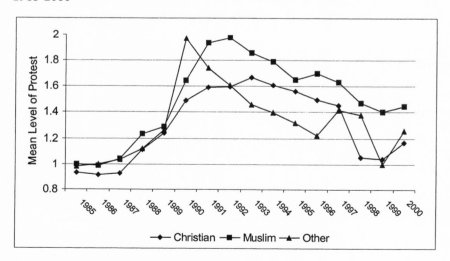

-Significance (t-test) between Christian and Muslim < .1 in 1999
-Significance (t-test) between Christian and Muslim < .05 in 1998
-Significance (t-test) between Christian and Other < .05 in 1990
-Significance (t-test) between Other and Muslim < .05 in 1996

Figure 5.15: Mean Level of Protest Controlling for Separatism, 1945-2000

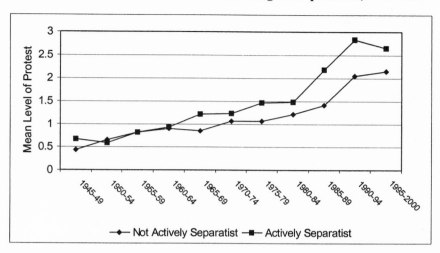

-Significance (t-test) between Separatist and Not Separatist < .05 in 1965-69 & 1975-79
-Significance (t-test) between Separatist and Not Separatist < .001 in 1985-2000

Figure 5.16: Mean Level of Protest Controlling for Separatism, 1985-2000

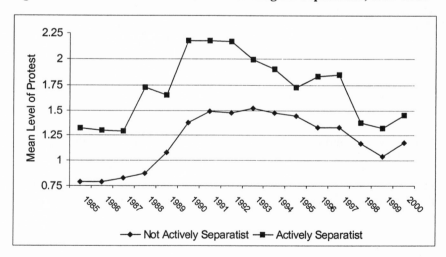

-Significance (t-test) between Separatist and Not Separatist < .1 in 1995
-Significance (t-test) between Separatist and Not Separatist < .05 in 1994
-Significance (t-test) between Separatist and Not Separatist < .01 in 1985-87, 1993, & 1996
-Significance (t-test) between Separatist and Not Separatist < .001 in 1998-92 & 1997

Figure 5.17: Mean Level of Protest Controlling for Separatism and Religion, 1945-2000

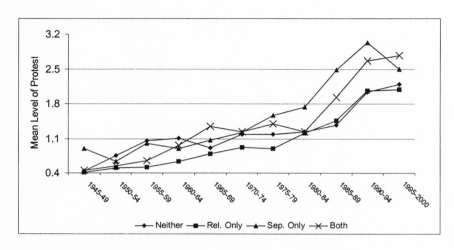

-Significance (t-test) between Neither and Rel. Only < .01 in 1955-64
-Significance (t-test) between Neither and Sep. Only < .1 in 1945-49 & 1980-84
-Significance (t-test) between Neither and Sep. Only < .001 in 1985-94
-Significance (t-test) between Neither and Both < .1 in 1955-59 & 1965-69
-Significance (t-test) between Neither and Both < .05 in 1985-89 & 1995-2000
-Significance (t-test) between Neither and Both < .01 in 1990-94
-Significance (t-test) between Rel. Only and Sep. Only < .05 in 1955-59 & 1975-84
-Significance (t-test) between Rel. Only and Sep. Only < .001 in 1985-94
-Significance (t-test) between Rel. Only and Both < .1 in 1975-79 & 1985-89
-Significance (t-test) between Rel. Only and Both < .05 in 1965-69 & 1990-94
-Significance (t-test) between Rel. Only and Both < .01 in 1995-2000

while groups of Abrahamic religions are more likely to protest, when protest occurs, the specific type of religion does not seem to have a significant impact on the intensity of the protest. The only exception to this is a relative increase in the intensity of protest by Muslim groups in the 1990s. This is consistent with a pattern, described in the previous chapter, of an increase in conflict by Muslim groups during the 1990s.

Religion and Separatism

As discussed in the previous chapter, separatism is, perhaps, the single best predictor of ethnic rebellion and the combination of religion and separatism has become an increasingly important cause of ethnic rebellion since 1980. This section

Figure 5.18: Mean Level of Protest Controlling for Separatism and Religion, 1985-2000

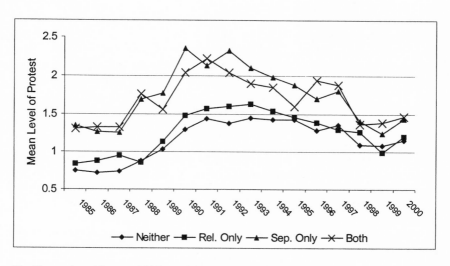

-Significance (t-test) between Neither and Sep. Only < .1 in 1995
-Significance (t-test) between Neither and Sep. Only < .05 in 1985-87 & 1994
-Significance (t-test) between Neither and Sep. Only < .01 in 1988, 1989, 1991, & 1993
-Significance (t-test) between Neither and Sep. Only < .001 in 1990 & 1992
-Significance (t-test) between Neither and Both < .1 in 1994
-Significance (t-test) between Neither and Both < .05 in 1985, 1987, 1989, 1993, & 1997
-Significance (t-test) between Neither and Both < .01 in 1986 & 1992
-Significance (t-test) between Neither and Sep. Only < .001 in 1988, 1990, & 1991
-Significance (t-test) between Rel. Only and Sep. Only < .1 in 1985 & 1993-95
-Significance (t-test) between Rel. Only and Sep. Only < .05 in 1989, 1991, & 1997
-Significance (t-test) between Rel. Only and Sep. Only < .01 in 1988, 1990, & 1992
-Significance (t-test) between Rel. Only and Both < .1 in 1986, 1990, & 1992
-Significance (t-test) between Rel. Only and Both < .05 in 1985, 1989, 1991, & 1996-97
-Significance (t-test) between Rel. Only and Both < .001 in 1988

examines whether this is also true of ethnic protest. The impact of separatism on protest, presented in Figures 5.15 and 5.16, is simple and clear. Until the 1965 to 1969 period there was no impact but from this period onward there was more protest in separatist conflicts.

When religion is added to the equation, the results become considerably more complicated. The results, presented in Figures 5.17 and 5.18, show that religion has no consistent impact on protest. Until 1985 there was no consistent relationship. However from 1985 onward protest by groups in the two separatist categories were consistently higher than protest by groups in the two nonseparatist categories. However, whether religious or nonreligious minorities within each category engaged in more protest differed from year to year.

All of this means that adding religion to separatism does not in any way increase our ability to predict the level of protest. Thus, while separatism influences the level of protest, the combination of separatism and religion does not. This stands in stark contrast to the finding in the previous chapter that since 1980 religion can intensify separatist rebellions. Therefore, it can be concluded that the influence of religion on protest differs from its influence on rebellion in this respect.

General Causes of Ethnic Protest

While the previous section shows that separatism, and not religion, is a significant cause of ethnic protest, it is important to remember that separatism and religion are only two among many potential influences upon ethnic protest. Accordingly, in this section we examine the influence of multiple potential causes of ethnic protest, other than religious causes. The religious causes are examined later. This is because it is important to assess the general causes of protest before factoring in religion.

The variables used here are mostly the same as those used to predict ethnic rebellion in the previous chapter. This is because the causes of different types of ethnic conflict are similar. A number of factors including regime type (which is included in the analysis here) influence whether an ethnic conflict will manifest itself as protest or rebellion. As the reasoning for using these variables is similar, if not identical, to the reasoning for using them in the analysis in the previous chapter, there is no need to reiterate the explanations for this inclusion in the analysis in this chapter. However, some additional variables are used in this chapter which are described below.[3]

International political support: This variable is similar to the variable for international military support described in the previous chapter except, rather than measuring military support, it measures more peaceful types of support by foreign states. This type of support includes ideological encouragement, nonmilitary financial support, access to external markets and communications, peacekeeping forces, and economic sanctions.

The spread of protest across borders: These variables are similar to the spread of conflict across borders in the previous chapter except, while the variables in the previous chapter measured the spread of rebellion across borders, these variables measure the spread of protest across borders. As is the case with the rebellion variables, the protest variables measure both contagion and diffusion. Contagion is when a conflict spreads through a region. Diffusion is the demonstration effect that antiregime activity can have for ethnic kindred living elsewhere, whether they live in bordering states or on the other side of the world. Each of these processes is included in our study. They are both measured for two time periods, 1985 to 1989 and 1990 to 1995. As violent conflict can also inspire protest elsewhere, the contagion and diffusion of rebellion variables are also included in the analysis

Table 5.1: Correlations between Potential Causes of Protest and Protest for All Minorities

Independent Variables	Correlated with Protest in			
	1990	1993	1996	2000
Separatism	.264****	.164***	.183***	.088
Autonomy Grievances	.298****	.304****	.366****	.327****
Cultural Grievances	.243****	.225****	.137**	.246****
Economic Grievances	.244****	.267****	.188***	.229****
Political Grievances	.315****	.280****	.181***	.243****
Cultural Differences	.160***	.115*	.105*	.221****
Polity Score	.253****	.310****	.180***	.232****
Repression	–	–	.271****	.218****
Int. Political Support	.132**	.097	.056	.056
Contagion of Prot. 1980s	.151**	.100	.032	.234****
Contagion of Prot. 1990-95	–	.187***	.092	.161***
Diffusion of Prot. 1980s	.212****	.189***	.186***	.327****
Diffusion of Prot. 1100-95	–	.100*	.094	.157***
Contagion of Reb. 1980s	.015	-.041	.007	.076
Contagion of Reb. 1990-95	–	-.067	.025	.044
Diffusion of Reb. 1980s	.137**	.107*	.055	.155***
Diffusion of Reb. 1990-95	–	.117*	.048	.120**
# of Political Orgs. 1990-95	.285****	.388****	.280****	.244****
Support, Pol. Orgs. 1990-95	.287****	.314****	.263****	.145**

* = Significance < .1, ** = Significance < .05, *** = Significance < .01, **** = Significance < .001

presented in this chapter.

Mobilization for protest: These variables are similar to the mobilization variables used in the previous chapter except they measure the number and support for peaceful political organizations rather than violent military ones. Two variables are used here to measure mobilization for protest. The first measures the number of peaceful organizations. The second measures the scope of support for peaceful organizations. Both variables are measured for the 1990 to 1995 period.

All analyses in this section are performed three times, once for all 285 groups in the analysis, once for the 107 religious minorities, and once for the 178 other minorities in the analysis. This is in order to determine whether the patterns of protest differ between religious and nonreligious minorities. For the purposes of the analyses performed in this section, religious minorities are those who belong to a different religion than the majority group in their state.

Two types of analyses are performed here. The first is bivariate correlation analysis which is designed to see which of the variables have an individual impact on rebellion. The second is multiple regression analysis which is designed to measure the combined impact of these variables on protest. In the multiple regression analyses, those variables which did not have a statistically significant impact

Table 5.2: Correlations between Potential Causes of Protest and Protest for Religious Minorities

Independent Variables	Correlated with Protest in			
	1990	1993	1996	2000
Separatism	.214**	.113	.210**	.093
Autonomy Grievances	.230**	.240**	.200**	.217**
Cultural Grievances	.150	.175*	-.014	.032
Economic Grievances	.214**	.298***	.048	.236**
Political Grievances	.327****	.247**	.198**	.220**
Cultural Differences	.183*	-.015	-.017	.098
Polity Score	.226**	.292***	.210**	.333****
Repression	–	–	.370****	.281***
Int. Political Support	.195*	.113	.026	.009
Contagion of Prot. 1980s	.206**	.135	.069	.317****
Contagion of Prot. 1990-95	–	.088	.026	.222**
Diffusion of Prot. 1980s	.294***	.228**	.151	.337****
Diffusion of Prot. 1990-95	–	.154	.105	.207**
Contagion of Reb. 1980s	.065	.064	.029	.111
Contagion of Reb. 1990-95	–	.008	.031	.102
Diffusion of Reb. 1980s	.202**	.168*	.061	.118
Diffusion of Reb. 1990-95	–	.100	.035	.053
# of Political Orgs. 1990-95	.345****	.308***	.145	.146
Support, Pol. Orgs. 1990-95	.284***	.236**	.137	.071

* = Significance < .1, ** = Significance < .05, *** = Significance < .01, **** = Significance < .001

on protest were removed from the analysis. In general this did not significantly reduce the extent to which the analyses were able to explain rebellion. This strength is measured by its Adjusted R^2 which is expressed as a decimal between 0 and 1 and measures the proportion of the variance in protest which the regression explains. Thus, this methodology allows us to focus on those variables which impact upon rebellion and eliminate those that do not.

All tests here examine protest in 1990, 1993, 1996, and 2000. While the protest variable was collected yearly for 1985 to 2000 and for every five-year period form 1945 to 2000, the analysis is limited to the 1990s because nearly all of the independent variables were not collected before 1990. Also, these four years are considered sufficient to examine whether the causes of protest change over time during the 1990 to 2000 period.

The bivariate analysis between the causes of protest and protest for all minorities, presented in Table 5.1, shows that separatism, the grievance variables, repression, cultural differences, regime type, and the mobilization variables all have a consistent impact on protest. However, international political support and the spread of conflict across borders, while influencing protest, have a less consistent impact. Among these variables, only diffusion of protest in the 1980s is significant for all

Table 5.3: Correlations between Potential Causes of Protest and Protest for Nonreligious Minorities

Independent Variables	Correlated with Protest in			
	1990	1993	1996	2000
Separatism	.290****	.190***	.161**	.080
Autonomy Grievances	.377****	.388****	.289****	.527****
Cultural Grievances	.342****	.384****	.160**	.257****
Economic Grievances	.252****	.244****	.255****	.331****
Political Grievances	.307****	.293****	.172**	.259****
Cultural Differences	.138*	.183**	.170**	.298****
Polity Score	.268****	.325****	.181**	.177**
Repression	–	–	.176**	.157**
Int. Political Support	.086	.071	.056	.068
Contagion of Prot. 1980s	.125	.086	.019	.189**
Contagion of Prot. 1990-95	–	.231**	.126	.143*
Diffusion of Prot. 1980s	.165**	.160**	.204***	.318****
Diffusion of Prot. 1990-95	–	.017	.091	.127*
Contagion of Reb. 1980s	-.020	-.121	-.022	.042
Contagion of Reb. 1990-95	–	-.133*	-.002	-.013
Diffusion of Reb. 1980s	.093	.049	.031	.173**
Diffusion of Reb. 1990-95	–	.122	.045	.163**
# of Political Orgs. 1990-95	.255****	.438****	.369****	.292****
Support, Pol. Orgs. 1990-95	.292****	.365****	.352****	.199***

* = Significance < .1, ** = Significance < .05, *** = Significance < .01, **** = Significance < .001

Table 5.4: Correlation between Potential Causes of Protest and Mobilization

Independent Variables	Correlated with					
	# of Peaceful Orgs. 1990-95			Support, Peace. Orgs. 1990-95		
	All Min.	Rel. Min.	Other Min.	All Min.	Rel. Min.	Other Min.
Separatism	.083	.089	.080	.097	.130	.078
Autonomy Grievances	.168***	.198**	.153**	.088	.039	.128*
Cultural Grievances	.284****	.406****	.219***	.145**	.070	.193**
Economic Grievances	.203****	.316****	.154**	.125**	.184*	.103
Political Grievances	.258****	.379****	.203***	.071	.115	.052
Cultural Differences	.162***	.211**	.138*	-.015	-.046	.014
Polity Score	.318****	.412****	.278****	.144**	.218*	.111
Int. Political Support	-.057	-.221**	.038	.026	-.049	.074
Contag. of Prot. 1980s	-.009	.000	-.016	.075	-.054	-.090
Contag. of Prot. 1990-95	.154***	.128	.167**	-.011	.045	-.034
Diff. of Prot. 1980s	.157***	.212**	.123	.082	.047	.106
Diff. of Prot. 1990-95	.133**	.231**	.075	-.013	.142	-.107
Contag. of Reb. 1980s	-.283****	-.274***	-.291****	.093	-.080	-.100
Contag. of Reb. 1990-95	-.258****	-.331****	-.215***	.057	-.103	.011
Diff. of Reb. 1980s	.034	.110	-.018	.029	.017	.044
Diff. of Reb. 1990-95	.050	.079	.034	-.051	-.013	-.075

* = Significance < .1, ** = Significance < .05, *** = Significance < .01, **** = Significance < .001

Table 5.5: Multiple Regression for General Causes of Protest for All Minorities

Independent Variables	Regressions for Protest in			
	1990	1993	1996	2000
Separatism	.136**	(.009)	(.014)	(-.070)
Autonomy Grievances	.157***	.207****	.218	.216****
Cultural Grievances	(.039)	(-.007)	-.106*	(.014)
Economic Grievances	(-.006)	(.029)	(.017)	.144***
Political Grievances	.238****	.157***	.096*	(.063)
Cultural Differences	(.025)	(-.040)	(-.002)	(.049)
Polity	.186****	.194****	.137**	.207****
Repression	–	–	.290****	.211****
Int. Political Support	.117**	.116**	(.041)	(.028)
Contagion of Prot. 1980s	(.029)	(-.072)	-.106	(.061)
Contagion of Prot. 1990s	–	(-.022)	(.033)	(.019)
Diffusion of Prot. 1980s	(.077)	(.028)	.123***	.238****
Diffusion of Prot. 1990s	–	(-.012)	(-.054)	(-.042)
Contagion of Reb. 1980s	.115**	.121**	(.068)	(.007)
Contagion of Reb 1990s	–	(-.047)	(.064)	.157***
Diffusion of Reb. 1980s	(.059)	(.027)	(-.055)	(-.051)
Diffusion of Reb. 1990s	–	(.053)	(-.086)	(-.009)
# of Political Orgs. 1990-95	(.080)	.214***	.120*	.126**
Support, Pol. Orgs. 1990-95	.219****	.141**	.151**	(.020)
df	284	284	284	284
Adjusted R^2	.258	.275	.252	.303

* = Significance < .1, ** = Significance < .05, *** = Significance < .01, **** = Significance < .001
All values in table are beta values. Means are substituted for missing data. Values in parentheses were excluded from the regression due to the fact they proved to be insignificant. The values in the parentheses are what the beta of the variable would have been if it were included in the regression.

years analyzed here.

It is important to note that protest is positively correlated with the polity score. This means protest is more likely in democratic regimes. This is consistent with the argument that, as democracies allow multiple legal and peaceful avenues for addressing grievances, ethnic conflict in democracies is more likely to take the form of peaceful protest than rebellion. That the polity variable is negatively correlated with rebellion (Table 4.1) also supports this conclusion.

The results of the separate analyses for religious and nonreligious minorities, presented in Tables 5.2 and 5.3, are similar to the general results but are different in one important way. The correlations for religious minorities in general are weaker and the correlations for nonreligious minorities are stronger. Thus, the factors that influence protest by both types of groups are similar, but they seem to influence religious minorities less than they do nonreligious minorities.

It is also important to examine the impact of these potential causes of protest

Table 5.6: Multiple Regression for General Causes of Protest for Religious Minorities

Independent Variables	Regressions for Protest in			
	1990	1993	1996	2000
Separatism	(.076)	(-.031)	(.098)	(.033)
Autonomy Grievances	.169*	.166*	(.072)	(.137)
Cultural Grievances	(-.159)	(-.025)	(.025)	(.045)
Economic Grievances	(-.081)	(.112)	(.004)	(.114)
Political Grievances	.173*	.188*	(.123)	(.126)
Cultural Differences	(.061)	-.192**	(-.059)	(.013)
Polity	(.039)	.175*	.294****	.268***
Repression	–	–	.431****	.279****
Int. Political Support	.305****	.218**	(.060)	(.071)
Contagion of Prot. 1980s	.181**	(.046)	(-.110)	.221**
Contagion of Prot. 1990s	–	(-.063)	(-.040)	(.086)
Diffusion of Prot. 1980s	(.137)	(.002)	(.057)	.210**
Diffusion of Prot. 1990s	–	(-.063)	(.058)	(.060)
Contagion of Reb. 1980s	(.097)	(.086)	(-.070)	(-.108)
Contagion of Reb. 1990s	–	(.048)	(-.058)	(.051)
Diffusion of Reb. 1980s	(.140)	.154*	(.009)	(-.109)
Diffusion of Reb. 1990s	–	(.086)	(.053)	(.017)
# of Political Orgs. 1990-95	.307****	.203**	(.078)	(.024)
Support, Pol. Orgs. 1990-95	(.157)	(.090)	(.147)	(.084)
df	106	106	106	106
Adjusted R²	.254	.187	.202	.278

* = Significance < .1, ** = Significance < .05, *** = Significance < .01, **** = Significance < .001
All values in table are beta values. Means are substituted for missing data. Values in parentheses were excluded from the regression due to the fact they proved to be insignificant. The values in the parentheses are what the beta of the variable would have been if it were included in the regression.

on mobilization. This is because the same factors that cause people to protest also cause them to mobilize and mobilization has been shown here to be strongly correlated with protest. The results of this analysis, presented in Table 5.4, show that the causes of peaceful mobilization are similar but not identical to the causes of protest. The cultural differences, regime type, and the grievance variables, including autonomy grievances, cause more protest but the separatism variable does not. International political support actually makes protest less likely among religious minorities. Finally, while the spread of protest across borders makes protest more likely, rebellion in bordering states makes protest less likely.

Thus, the international factors that tend to make protest more likely actually inhibit peaceful mobilization. One potential reason for this is that, as shown in the previous chapter (Table 4.4), all of these factors make mobilization for rebellion more likely. Thus, to the extent that cross-border factors influence mobilization,

Table 5.7: Multiple Regression for General Causes of Protest for Nonreligious Minorities

Independent Variables	Regressions for Protest in			
	1990	1993	1996	2000
Separatism	.158**	(.023)	(.010)	(-.073)
Autonomy Grievances	.184**	.241****	.324****	.299****
Cultural Grievances	(.062)	(-.004)	-.143**	(-.012)
Economic Grievances	(.034)	(.013)	.151**	.185***
Political Grievances	.260****	.206****	(.060)	(.023)
Cultural Differences	(-.028)	(.019)	(.030)	(.082)
Polity	.131*	.142**	(.032)	.120*
Repression	–	–	.129*	.196***
Int. Political Support	(.041)	(.031)	(.018)	(.002)
Contagion of Prot. 1980s	(.067)	(-.009)	(-.115)	(.001)
Contagion of Prot. 1990s	–	(.023)	(-.009)	(-.100)
Diffusion of Prot. 1980s	(.033)	(.030)	.202**	.218****
Diffusion of Prot. 1990s	–	(.004)	(.063)	(-.041)
Contagion of Reb. 1980s	(.100)	(.075)	(-.014)	(.077)
Contagion of Reb. 1990s	–	(.044)	(.017)	(.096)
Diffusion of Reb. 1980s	(.049)	(.016)	-.151*	(-.006)
Diffusion of Reb. 1990s	–	(.081)	(.027)	(.014)
# of Political Orgs. 1990-95	(.001)	.222***	.172**	.143**
Support, Pol. Orgs. 1990-95	.220****	.175**	.172**	(.017)
df	177	177	177	177
Adjusted R²	.260	.325	.303	.317

* = Significance < .1, ** = Significance < .05, *** = Significance < .01, **** = Significance < .001
All values in table are beta values. Means are substituted for missing data. Values in parentheses were excluded from the regression due to the fact they proved to be insignificant. The values in the parentheses are what the beta of the variable would have been if it were included in the regression.

they tend to increase the likelihood of militant mobilization while decreasing the likelihood of peaceful mobilization.

The multivariate analysis is similar to the bivariate analysis. The results for all ethnic minorities, presented in Table 5.5, show that the variables which most often impact on protest are mobilization, autonomy grievances, political grievances, repression, and regime type. At least one of the spread of conflict across borders variables is significant for all of the years analyzed here, though rebellion in bordering states is significant more often than the spread of protest across borders variables. International political support is also important in 1990 and 1993 but not in 1996 and 2000.

The results of the separate analyses for religious and nonreligious minorities, presented in Tables 5.6 and 5.7, follow similar patterns with some differences. The results for both of these analyses tend to be weaker. The results for religious

Table 5.8: Multiple Regression for Causes of Protest for All Minorities, Including Religious Identity Variables

Independent Variables	Regressions for Protest in			
	1990	1993	1996	2000
Different Religions	(-.009)	(.004)	.155**	(-.011)
Minority Christian	-.220**	(.089)	.158**	(.036)
Minority Muslim	-.130*	.096*	.186***	(.008)
Separatism	.157***	(.009)	(-.010)	(-.070)
Separatism * Diff. Religion	(-.041)	(-.007)	(-.002)	(-.073)
Autonomy Grievances	.364***	.190****	.476***	.216****
Aut. Griev. * Diff. Relig.	-.237*	(-.120)	-.315*	(-.175)
Cultural Grievances	(.008)	(.008)	(-.075)	(.014)
Economic Grievances	(-.026)	(.026)	(.033)	.144***
Political Grievances	.217****	.156***	(.061)	(.063)
Cultural Differences	(.015)	(-.044)	(-.024)	(.049)
Polity	.154***	.205****	.107*	.207****
Repression	–	–	.294****	.211****
Int. Political Support	.121**	.108**	(.017)	(.028)
Contagion of Prot. 1980s	(.029)	(-.056)	(-.075)	(.061)
Contagion of Prot. 1990s	–	(-.034)	(-.072)	(.019)
Diffusion of Prot. 1980s	.091*	(.016)	(-.026)	.238****
Diffusion of Prot. 1990s	–	(-.035)	.151**	(-.042)
Contagion of Reb. 1980s	(.055)	.096*	(.048)	(.007)
Contagion of Reb 1990s	–	(-.037)	(.074)	.157***
Diffusion of Reb. 1980s	(.053)	(.013)	-.109*	(-.051)
Diffusion of Reb. 1990s	–	(.038)	(-.002)	(-.009)
# of Political Orgs. 1990s	(.044)	.217****	.121*	.126**
Support, Pol. Orgs. 1990s	.194****	.144**	.155**	(.020)
df	284	284	284	284
Adjusted R²	.279	.280	.262	.303

* = Significance < .1, ** = Significance < .05, *** = Significance < .01, **** = Significance < .001
All values in table are beta values. Means are substituted for missing data. Values in parentheses were excluded from the regression due to the fact they proved to be insignificant. The values in the parentheses are what the beta of the variable would have been if it were included in the regression. Religious conflicts are those where the two groups belong to different religions.

minorities are weaker with regard to the grievance variables. The results of both analyses are weaker with regard to the spread of conflict across borders variables. This can be explained by the fact that there are fewer cases in each analysis.

Adding religious identity variables to the regression, presented in Table 5.8, produces interesting results. Whether the minority is Muslim or Christian influences the level of protest but this influence is inconsistent. In 1990, minorities which were Muslim or Christian protested less but Muslim minorities were more likely to protest in 1993 and 1996 and Christian minorities were more likely to protest in

1996. More importantly, when the variables for whether the groups belong to different religions were significant, they resulted in lower levels of protest. That is, religious difference makes protest less likely. In 1993 the combined autonomy grievances and religious differences variable was negative but the individual autonomy grievances variable was positive. In 1996 both the individual religious differences and autonomy grievances variables were positive but the variable which combined the two was negative. Both of these results mean that autonomy griev-ances among nonreligious minorities made protest more likely, but among religious minorities the influence of autonomy grievances on protest was weak at best.

This result is highly counterintuitive. We would expect religion to increase protest rather than detract from it. It is demonstrated later in this chapter that the explanation for this phenomenon is found in the more specific religious causes of protest.

Religious Causes of Protest

The above analysis examines the impact of general causes of ethnic conflict and religious identity on protest. However, the religious aspects of that analysis only take into account whether the two groups involved in a conflict belong to different religions. It does not deal with whether the conflict involves religious factors. That is, when religious and nonreligious conflicts are found to be different, it is assumed that it is because of religion. While this is an assumption that is supported by the analysis, it is still an assumption.

Accordingly, this section analyzes the impact of more specific religious factors on ethnic protest by a subset of 105 ethnoreligious minorities from the MAR dataset on which more detailed information is available. All of these conflicts involve religious minorities which belong to different religions or different denominations of the same religion as the majority group in their state. They were selected from an earlier verison of the MAR dataset which contained 267 religious minorities and include all groups which met any of the following criteria: (1) the groups belong to different religions; (2) the groups belong to different branches of Islam; or (3) both groups are Christian but one is Catholic and the other Protestant.

As the data was collected for the 1990 to 1995 period, it is inappropriate to extend it too far away from that period. However, as there is little change in the codings from that period, it is fair to extend the codings five years on either end, thus allowing comparisons for the 1990 to 2000 period. It can be extended past 1995 because most of the relevant groups which were active in 1995 continued to be active until 2000. However, before 1990 many of the relevant groups, especially those in the former Soviet bloc, were not active, so extending the analysis to before 1990 is not appropriate.

The following analysis analyzes four aspects of religion: religious grievances, religious demands, religious legitimacy, and religious institutions. Religious

Figure 5.19: The Influence of Religious Grievances on Protest, 1990-2000

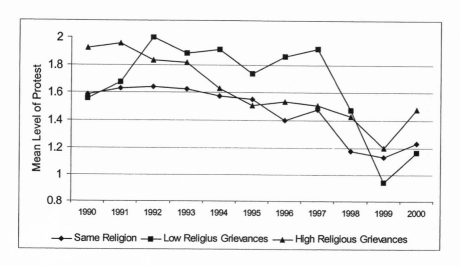

Figure 5.20: The Influence of Religious Demands on Protest, 1990-2000

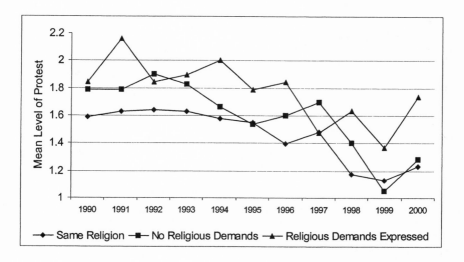

Figure 5.21: The Influence of Religious Legitimacy on Protest, 1990-2000

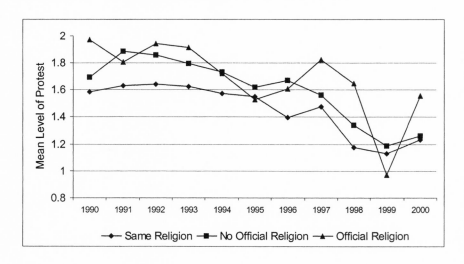

Figure 5.22: The Influence of Religious Institutions on Protest, 1990-2000

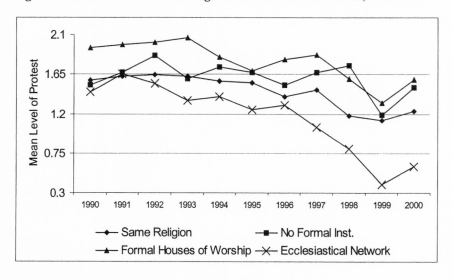

-Significance (t-test) between No Formal Houses and Eccl. Net. < .1 in 1998-2000
-Significance (t-test) between Formal Houses and Eccl. Net. < .05 in 1993, 1997, & 1998
-Significance (t-test) between Formal Houses and Eccl. Net. < .01 in 1999 & 2000

grievances are complaints expressed over religious discrimination. Religious demands are demands for additional rights or privileges for a minority's religion. Religious legitimacy is measured here by whether or not the state has an official religion. Religious institutions are measured here as the extent to which religious institutions are formal ones.

The theoretical reasons for believing that these factors influence ethnic conflict are described in the previous chapter. As a control, all of the bivariate analyses below also include the extent of protest by nonreligious minorities taken from Figure 5.6.

The analysis of the influence of religious grievances on protest, presented in Figure 5.19, shows an inconsistent influence. In four of the eleven years analyzed, ethnoreligious minorities expressing high religious grievances engaged in higher levels of protest but in seven they engaged in lower levels of protest. Thus, if anything, religious grievances are associated with lower levels of protest. None of these results are statistically significant.

The analysis of the influence of religious demands on protest, presented in Figure 5.20, shows a more consistent influence. In nine of eleven years analyzed, ethnoreligious minorities expressing religious demands engaged in higher levels of protest. However, none of these results are statistically significant.

The results for religious legitimacy, presented in Figure 5.21, are also inconsistent. In seven of eleven years analyzed, religious legitimacy is associated with higher levels of protest. Like the other analyses, these results are not statistically significant.

The results for religious institutions, presented in Figure 5.22, do show some influence. While none of the categories examined here are positively correlated with protest, the presence of an ecclesiastical network is negatively associated with protest, with this relationship having statistical significance in several of the years examined here. That is, formal ecclesiastical networks linking the houses of worship of an ethnic minority make protest less likely. This is consistent with the results from the previous chapter in which a similar link is found between ecclesiastical networks and rebellion. Also, formal houses of worship are associated with the highest levels of protest in all but one of the years analyzed here, but this relationship is not statistically significant.

The multivariate analysis of the religious causes of protest, presented in Table 5.9, includes all of the above religious variables both individually and in combination with separatism. This was done in order for the regression to be consistent with the one for rebellion presented in the previous chapter (Table 4.10) even though in analyses not presented the combination of these religious factors and separatism had no consistent impact on protest.

The results show that religion has a dual impact on protest. That is, some religion variables make protest more likely and others make it less likely. All of the religion variables are significant, either by themselves or in combination with separatism, for at least one of the years analyzed. Formal houses of worship is significant in 1990 and 1993. In 1990, the individual variable is positive but the

Table 5.9: Multiple Regression for Religious Causes of Protest

| | Regressions for Protest in | | | |
Independent Variables	1990	1993	1996	2000
Religious Grievances	(-.077)	-.204*	-.212**	(.001)
Religious Demands	(.047)	.161*	(.111)	.171*
Religious Legitimacy	(-.012)	(-.101)	(.090)	(-.019)
Formal Houses of Worship	.294***	.265***	(.133)	(.144)
Separatism	.823**	(.133)	(.084)	(-.074)
Separatism * Relig. Griev.	(-.159)	-.239*	(.031)	(.010)
Separatism * Relig. Demands	(.090)	(.002)	(.128)	(-.112)
Separatism * Relig. Legit.	(.098)	.369***	(.079)	(-.077)
Separatism * Formal Houses	-.562*	(.039)	(.105)	(-.043)
Autonomy Grievances	(.081)	(.103)	(.011)	(.079)
Cultural Grievances	(-.057)	(.077)	(.136)	(.075)
Economic Grievances	(.034)	.206**	(-.043)	(.105)
Political Grievances	.222**	.170*	(.012)	(.121)
Cultural Differences	(.062)	-.213**	(-.100)	(.084)
Polity	(.063)	.191**	.271***	.216**
Repression	–	–	.545****	.276***
Int. Political Support	(.107)	(.134)	(-.048)	(-.028)
Contagion of Protest 1980s	(.058)	-.175	-.208**	.227**
Contagion of Protest 1990s	–	(.092)	(.073)	(-.075)
Diffusion of Protest 1980s	.246***	(.053)	(.075)	.336****
Diffusion of Protest 1990s	–	(-.080)	(.009)	(-.083)
Contagion of Reb. 1980s	(-.051)	(-.084)	(.097)	-.421**
Contagion of Reb. 1990s	–	(.027)	(.092)	.378**
Diffusion of Reb. 1980s	(.056)	(.037)	(-.008)	(-.124)
Diffusion of Reb. 1990s	–	(-.080)	(.018)	(-.073)
# of Political Orgs. 1990s	(.109)	(.109)	(-.021)	(.130)
Support, Pol. Orgs. 1990s	.221**	(.039)	(.023)	(.119)
df	102	102	102	102
Adjusted R^2	.281	.286	.292	.324

* = Significance < .1, ** = Significance < .05, *** = Significance < .01, **** = Significance < .001
All values in table are beta values. Means are substituted for missing data. Values in parentheses were excluded from the regression due to the fact they proved to be insignificant. The values in the parentheses are what the beta of the variable would have been if it were included in the regression.

combined formal houses of worship and separatism variable is more strongly negative. In 1993 only the individual formal houses of worship variable is significant. Thus, the impact of religious institutions on protest is inconsistent.

Fox (1999a), when examining the impact of religious institutions on ethnic protest, also found that they sometimes increased and sometimes decreased protest. The explanation was that when religion was not important to a conflict religious institutions inhibited protest, but when religion was important to the conflict religious institutions exacerbated protest. Thus, in general, religious institutions were found to support the status quo unless some religious principle was at stake, in which case they facilitated protest against the government.

Religious legitimacy is only significant in 1993 when in combination with separatism and has a positive influence on protest. Religious demands is significant only in 2000 as an individual variable and also has a positive influence on protest. Religious grievances, however, is significant in 1993 and 1996, consistently causing less protest.

Thus, all of the religion variables have an impact on protest and in all years analyzed here at least one of the religion variables influences protest. However, their overall impact is less than it is in the case of rebellion. Also, unlike the relationship between religion and rebellion, that impact of religion on protest is often a negative one.

Conclusions

The general finding of this chapter is that while the general causes of ethnic protest are similar, but not identical, to the causes of ethnic violence, the impact of religion on the conflict process for rebellion and protest are very different. In other words, there are several differences between the process causing rebellion and the process causing protest.

First, nonreligious grievances impact on protest more than they do on rebellion. Second, separatism is a stronger influence on rebellion than on protest. These two results make sense. The expression of grievances means that the group would like to address their complaints within the context of the political system. Protest is a way of doing this. Ethnic rebellion presumes that sufficient change is not possible within the context of the current political system and the best choice is to exit that system. This desire is expressed through separatism.

Third, rebellion is more common in autocracies and protest is more common in democracies. This finding is not a new one. It is also consistent with the fact that democracies generally allow minorities to peacefully express their complaints and often address at least some of them. Autocracies are more likely to repress minorities rather than address their complaints, forcing the minorities to rebel if they wish to have their grievances addressed.

Fourth, the spread of conflict across borders has a much greater impact on rebellion than it does on protest. Fifth, to the extent that cross-border factors influence mobilization, they tend to increase the likelihood of militant mobilization while decreasing the likelihood of peaceful mobilization. One explanation for these findings is that, being more emotional in nature, violence spreads more easily across borders and is much more likely to inspire violence than protest. Protest, however, is a more conscious planned activity that, as noted above, is strongly influenced by domestic factors. Also, groups who engage in protest most likely live in states where there is a good chance of having their grievances addressed. Thus, they do not need outside support. In fact, this outside support may hurt their cause in that it is likely to antagonize the government of the state in which they live. Given this, instances of outside support for a group likely indicate that a peaceful solution is difficult to achieve, making it likely that the conflict will turn violent, if it is not already violent.

Sixth, religious factors have a lower and more inconsistent impact on protest than they do on rebellion. While some religious factors are associated with higher levels of protest, both whether the conflict involves groups of different religions and the expression of religious grievances are associated with lower levels of protest.

This leads to a series of questions. Why are religious minorities less likely to protest? Why do religious grievances cause less protest, especially when all other types of grievances, when they are significant, cause more protest? In other words, why do people protest less when they are upset over religious issues? We would expect the opposite to be the case.

One possible explanation is that religious issues may be so important and emotive that protest is simply not enough to deal with them and, therefore, groups resort directly to violence. Unfortunately, this explanation has limited value because religious grievances are only associated with higher levels of rebellion when they are combined with separatism. Thus, this explanation only holds for separatist conflicts. Even more unfortunately, no better explanation comes to mind.

In all, the results of this chapter show that while religion does impact on ethnic protest this influence is weaker than it is for rebellion. Also, religion is not the most significant cause of either protest or rebellion. Thus, the results of this chapter confirm the results of the previous one which show that religion is an important intervening variable in ethnic conflict, but is not a primary cause. Furthermore, its impact is more evident in the violent manifestations of ethnic conflict than it is in the more nonviolent manifestations.

Notes

1. For the purposes of this analysis, religion is considered relevant to the conflict if the variable for religious relevance in 1990 is coded as 2 or higher. This means that religious issues must be salient to the conflict, though they need not be as important as other issues.
2. See previous note.
3. All of the variables described below are based on descriptions in the Minorities at Risk codebook which is available at www.cidcm.imd.edu/inscr/mar.

Chapter 6

The Clash of Civilizations?

This chapter and the following two chapters deal with Samuel Huntington's "Clash of Civilizations" (CoC) theory. This chapter deals with the theoretical issues involved in the theory and the next two provide tests of the theory both by itself and in comparison to religion as an explanation for conflict. As will be seen from the discussion in this chapter as well as the analysis in the following chapter, there is considerable overlap between Huntington's CoC theory and religion. Accordingly, no evaluation of the impact of religion on conflict would be complete without addressing the CoC theory.

Samuel Huntington's CoC theory sparked what was likely one of the most important continuing debates among international relations scholars during the 1990s and the new millennium. It is certainly among the most voluminous. While the theory itself is extremely controversial and problematic, it is nonetheless of considerable import because it was among the key triggers of a debate over what will be the nature of international politics and conflict in the post-Cold War era.

The debate began with Huntington's 1993 article in *Foreign Affairs* entitled "The Clash of Civilizations?" which was immediately followed by a number of critiques in the same journal, and eventually other journals. Huntington expanded his arguments into a 1996 book entitled *The Clash of Civilizations and the Remaking of the World Order*. This book both elaborated upon his previous arguments and addressed many of his critics. It also sparked a new round of debate over his theory with many of his critics taking the opportunity to write book reviews critiquing his theory. Some of his critics wrote entire books criticizing the CoC theory.

This chapter is intended to provide the general outlines of this debate including Huntington's theory and the basic arguments of his critics. As the volume of this debate runs into the thousands, if not tens of thousands, of pages, it is not possible to discuss all of the individual critics. Nor is it possible to discuss all of the details of Huntington's arguments considering that his writings on the topic include several

155

articles and a book. However, despite this volume of writing on the topic, Huntington's basic arguments are simple. Likewise, despite the number of critics, there are a limited number of general critiques of the CoC theory. Thus, it is possible to provide a good description of the important aspects of the CoC debate in the context of this chapter.

The Clash of Civilizations Theory

Huntington's (1993a; 1996a) basic argument is that with the end of the Cold War, the ideological conflicts between the East and the West have been replaced by identity-based conflicts between groupings he calls civilizations. Huntington (1993a) defines a civilization as

> the highest cultural grouping of people and the broadest level of cultural identity people have short of what distinguishes humans from other species. It is defined by both common language, history, religion, customs, institutions and by the subjective self identification of people.

This definition is similar to many definitions of ethnicity. For example, Gurr (1993a: 3) defines ethnicity as

> in essence, communal [ethnic] groups [which] are psychological communities: groups whose core members share a distinctive and enduring collective identity based on cultural traits and lifeways that matter to them and to others with whom they interact.
>
> People have many possible bases for communal identity: shared historical experiences or myths, religious beliefs, language, ethnicity, region of residence, and, in castelike systems, customary occupations. Communal groups–which are also referred to as ethnic groups, minorities and peoples–usually are distinguished by several reenforcing traits. The key to identifying communal groups is not the presence of a particular trait or combination of traits, but rather in the shared perception that the defining traits, whatever they are, set the group apart.

The similarity between these two definitions is that both are based on a sense of identity that is linked to ascriptive traits. These shared traits build the perception among a group that they are a group. Put differently, both ethnic groups and civilizations are defined by a shared identity based upon common traits. These common traits are only significant to the extent that they contribute to this shared perception of being members of a group. The key difference between these two concepts is the level of inclusiveness of the identity group. Civilizational groups are more broadly defined than ethnic groups. In fact, civilizations can be described as the amalgamation of more narrowly defined ethnic identities into a broader identity group based on more generally defined common traits. Thus, if two groups belong to different civilizations, they most likely also belong to different ethnic groups, but

Figure 6.1: Civilizations and Ethnic Groups

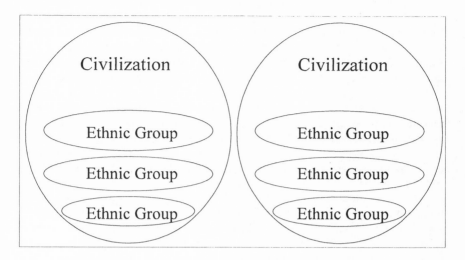

the reverse is not true because the broader definition of civilizations allows for multiple ethnic groups to share in the same civilization. This relationship is shown in Figure 6.1.

Civilizations and Religion

Huntington lists a number of civilizations. These include the Western, Sino-Confucian, Japanese, Islamic, Hindu, Slavic-Orthodox, Latin American, and "possibly" African civilizations. Most of these civilizations include at least some aspect of religion in their definition and even are named after religions. The Islamic civilization seems to be wholly defined by religion. If group members belong to the religion of Islam, their group is part of the Islamic civilization. Ethnically and culturally distinct groups within the Islamic civilization, like Arabs, Persians, and Malays, are considered by Huntington to constitute subcivilizations. (Huntington, 1996a: 45) The Hindu civilization is similarly defined mostly by membership in the Hindu religion. (Huntington, 1996a: 45)

However, most of the civilizations also include a nonreligious component. The Slavic-Orthodox civilization combines religious, historical, and political elements. On one hand, it is based on religious factors like the divide between the European Catholic and Orthodox Christian churches as well as the limited influence of the Reformation on the Orthodox communities. On the other hand, it is differentiated from the Western civilization by secular cultural and historical factors like its limited exposure to the Renaissance, Enlightenment, and "other central Western experiences" as well as "200 years of Tatar rule" and "bureaucratic despotism." (Huntington, 1996a: 45-46) It also includes the ethnic element of Slavic descent, though this was downplayed in Huntington's book. The Latin American civilization is also distinguished from the Western civilization in part by religion because it is primarily Catholic and had limited exposure to the Reformation. It also includes nonreligious elements like a corporatist authoritarian culture and the inclusion of indigenous elements into the culture. (Huntington, 1996a: 46) The Western civilization is distinguished by its combined Catholic and Protestant culture as a result of the Reformation and its adherence to the concept of separation of church and state. It is also distinguished by nonreligious traits including its classical legacy, multiplicity of languages, social pluralism, adherence to the rule of law, near-universal acceptance of representative government, and sense of individualism. (Huntington, 1996a: 46, 68-72)

The Sino-Confucian civilization includes Confucianism as a major component. Huntington also alludes that the civilization includes other common cultural elements but never describes them. He is also unclear as to whether Buddhist groups are included in the civilization or constitute a separate civilization. On one hand, the Buddhist civilization appears on his map of "The World of Civilizations: Post-1990." (Huntington, 1996a: 26-27) He also infers that there is a Buddhist civilization in table 10.1 of his book (Huntington, 1996a: 257) where he argues that the Chinese-Tibetan conflict is intercivilizational "since it is clearly a clash between Confucian Han Chinese and Lamaist Buddhist Tibetans." On the other hand, he does not include Buddhism in his listing of civilizations in his original *Foreign Affairs* article and in his book and overtly states that "Buddhism, although a major religion, has not been the basis of a major civilization." (Huntington, 1996a: 48). He also includes "the related cultures of Vietnam and Korea," which are countries with Buddhist majorities, in the Sino-Confucian civilization. (Huntington, 1996a: 45) Thus, for the purposes of this study, we include Buddhist groups in the Sino-Confucian civilization.

The Japanese civilization is distinguished from the Sino-Confucian civilization by its adherence to Shintoism as well as its long separation from the Chinese mainland. (Huntington, 1993a; 1996a: 45)

The only civilization which includes no obvious religious component is the African civilization. It is, rather, based on a sense of common identity. (Huntington, 1996a: 47) The fact that there is no religious component to the African civilization is likely the reason that Huntington is unsure whether this civilization is truly a separate civilization.

It is important to emphasize that Huntington's list of civilizations is not universally accepted. Many, including Nussbaum (1997), Tony Smith (1997), and Tipson (1997), disagree with Huntington's division of the world into civilizations, both in principle and with the specifics of these divisions.

There is no shortage of additional evidence that Huntington bases his concept of civilization on religion. First, he argues that political and social modernization has separated people from their local identities and weakened the nation-state. In much of the world, religion has filled this gap for people separated from their roots by modernity. (Huntington, 1993a: 25-29; 1996a: 95-99) Many like Sahliyeh (1990: 9), Haynes (1994: 7, 34), Shupe (1990: 22-26), and Juergensmeyer (1993) echo Huntington's arguments that modernization has, in fact, caused a resurgence of religion in recent times. Second, Huntington (1996a: 100-101) argues that the failure of Communism, socialism, and other Western (economic) ideas have created an ideological vacuum, which religion has begun to fill. These arguments are echoed by a number of other academics.[1]

Finally, he makes a number of statements which explicitly say that he based his concept of civilizations on religion. For example, when discussing the nature of civilizations he argues that "the major civilizations of human history have been closely identified with the world's great religions." (Huntington, 1996a: 42) When listing the different civilizations he states that "religion is a central characteristic in defining civilizations." (Huntington, 1996a: 47) On the formation of civilizational differences he argues that when people are in crisis, they "rally to those with similar ancestry, religion, language, values, and institutions, and distance themselves from those with different ones." (Huntington, 1996a: 123) When discussing civilizational wars he notes that "Since religion . . . is the principle [sic] defining characteristic of civilizations, fault line wars are almost always between peoples of different religions." (Huntington, 1996a: 253)

Huntington's Predictions

Huntington's most basic prediction is that conflict will increase between these civilizations and conflicts within these civilizations will decrease in the post-Cold War era. Huntington defines three types of civilizational conflicts. The first two are types of international conflict. Core state conflicts are international conflicts between those states which are the most powerful within their respective civilizations. He argues that most of these civilizations have core states which are the most powerful states in their civilization and, thus, tend to lead them. He expects conflicts between these core states to become one of the defining elements of international politics. The United States vs. China would be an example of a core state conflict. International fault-line conflicts, the second type of conflict, are conflicts between states belonging to different civilizations which happen to border each other. Thus, where states of different civilizations border each other, he predicts that there is likely to be increased tension. The India-Pakistan conflict is an example of this type of conflict. The third type of conflicts are domestic fault-line conflicts which are conflicts within states that have heterogeneous populations including groups of different civilizations. The civil wars in the former Yugoslavia and between the Chechens and Russians are examples of this type of conflict. This study focuses exclusively on the latter of these types of conflicts which Huntington himself argues are the most common type of post-Cold War conflict and, accordingly, the most important to study. (Huntington, 2000: 609-610)

Huntington's second major prediction is that the end of the Cold War has accelerated a preexisting trend of the decline of Western (American) power. This makes a major rethinking of Western foreign policy necessary because

> as Western power recedes, so too does the appeal of Western values and culture, and the West faces the need to accommodate itself to its declining ability to impose its values on non-Western societies. In many fundamental ways, much of the world is becoming more modern and less Western. (Huntington, 1996b: 38)

According to Huntington (1996b) the conceit of the West takes two forms. First, the West, and particularly the United States, believes that its culture is enveloping the world through its media and consumer goods. He calls this the Coca-Colonization thesis. Yet the essence of culture is based on language, religion, values, traditions and customs, which resist the incursions from the West, and are perhaps strengthened by the vigorous and conscious defense against these incursions. This argument mirrors the arguments by Marty and Appleby (1991) and Juergensmeyer (1993) that religious fundamentalism and religious nationalism are often reactions against the penetration of nonindigenous cultural and political ideas and values.

The second conceit of the West is the belief that because the West has led the world in modernization, non-Western countries will Westernize as they modernize. Clearly, there are differences between modern and traditional cultures. "It does not necessarily follow, however, that societies with modern cultures should be any more similar than are societies with traditional cultures." (Huntington, 1996b: 29)

In fact, modernization tends to produce renewed commitment to indigenous cultures. The social and cultural disruption caused by modernization causes many to actively seek out and strengthen their cultures in order to protect and preserve them. The wealth and power that comes from successful modernization gives people more confidence in the value of their culture.

All of this implies that conflict involving the West will be increasingly civilizational as the West defends its declining power in the world arena.

Huntington's final predictions, dealing with specific civilizations, are discussed later in this chapter.

The CoC theory has significance beyond its predictions of the nature of conflict in the post-Cold War era. It defines a new world order where the basic unit of analysis is no longer ethnic groups or the state. Rather, the larger identity group of civilizations is predicted to become the most important unit of analysis. This means that not only conflict, but diplomacy, trade, treaties, and alliances will be based along civilizational lines. If Huntington's predictions are correct, this would be a revolutionary change in the international system on the order of the Treaty of Westphalia (1648) which defined the role of sovereign states in the modern era. This change would replace sovereign states with larger civilizational units which could impinge upon the previously inviolable sovereignty of states.

Huntington's Critics

Huntington's CoC theory has no shortage of critics. Interestingly, about the only thing these critics can agree upon is that Huntington was wrong. The specific criticisms made by Huntington's detractors are often not consistent with those of other critics. In some cases individual critics even contradict themselves. Accordingly, rather than provide an internally consistent critique of the CoC theory, the purpose here is to provide a description of the various criticisms of the theory that exist in the literature.

This discussion divides the various criticisms of the CoC theory into several categories. First, many argue that those factors that defined conflict during the Cold War will continue to do so after it. However, there is little agreement as to the nature of these traditional lines of conflict. Realists argue that traditional realpolitik theories, based on the state as the basic unit of international relations, still provide the best explanation for international conflict. For example Ajami, (1993: 6) argues that the state system and the concept of balance of power are too internalized to dissipate. Gray (1998) argues that the real conflicts will continue to be based on the conflicting interests of states. Pfaff (1997) argues that Huntington's civilizations are only relevant to the extent that they represent major power groupings of individual states. Some make more liberal arguments. For example, Ajami (1993:5) argues that people are more interested in economic prosperity than maintaining their traditions. Others base their predictions on more Marxist considerations. For example, Hunter (1998) argues that the real clash is caused by unequal distribution of wealth and power.

Another version of this type of argument is that the civilizations Huntington describes were not united during the Cold War and are not united now. Accordingly, most conflicts, both international and domestic, will be between members of the same civilizations, mostly between states or ethnic and national groups. Halliday (1997) argues that cultures are not homogeneous entities and have within them varying interpretations and subdivisions. Kirkpatrick et al. (1993: 23) similarly make the general argument that in the past civilizational clashes were not the worst conflicts and there is no reason to believe that this will change. Beedham (1999) argues that it takes very little to differentiate one state from another and that civilizations are too loose and untidy to behave like states. Yamazaki (1996) argues that Asia can be broken up into several regions based on political, cultural, and religious structures. Walt (1998) argues that nationalism remains the most important factor in the post-Cold War era, making conflicts within civilizations as likely as conflicts between them. Gurr (1994) argues that ethnicity is a better explanation for domestic conflict than is civilization. Others who predict more conflicts within civilizations than between them include Heilbrunn (1998), Kader (1998), Kirth

(1994), Rosecrance (1998), and Tipson (1997).

The second type of critique of the CoC theory is the argument that the world is becoming more united and interdependent, thus causing a general reduction of conflict in the post-Cold War era. Anwar (1998) and Tipson (1997), for example, argue that factors like economic interdependence, communications, and world integration will lead to a world civilization which will rise above conflicts. Ahari (1997) makes a normative version of this argument, saying that the only culture that should occupy the world is the human culture. Ikenberry (1997) believes that the process of globalization does not even need to reach a very high level, arguing that "a belief in universalism and global cultural homogenization is not necessary to pursue an order that goes beyond the West. All that is needed are states with commitments to democracy, free markets and the rule of law." Halliday (1997) notes that there has been a historical borrowing and mixing among cultures, making it difficult to argue that the civilizations Huntington describes are distinct. Although it predates the CoC theory, Fukayama's (1989) argument that the collapse of Soviet Communism will result in the "end of history" with the universalization of Western liberal democracy is also related to this type of critique of Huntington.

The third type of critique is the contention that Huntington ignored an important post-Cold War phenomenon that will impact on conflict, thereby making his theory irrelevant. That is, many argue that some factor other than civilizations will be the basis for world conflict or the lack thereof. Viorst (1997) argues that Huntington ignores the fact that the world is better at managing conflict than it used to be. He also believes that population and environment issues will define world politics in the future. Barber (1997/1998) argues that power in the post-Cold War era will be defined by control over information technology. Senghass (1998) argues that most ethnopolitical conflicts result from protracted discrimination rather than cultural roots. Rosecrance (1998) points out that military power overshadowed civilizations in the past and there is no reason it cannot do so in the future. He also argues, as do Hunter (1998) and Nussbaum (1997), that economic power is the most important type of power today. Ajami (1993) similarly argues that Huntington underestimates the power of modernity and secularism and that people are more interested in economic prosperity than maintaining their traditions. Kirkpatrick et al. (1993) believe that since other civilizations want to be like the West, the predicted West vs. non-West conflicts will not occur. Similarly, Mahbubani (1993) argues that the non-West wants Western leadership and is, in fact, afraid that the West is weakening. Howell (1997) argues for an opposite trend of the West becoming Easternized.

Fourth, many argue that Huntington has his facts wrong. Some, like Anwar (1998), Hassner (1997a), Heilbrunn (1998), Kader (1998), Neckermann (1998), and Walt (1997), simply argue that the facts do not fit Huntington's theory. Pfaff (1997) accuses Huntington of ignoring facts. Some, like Hassner (1997b), even go as far as to accuse Huntington of bending the facts to fit his theory.

Fifth, many critique Huntington's methodology. Hassner (1997a) and Pfaff (1997) accuse Huntington of oversimplification. Beedham (1999), Pfaff (1997),

Tony Smith (1997), and Tipson (1997) question Huntington's assessment of what are the world's civilizations. Ikenberry (1997) similarly argues that the features that Huntington feels make the West unique are, in fact, not cultural factors nor are they unique to the West. Heilbrunn (1998) notes that Huntington, in his various writings, contradicts himself. Naff (1998) argues that Huntington is too dependent on English-language sources. Gurr (1994) and Halliday (1997) note that Huntington's evidence is completely anecdotal, leaving room for many to cite counterexamples. Similarly, Senghass (1998), Rosecrance (1998), and Walt (1997) argue that Huntington provides no systematic analysis of the link between civilizational controversies and political behavior. That is, a quantitative, or at least a more systematic, analysis of Huntington's is necessary before it can be properly evaluated. (The same argument is made here.) However, Pfaff (1997) accuses Huntington of the opposite. He argues that political science in general, and Huntington specifically, have wrongly made the behavioral assumption that political behavior can be explained scientifically.

Sixth, many argue that because of his popularity among policy makers, Huntington's theory is a self-fulfilling prophecy. (Hassner, 1997a; Pfaff, 1997; Singhua, 1997; Tony Smith, 1997; Tipson, 1997; and Walt, 1997). Similarly, Anwar (1998) and Gungwu (1997a) accuse Huntington of making unwarranted doomsday predictions.

Seventh, Aysha (2003) argues that even Huntington himself does not believe his theory. Rather, Huntington's true intent in forming and publicizing the theory was to address four problems in U.S. domestic politics. First, Huntington wanted to fight multiculturalism which he sees as a threat to America's commitment to individualistic liberalism. Second, the collapse of communism has led to an identity crisis in the United States. The United States needs an enemy in order to shore up its identity. Third, there is a need to strengthen the ties between citizens and the federal government to counter a rising tide of anti-federalism. Finally, there is a need to counter the erosion of U.S. nationalism caused by economic globalization. Getting people to believe in the CoC theory will help to unify the United States, give it focus, and build stronger links between citizens and the federal government.

The eighth type of critique of the CoC theory are ad hominem arguments against Huntington himself. Hassner (1997a; 1997b) provides a good example of this. He calls Huntington and his CoC theory "delusional," "inflammatory," "excessive simplification," "deeply wrong," "indefensible," "distorted," "appalling," "odd," "objectionable," and "dangerous." He further argues that "Huntington's descriptions and predictions are a collection of unilateral statements that have, at best, half a chance of being proven true."

Ninth, a number of quantitative studies contradict Huntington's predictions. In a study of militarized interstate disputes from 1950 to 1992, Russett et al. (2000) find, among other things, that intracivilizational conflicts were more likely than intercivilizational conflicts. They also found that civilizational conflicts, if anything, waned as the Cold War ended and that while civilizational variables are not important, aspects of the realist and liberal theories are important predictors of international conflict.[2] These findings are consistent with those of Henderson (1997; 1998) that cultural factors do not have a unidirectional impact on international war. Henderson and Tucker (2001) find that, if anything, civilizational differences make states less likely to go to war. Ellingsen (2002) found no link between civilizations and UN voting behavior.

However, Davis and Moore (1997) and Davis, Jaggers, and Moore (1997) find a connection between international ethnic alliances and international conflict. While this is consistent with Huntington's predictions of civilizational influence in conflicts, it is only limited confirmation for two reasons. First, this study does not address whether the strength of this link between ethnicity and intervention increased or decreased since the end of the Cold War. Second, the evidence refers to ethnic conflict and not civilizational conflict.

Studies of domestic conflict also tend to contradict the CoC theory. Henderson and Singer (2000) find that cultural factors are less important than political ones when examining civil wars. Gurr (1994), in an examination of major ethnic conflicts, found no support for Huntington's theory. Ellingsen (2000) found that there is no real change in the dynamics of ethnic conflict from the Cold War to the post-Cold War eras. Fox (2001f; 2002b; 2003) also found that globally there has been little change in the ratio of civilizational vs. noncivilizational domestic conflict, including ethnic conflict, genocidal wars, and revolutionary wars, since the end of the Cold War and that the majority of domestic conflict is within civilizations.

However, a series of studies on terrorism, by Weinberg and Eubank (1999) and Weinberg et al. (2002) does provide some evidence in support of the CoC theory. They found that in the 1980s and 1990s, terrorism was becoming more civilizational. In particular most terrorism was by Islamic groups against non-Muslims and most new terrorist organizations were Islamic. However, this is by no means conclusive in that it shows only that Muslim groups tend to choose terrorism as a tactic. It does not include other types of violence including guerrilla warfare and high intensity civil war. That the studies mentioned above (as well as the results of this study) which include several types of domestic conflict do not confirm this result indicates that domestic conflict, in general, is not civilizational.

While these studies are informative, they in no way make the analysis presented here redundant for several reasons. First, none of them analyzes the specific data examined here. Second, most of them analyze different types of conflicts than those examined in this study. This study examines the updated versions of the MAR and SF datasets. Russett et al. (2000), Henderson (1997, 1998), Henderson and Tucker (2001), Davis and Moore (1997), and Davis, Jaggers and Moore (1997) analyze international wars. Weinberg and Eubank (1999) and Weinberg et al. (2002) analyze only terrorism. Fox (2001f; 2002b; 2003) and Gurr (1994) analyze earlier versions of the MAR or SF datasets individually. Ellingsen (2000) examines only ethnic wars. Ellingsen (2002) examines only UN voting behavior. Third, many of the studies do not cover a significant amount of the post-Cold War era. For example, Russet et al. (2000) and Henderson and Tucker's (2001) studies do not include data from after 1992 and Henderson (1997) does not include data from after 1989.

Despite all this, Huntington is not without his supporters. Gregg (1997), Gungwu (1997a; 1997b), Hardjono (1997), Harris (1996), Murphey (1998), Naff (1998), Seamon (1998), and Walid (1997), among others, agree with his argument and use it to make policy prescriptions. Paul Marshall (1998) agrees with Huntington's thesis, arguing that the majority of conflicts are occurring along religious divides.

Another interesting aspect of the debate is that while Huntington's civilizations are to a large extent based on religion, there is almost no discussion of these religious aspects in the debate. This is likely a result of the fact that international relations theories assign little import to religion. Paradigms like realism, liberalism, and globalism placed their emphasis on military and economic factors as well as rational calculations, all of which left little room for religion. Thus, rather than having a theory as to why religion was not important, international relations theories tend to focus on factors that did not include religion. Huntington and his critics mostly argue over at what level of analysis these factors play a key role. That one of these levels of analysis, Huntington's civilizations, is largely based on religion is ignored. This is not unusual for the study of international relations. Philpott (2002: 69) demonstrates that between 1980 and 1999 major international relations journals rarely published articles which included religion as a primary explanation for international phenomena.[3] This trend can be traced to the fact that the academic study of international relations was founded upon, among other things, the belief that the era of religion causing wars was over. (Laustsen and Waever, 2000: 706; Philpott, 2002) This is analogous to the formation of sociology by people who believed that they were the vanguard of a movement to replace all the evils caused by religion with a more benign modern rational and scientific society. (Hadden, 1987b)

It is important to note that many of the arguments against the CoC theory do not contradict the argument that religion is an important factor in conflict. For example, those that argue that the salient level of identity will be subcivilizational do not make any arguments that directly contradict the contention that religion plays a role in identity. In fact, there are many who argue that ethnic and national identities include religious elements. (Gurr, 1993a: 3; Anthony Smith, 1999; 2000) However, some of Huntington's critics do dispute religion's importance to identity in the post-Cold War era. Those who argue the world is developing a single identity have a vision of identity that is beyond any single religion. Also, those who make particularly realist arguments remain within the tradition described above of denying non-material factors are important. Thus, denying that civilizations and religion are important are not exactly the same thing.

Huntington's Reply

Huntington's (1993b; 1996a: 21-39; 58-78) reply to some of these critiques can be best summed up by his statement: "Got a better idea?" He argues, based on Kuhn's (1970) famous work on scientific paradigms, that a paradigm need only be better than its competitors; it doesn't have to explain everything. He points out that the Cold War paradigm, the dominant international relations theory for forty years, did not explain everything and often blinded scholars to important events such as the Sino-Soviet split. Yet, it explained more world events than did any of its competitors. The reason it could not explain everything is because, just like the CoC theory, it is a simplification of a complex reality. This is the role of a paradigm and, as a result, no paradigm can explain everything. The true test of a paradigm is how it performs compared to other paradigms. Which explains more? Thus, the CoC theory need not explain everything; it simply needs to be a better explanatory tool than any of its competitors.

He continues this argument by critiquing alternate theories. First, the paradigms from the Cold War era are no longer useful. The two most prominent of these divide the world into two blocs, either East vs. West or the rich vs. the poor. But global politics are now too complex to be "pigeonholed" into two simple categories. Many recent events do not fit into these two-dimensional paradigms but are explainable by the CoC theory. These include the breakup of the former Soviet Union and Yugoslavia, the rise of world fundamentalism, conflicts within Russia, Turkey, and Mexico over identity issues, trade conflicts between the United States and Japan, and the increasing activity of Sino-Confucian and Islamic states on the world scene. He cited the then prominent peace process between Israel and the Palestinians as an anomaly but predicted, as it turns out correctly, that this was likely a temporary truce and that the violence would likely resume. Intercivilizational issues, he argues, are becoming more important. These include arms control, especially of weapons of mass destruction, human rights, and immigration. These issues are expected to pit the West against the other civilizations.

Although they occurred after Huntington made these arguments, it is arguable that the events of September 11, 2001, and their aftermath strengthen his case. The terrorist threat to the United States clearly comes from the Islamic civilization. Huntington (2002: 5) makes this point when he argues that "undeniably, the terrorist actions of Osama bin Laden have reinvigorated civilizational identity. Just as bin Laden sought to rally Muslims by declaring war on the West, he gave back to the West its sense of common identity in defending itself."

Issues of human rights and weapons of mass destruction, issues most associated with Western states, were among the justifications cited by the Bush administrations for the U.S.-led occupation of Iraq. However, much of the opposition to U.S. policy on Iraq came from Western states like France and the United States has found allies among Islamic states in opposing the terrorist threat. Thus, events are not fully consistent with the CoC theory.

The second theory he critiques is the argument that states remain the primary unit of international relations and their foreign policies are based solely on power considerations. He argues that states do include power in their calculations of their interests but there have always been other considerations. For example, if balance of power was the only consideration, Western Europe would have joined forces with the former Soviet Union in order to balance U.S. power in the late 1940s. Values and culture also influence how states determine their interests. The conflict in values between the East and the West during the Cold War certainly explains why Western Europe sided with the United States rather than the USSR.

Nevertheless, nation-states will remain important actors, but they will act jointly with their civilizational partners. Just like during the Cold War, states acted together as part of the Western or Soviet blocs in the post-Cold War era, they act in civilizational blocs joined by shared religion, culture, language, and history. This is because states will increasingly define their interests in civilizational terms.

Put differently, nation-states will remain the principal actors in world affairs but their alliances will be civilizational and the civilizational nature of these alliances will dominate world politics. This is because cultural commonalities shape the interests that realists hold to be of paramount importance. Accordingly, most world conflict will be between entities from different civilizations, though the particular actors may be states or even substate entities.

The third theory Huntington critiques is the "one-world paradigm" in which the world is uniting into a single unit. Clearly, people have common factors which bind them, they always have, but this never precluded the existence of different and opposing cultures. The argument that the collapse of the Soviet Union means the entire world will become democratic assumes that democracy is the only alternative to Communism, which is obviously not the case as there are many other forms of authoritarianism, including religious ones. The assumption that increased interaction and communication leads to a common culture is sometimes true but it often leads to the mutual reenforcement of different cultures.

Similarly, while modernization does have some uniform effects on societies, it is not the same thing as Westernization or democratization. The argument that modernization makes people more Western is simply "arrogant." Only universal power can produce a universal civilization, and no universal power exists today. The West is currently the most powerful civilization, but Huntington believes that this power is in decline.

Huntington argues that the source of this type of theory is the euphoria from the end of the Cold War dominated by images like the fall of the Berlin Wall. In the past, when wars ended there was a similar euphoria, but it never led to a united world. World War I was seen as the war to end wars, but turned out to be one of the causes of World War II. World War II was expected to make the world safe for democracy but was immediately followed by the Cold War. Thus, history shows that this one-world euphoria is unjustified.

This set of replies by Huntington to his critics, addresses the first three types of criticism listed above. However, it does not address the rest of them. The arguments that he got his facts wrong, that his methodology is suspect, that he has ulterior motives for this theory, and that his predictions are self-fulfilling are never truly addressed. Nor are the ad hominem arguments, but that type of argument does not really need to be addressed. He also does not really address the contention that conflict within civilizations will be more prominent than conflict between them.

He does address a few of the quantitative studies which contradict his theory, but he does so on a case-by-case basis. For example Huntington (2000) critiques Russett et al.'s (2000) analysis of international conflict. He points out that the data ends in 1992, not very far into the post-Cold War era and that the data is limited to military disputes and not other forms of international conflict. He also argues that, as domestic conflict is becoming more important in the post-Cold War era, this should be the true test of the CoC theory. However, as discussed above, many of the qualitative studies which contradict Huntington's predictions meet the criteria of extending farther into the post-Cold War era and dealing with domestic conflict. As a whole, this body of critics covers most forms of conflict, international and domestic. Thus, Huntington has no real answer to this form of critique other than the argument that his theory will prove to be true in the future.

The Debate over Islam

Perhaps the most controversial prediction made by Huntington is his argument that the Islamic civilization will be the most violent civilization and the primary threat to the West in the post-Cold War era. Huntington (1996a: 183) sums up this argument when he states that some civilizational conflicts

> are more conflict-prone than others. At the micro level, the most violent fault lines are between Islam and its . . . neighbors. At the macro level, the dominant division is between "the West and the rest," with the most intense conflicts occurring between Muslim and Asian societies on one hand, and the West on the other. The dangerous clashes of the future are likely to arise from the interaction of Western arrogance, Islamic intolerance, and Sinic assertiveness.

The Western "arrogance" which Huntington (1996a: 183-206, 1996b: 28-29) feels is likely to cause conflict is the belief that Western values like democracy and capitalism are universally valid combined with the Western willingness to defend its values and interests as the values of the world community. In addition, the West believes that it has led the world into modernity, giving it the right to lead the world. While democracy and human rights tend to be accepted in Christian states, other civilizations are less interested and tend to resist Western influence. On a more micro level, immigrants in Western states from the non-West are not integrating well into Western society and, accordingly, are perceived as an internal challenge.

The Islamic civilization, while accepting modernity according to Huntington (1996a: 32, 109-120, 185, 209-218), rejects Western culture and prefers to search for the answers to its problems in Islam. This is, to some extent, fueled by the increase in Islamic wealth from oil, but it is more probably due to the failure of governments in Islamic states that were guided by Western ideologies to successfully address social problems, causing a return to Islam.[4] Furthermore, Islam and the West, historically, have mutually feared each other and rejected each other's culture. This is exacerbated by the fact that the Islamic civilization considers itself superior to others and the Islamic religion divides the world into those who follow Islam and those who do not.

Huntington also expects an alliance between the Islamic and Sino-Confucian civilizations against the West.

Many critique this argument. For example, some argue that Huntington mistakes growing pains caused by economics and modernity with civilizational conflict. For example, Ajami (1993) argues that Huntington underestimates the power of modernity and secularism to reshape world politics and that the Confucian-Islam alliance is economic rather than civilizational. Similarly, Bartley (1993) argues that democracy is a result of economic development and not of the ideological agenda of the West and that Islamic fundamentalists are clashing with modernity, not other civilizations. Fuller and Lesser (1995) add that this clash may eventually result in the secularization of Islam. Pfaff (1997) adds that Islamic fundamentalism is controversial even within the Islamic civilization. Esposito (1995) and Halliday (1996) take this one step further and argue that Islamic fundamentalism is more of a threat to the authoritarian regimes in Islamic states than it is to the West. Also, many, like Esposito (1995), Fuller and Lesser (1995), and Monshipouri (1998), argue that any clashes between Islam and the West are due to secular causes and not religious ones. These secular causes include economic, national, political, cultural, psychological, postcolonial, and strategic issues.

Others argue that the West, rather than being rejected, is being embraced by other civilizations. Kirkpatrick et al. (1993) argue that other civilizations aspire to the Western model. Mahbubani (1993) argues that, while power among civilizations is shifting, much of the non-West fears the retreat of Western leadership and that while the West fears Islam, the Islamic civilization is weak and poses no real threat. Still others, including Beedham (1999), Kader (1998), and Monshipouri (1998), argue that the Islamic civilization is divided and conflicts occur more often within it than between it and other civilizations.

Hunter (1998) combines most of these arguments as well as others into a full-scale attack on Huntington's predictions regarding the Islamic civilization. She argues that the Islamic civilization is not monolithic. Nationalism is a potent factor within the Islamic civilization causing many divisions within it. As a result, there are both many clashes within the Islamic civilization and Islamic states often have better relations with non-Islamic states, as was the case during the Gulf War. The rise in Islamic fundamentalism, that Huntington perceives as a threat to the West, is not a civilizational issue. It is rather caused by the same economic and social causes that have resulted in fundamentalist movements within the West.[5] Thus, the conflict between faith and secularism is not civilizational at all. Furthermore, the enthusiasm for Islamic fundamentalism is waning due to the failures of Iran's Islamic state. While there may be some tensions between the Western and Islamic civilizations, these tensions have more to do with the unequal distribution of wealth, power, and influence than cultural issues.

On the other hand, many agree with this argument. Lewis (1993), in agreement with Huntington, argues that Islam and Christianity are both exclusive, not merely universal, religions, thus almost guaranteeing a clash between them. Even some of Huntington's critics like Hassner (1997a; 1997b) and Heilbrunn (1998) believe that there may be something to Huntington's arguments with regard to clashes between the Western and Islamic civilizations.

Several quantitative studies also contradict this element of Huntington's theory. Fox (2000a; 2001b; 2001c; 2003) found that Muslim groups are no more violent than non-Muslim groups, the amount of conflict involving Muslim groups which is civilizational did not change substantially with the end of the Cold War, and that the majority of conflict involving Muslim groups is intracivilizational.

However, some quantitative studies also support Huntington's arguments regarding Islam. As noted above, Weinberg and Eubank (1999) and Weinberg et al. (2002) found that terrorism is particularly Islamic. Also, as noted above, this finding is not significant when placed in the context of the wider range of conflict of which terrorism is only a subset. To use Huntington's own arguments, civilizations are culturally different. The greater Islamic tolerance for the use of terrorism is just one of these differences. Also, the results of the analysis in Chapter 3 of this book show that, when taking their proportion of the world's population into account, Muslims are more likely to engage in violent conflict.

Operationalizing the Clash of Civilizations

A final issue which must be addressed is how to operationize the CoC theory. That is, how do we assign civilizational categories to specific countries and minority groups? This is necessary for this study, as in the next two chapters we statistically compare civilizational conflicts to noncivilizational conflicts as well as the characteristics of different civilizations. This process of making a final decision on how to code each of these countries and minority groups has other advantages. It prevents one from categorizing specific groups differently in different parts of that analysis, as Huntington sometimes does. It is also a practical way to test whether a theory is truly specific and internally consistent.

There were several problems in translating Huntington's theory into practical codings. First, Huntington divides the world into eight major civilizations: Western, Sino-Confucian, Japanese, Islamic, Hindu, Slavic-Orthodox, Latin American, and "possibly" African. However, as noted above, he is unclear as to whether a Buddhist civilization exists separately from the Sino-Confucian civilization. For operational purposes here, Buddhists are considered part of the Sino-Confucian civilization for several reasons. First, there is no mention of the Buddhist civilization in his 1993 *Foreign Affairs* article. Second, more often than not, Huntington did not include them in his list of civilizations. Third, in the actual listing and description of civilizations in his book, Huntington stated that Buddhists are included in the Sino-Confucian civilization.

A second problem in operationalizing the CoC theory is that Huntington's list and description of civilizations is in many places not nearly specific enough for use in categorizing groups, especially minority groups. As discussed above, for the most part, as Huntington admits, his definitions are, to a great extent, based on religion. Thus, when religion can be used to identify a civilization, it is used for that purpose. This rule, along with the general descriptions of the civilizations provided by Huntington, taken at face value, are generally adequate to define the civilization of majority groups in states, with two exceptions, Israel and the Philippines. Although Huntington to a great extent bases his civilizations on religion, he does not deal with Judaism. Although Israel is geographically located in the Middle East, an Islamic region, and much of Israel's Jewish population came from Islamic countries, it is more appropriate to include Israel in the Western civilization for four reasons. First, in the past, and to a lesser extent presently, many Middle Eastern Muslims have perceived Israel as a Western imperialist intruder in the Middle East. Second, many of the traits of the Western civilization described by Huntington apply to Israel. (Huntington, 1996a: 69-72) Third, Israel was established primarily by European Jews, with most Eastern Jews coming after the state's establishment. Finally, when Huntington (1996a: 71) does address Israel, he implies that it is part of the Western civilization. In the Philippines, the majority group is Asiatic but they are mostly Westernized and Christian. In this case, religion was the deciding factor and they were coded as Western.

The application of these definitions of civilizations to minority groups is considerably more problematic. That is, these definitions are vague and leave many questions open when applying them to many minority groups. The Afro-Americans in the United States and several Latin American states bring up such a question. Are they part of the African identity group or are they sufficiently assimilated into their local cultures to be considered part of the African civilization? Reasonable arguments can be made for either case. For operational purposes, these groups are considered part of the African civilization because there are many indications, especially in the United States, that many Afro-Americans consider themselves to have a distinct identity which is, in part, tied to their African origins. This common identity seems to be the key factor in Huntington's definition of the African civilization which is unique from his definitions of the other civilizations in that it is wholly based on identity and culture and has no obvious religious component. It is important to note, however, that this is an extension of Huntington's theory. It is argued here that this extension is necessary because Huntington did not address this issue.

A similar question arises for black Muslim groups in Africa. Are they part of the African or Islamic civilizations? Since Huntington seems to be ambivalent about the African civilization and defines the Islamic civilization wholly on the basis of religion, these and all other Muslim groups are considered part of the Islamic civilization. He also includes several African-Muslim states as part of the Islamic civilization in his map of world civilizations. (Huntington, 1996a: 26-27) The Druze, Baha'i, and Sikhs are groups that do not fit well into any of Huntington's categories. Since the Druze and Baha'i religions are considered Islamic offshoots and the Sikh religion combines elements of the Islamic and Hindu faiths, ethnic groups of these three religions are considered here part of the Islamic civilization. Another problematic group are the Gagauz in Moldova. They are Orthodox Christian but not European in origin. For operational purposes, religion was the deciding factor and they are included in the Slavic-Orthodox civilization. Finally, there are many minority groups that are of mixed origins. An excellent example are the Roma minorities in Europe. These groups were coded as "mixed" and clashes between them and other groups are considered noncivilizational conflicts.

A third problem in operationalizing Huntington's definitions is that there is a category of minority found throughout the world which does not fit into any of his civilizations, yet is clearly distinct from the others. This category is indigenous peoples. While their religion, race, and culture vary widely, indigenous peoples have a common historical experience that in many ways makes them more similar to each other than to any of Huntington's civilizations.[6] For this reason, while not considered a separate civilization, indigenous groups are, for the purposes of this study, considered a separate category from other civilizations and conflicts involving indigenous groups are not considered civilizational. Perhaps Huntington failed to account for indigenous peoples because the primary focus of his theory was originally international conflict. However, this argument is weak because he later claims the theory applies most to domestic conflict in response to a quantitative study showing his theory did not work for international conflict. (Huntington, 2000) Be that as it may, the failure to include a major portion of the world's ethnic minorities in his theory is a serious problem.

Finally, the MAR dataset is designed to assess the relationship between majority and minority groups within a state. The majority group is operationally defined as the group which controls the state. Accordingly, in cases of civil war, there is no such majority group. This only affects three cases: Afghanistan, Bosnia, and Lebanon. All cases in Afghanistan are coded as not civilizational because all four ethnic groups are Islamic. In Bosnia, the three ethnic groups, the Serbs, Croats, and Muslims, belong to three different civilizations (Slavic-Orthodox, Western, and Islamic, respectively). Accordingly, these three cases are coded as civilizational conflicts. Similarly, Lebanon is ruled by a combination of Muslims and Christians. Accordingly, all of the cases in Lebanon are considered civilizational clashes. As the SF dataset includes two sides for each conflict, these issues do not apply.

These difficulties in operationalizing Huntington's CoC theory reveal several weaknesses because the theory is often vague and inconsistent. It is argued here that these codings are a reasonable operationalization of Huntington's concept of civilizations, if not the only possible operationalization. Some compromises were certainly necessary in order to operationalize the theory. In general, wherever possible, religion was used as the deciding factor. In cases where this could not be done, as was the case with minorities of African origin in North and South America, indigenous peoples, and minorities of mixed origins, as well as the Jewish majority in Israel, other solutions were found.

These difficulties in operationalizing Huntington's concept of civilizations, in and of themselves, cause one to question the validity of Huntington's CoC theory. They lend credence to those that argue that Huntington's concept of civilizations is oversimplified, unclear, and not sufficiently systematic. His self-contradictory statements on whether Buddhism constitutes a civilization is an example of how the anecdotal approach can lead to situationally convenient explanations and arguments. Also his failure to account for indigenous peoples places the comprehensiveness of his thesis into question. While, to be fair, the coding of events data generally requires some questionable judgment calls, the combination of coding quandaries described above reveals a theory that has some serious inconsistencies and overlooks important facts for which it should account.[7] Then again, many grand theories are vague and inconsistent in the details, so rejecting the CoC theory solely on these grounds is unwarranted.

Conclusions

The debate over Huntington's CoC theory remains controversial. This has only been exacerbated by the terrorist attacks of September 11, 2001, and their aftermath. This review of the literature on the debate cannot settle the issue, though the body of quantitative evidence against the CoC theory is impressive and convincing. However, even this body of evidence can only show that in the past Huntington's theory was not correct for the time periods these studies analyze. It cannot prove that the CoC theory will not turn out to be correct in the future.

The following two chapters test the various aspects of Huntington's CoC theory with regard to domestic conflict using the MAR and SF datasets.

Notes

1. See, for example, Juergensmeyer (1993), Esposito (1998: 21), Haynes (1994: 7), Nasr (1998: 33), and Williams (1994: 803).
2. For a reply to this study see Huntington (2000).
3. Philpott (2002: 69) found that in about 1,600 articles in four major international relations journals only six articles "featured religion as an important influence." The journals in the study were *International Organization*, *International Studies Quarterly*, *International Security*, and *World Politics*.
4. Juergensmeyer (1993) similarly argues that in the Third World, in general, many states are returning to their indigenous religions due to the failure of governments guided by Western ideologies. Deeb (1992: 53-54), Piscatori (1994: 361-363), and Layachi and Halreche

(1992: 70) make similar arguments with respect to Islam.

5. Many, including Marty and Appleby (1991; 1993; 1994), echo the argument that the rise in fundamentalism is occurring internationally and is, at least in part, a reaction to modernity.

6. For a full discussion of the commonalities of indigenous peoples as well as the international mobilization of these groups see Alfred and Wilmer (1997) and Wilmer (1993).

7. Russett et al. (2000) also find difficulty in coding Huntington's civilizations. Because their analysis focuses on international war they encounter and deal with only those problems relevant to coding the civilization of a state. Their codings, while not identical to those used here, are strikingly similar. In cases of mixed population, they code based on the majority group's religion. Israel is coded as Western. The only major difference is that, while they agree with the assessment here that Huntington is ambivalent over whether or not there is a Buddhist civilization, they choose to include it as a separate civilization in their analysis.

Chapter 7

Is Conflict Civilizational?

The debate over Samuel Huntington's Clash of Civilizations (CoC) theory can be boiled down to several questions. However, only some of these questions can be addressed in a quantitative study such as this one. This chapter addresses a number of those questions which can be addressed in a quantitative study, focusing on those which can be answered with a bivariate analysis. The following chapter addresses a number of those questions which require a multivariate analysis.

This chapter analyzes ethnic conflict, mass killings, and revolutionary wars between 1945 and 2001 (1945 to 2000 for the MAR dataset and 1948 to 2001 for the SF dataset) in order to assess the validity of many of Huntington's claims. The analysis essentially attempts to answer several questions. First, did civilizational conflict become more common with the end of the Cold War? Second, did the conflict behavior of any specific civilizations change with the end of the Cold War? Third, did civilizational conflict become more violent in the post-Cold War era, especially in comparison to noncivilizational conflict? Fourth, has the level of violence by any particular civilization changed with the end of the Cold War? Finally, did conflict between the Islamic and Western civilizations become more common or violent in the post-Cold War era?

It is also important to reiterate that Huntington does not predict that religion and culture, in the form of his civilizations, will become more important in the post-Cold War era. Rather, he predicts that civilizations will become the dominant and defining political factor. In short, he predicts a paradigm shift where most conflict will be civilizational. Thus, to substantiate his theory, it is not enough to show that civilizational conflict increased in the post-Cold War era. It also must be shown that civilizational conflict became the dominant form of conflict after the end of the Cold War.

For the purposes of this study, the Cold War ends in 1989 and 1990 is considered the first year of the post-Cold War era.

Is Civilizational Conflict More Common?

This section examines whether civilizational conflicts are more common than non-civilizational ones and whether there was any change in the proportion of civilizational vs. noncivilizational conflicts with the end of the Cold War. The analysis of the MAR data, presented in Figure 7.1, shows a small increase over time in the amount of civilizational conflict. The proportion of civilizational conflict increases from 36.5 percent during the Cold War to 37.5 percent in the early 1990s and 38.6 percent in 2000. However, this slight increase is nowhere near the dramatic rise in civilizational conflict one would expect if there was truly a shift in paradigms as Huntington predicted. Furthermore, this small increase in civilizational conflict is well within the bounds of the small random changes one would expect to occur over time.

The analysis of the SF data also does not show the dramatic changes one would expect from a paradigm shift to the CoC theory. The analysis of the proportions of conflict which are civilizational in the SF data, presented in Figure 7.2, show some evidence of a rise in civilizational conflict. State failures in general as well as ethnic wars and mass killings became more civilizational beginning in the mid-1980s. However, only in the category of mass killings, the category with the smallest absolute number of conflicts, did civilizational conflicts become the majority of conflicts. In contrast, revolutionary wars were almost exclusively noncivilizational both during and after the Cold War.

Furthermore, an examination of the yearly number of all state failures which are civilizational and noncivilizational provides even less support for Huntington's theory. An examination of all state failures, presented in Figure 7.3, shows that until 1996 the rise and fall of civilizational and noncivilizational state failures roughly paralleled each other with civilizational state failures remain less common. From 1997, the number of noncivilizational state failures dropped from twenty-four to twelve a year while civilizational state failures dropped only from nine to eight. Thus, the rise in civilizational state failures in proportion to noncivilizational ones during the 1990s is not due to a dramatic increase in civilizational state failures but a drop in noncivilizational ones. Furthermore, during the entire time period examined here, civilizational state failures remained less common than did non-civilizational state failures.

Of all of the analyses of specific types of state failure, the analysis of ethnic wars, presented in Figure 7.4, comes the closest to supporting the CoC theory. Until 1999, the number of civilizational and noncivilizational state failures run roughly in parallel with noncivilizational conflicts becoming more common. In 1999, however, they become equally as common as each other at 9 and both drop to 7 in 2001. Thus, there is clearly a rise in the proportion of ethnic state failures which are civilizational but at no time did civilizational ethnic state failures become more common than noncivilizational ones.

The analysis of mass killing state failures, presented in Figure 7.5, shows little

Figure 7.1: Percentage of Ethnic Conflicts Which Are Civilizational

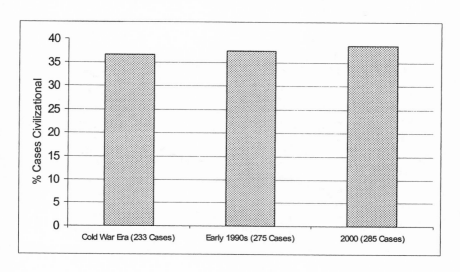

Figure 7.2: Percentage of State Failures Which Are Civilizational, 1965-2001

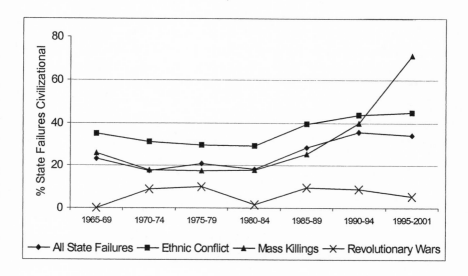

Figure 7.3: Number of State Failures Which Are Civilizational, 1965-2001

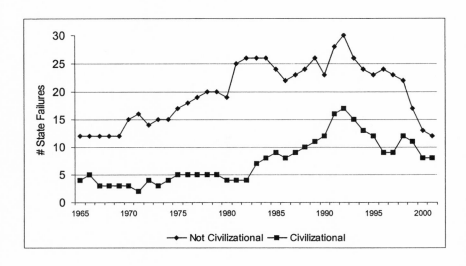

Figure 7.4: Number of Ethnic State Failures Which Are Civilizational, 1965-2001

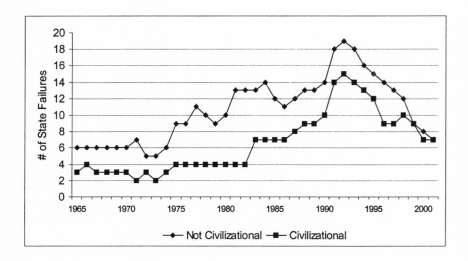

Figure 7.5: Number of Mass Killing State Failures Which Are Civilizational, 1965-2001

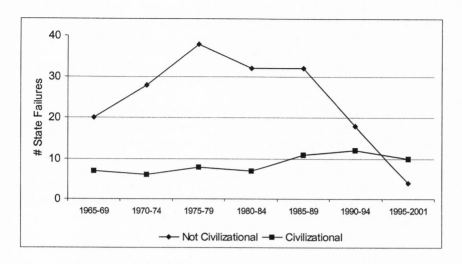

Figure 7.6: Number of Revolutionary War State Failures Which Are Civilizational, 1965-2001

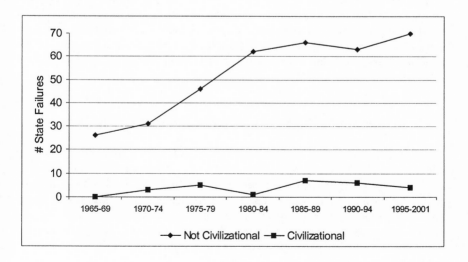

change over time in civilizational mass killings, as one would expect if the CoC theory was correct, though there is a slight rise in civilizational mass killings beginning in the mid-1980s. From 1965 to 1984 the number of mass killing state failures ranged between six and eight for every five-year period. From 1985 onward this rose to ten to twelve per period. This represents a rise from an average of 1.4 civilizational mass killings per year to 1.9 per year. However, for most of this period noncivilizational mass killings were far more common than civilizational mass killings. Civilizational mass killings became a majority of all mass killings in the late 1990s, not because of the slight rise in civilizational mass killings, but because of a dramatic drop in noncivilizational mass killings. While this is not inconsistent with Huntington's predictions, by itself it does not strongly support the theory. If the CoC theory were correct we would have expected a more dramatic rise in civilizational mass killings.

The analysis of revolutionary war state failures, presented in Figure 7.6, contradicts the CoC theory. Civilizational revolutionary wars are far less common than noncivilizational ones and do not become much more common with the end of the Cold War. Furthermore, noncivilizational revolutionary wars become slightly more common with the end of the Cold War.

In all, while some individual aspects of this analysis are not inconsistent with Huntington's CoC theory, the balance of the evidence weighs strongly against the prediction that civilizational conflicts will become the defining type of conflict in the post-Cold War era. In the general analyses of the MAR and SF datasets civilizational conflicts are less common than noncivilizational conflicts. In the analysis of specific types of conflict in the SF dataset, only mass killings become more common in the post-Cold War era and this is due to a drop in noncivilizational mass killings, not a rise in civilizational ones. Certainly, it is arguable that civilizational conflict is somewhat more common in the post-Cold War era than it was during the Cold War. However, this shift is nowhere near the type of shift one would expect if civilizational conflicts were the defining element of the international system, as Huntington predicts.

Specific Civilizations and Civilizational Conflict

This section analyzes whether the conflict pattern of specific civilizations changed with the end of the Cold War. Specifically, it assesses whether any particular civilizations engage in a different amount of conflict and whether there are any changes in the opponents groups of particular civilizations face. Based on Huntington's predictions, we would expect the amount of civilizational conflict involving all individual civilizations, and especially the Islamic civilization, to increase in the post-Cold War era. We would also expect more conflict between the West and both the Islamic and Sino-Confucian civilizations.

For the purposes of this portion of the analysis the unit of analysis is not a

Table 7.1: Participation of Specific Civilizations in Conflict, MAR Data

Civilization	% Civilizational			% of All Conflict		
	Cold War Era	Early 1990s	2000	Cold War Era	Early 1990s	2000
Western	65.62	69.01	69.44	13.73	12.91	12.63
Sino-Confucian	62.16	61.90	61.90	7.94	7.64	7.37
Slavic-Orthodox	66.67	65.62	65.62	7.73	11.64	11.23
Latin American	100.00	100.00	100.00	6.44	6.00	5.96
Hindu	73.33	71.43	71.43	3.22	3.82	3.68
Islamic	51.79	46.31	46.50	24.03	27.09	27.54
Japanese	100.00	100.00	100.00	0.22	0.36	0.35
African	22.58	26.13	27.27	26.61	20.18	21.23
Indigenous	–	–	–	8.37	7.45	7.19
Mixed	–	–	–	1.72	2.91	2.81
% Within Civ.	43.35	41.45	41.75	–	–	–
% Civilizational	36.48	37.45	38.60	–	–	–
% Indig. or Mix.	20.17	21.10	19.65	–	–	–
# of Cases	466	550	570	–	–	–

conflict but a side in a conflict. That is, the focus is on participants. For example, a conflict involving a Western and an Islamic group would be counted twice. Once for the Western group and once for the Islamic group. Similarly, a conflict between two Islamic groups would also be counted twice, each as an Islamic group involved in a conflict. For the MAR data this is done group by group and for the SF data this is done for each conflict year. This procedure is used in this section of the analysis because the emphasis is on determining the civilizational identity of the opponents of specific civilizations. As all conflicts in this study have two sides, each with a civilizational identity, it is necessary to look at each of these sides separately in order to address the issue at hand.

An examination of the percentage of ethnic conflicts involving specific civilizations in the MAR data, presented in Table 7.1, shows little change in the distribution of civilizational conflict. Of the eight civilizations analyzed with regard to the percent of ethnic conflict which is civilizational, only three change by more than 2 percent with the end of the Cold War. The proportion of conflicts involving the Western and African civilizations which are civilizational increase by about 5 percent and the proportion of conflicts involving the Islamic civilization which are civilizational drops by about 5%. Thus, there is no great change in who is fighting whom with the end of the Cold War. Also the Islamic civilization, the specific civilization Huntington predicted would engage in more civilizational conflict,

Table 7.2: Participation of Specific Civilizations in Conflict, SF Data

	% Civilizational		% of All Conflict	
Civilization	1948 to 1989	1990 to 2001	1948 to 1989	1990 to 2001
Western	53.03	82.05	9.44	9.58
Sino-Confucian	11.48	42.86	17.45	6.02
Slavic-Orthodox	60.00	66.67	0.36	4.42
Latin American	11.50	9.09	12.95	6.76
Hindu	100.00	70.00	1.97	4.92
Islamic	33.96	36.33	30.54	39.93
Japanese	–	–	0.00	0.00
African	22.74	14.81	22.96	26.54
Indigenous	–	–	3.72	1.60
Mixed	–	–	1.00	0.25
% Within Civilization	69.53	61.92	–	–
% Civilizational	21.03	34.89	–	–
% Indig. or Mix.	9.44	3.19	–	–
# of Cases	1398	814	–	–

actually engages in a lower proportion of civilizational conflict.

There are also few changes in the extent to which each civilization engages in ethnic conflict. The proportion of all conflict in which a particular category of group is involved changes by less than 2 percent for seven of the ten categories examined here. The increase in involvement in conflict by the Slavic-Orthodox civilization is explainable by the conflicts caused by the breakup of the former Soviet Union and the former Yugoslavia. The amount of conflict involving the Islamic civilization also increases significantly but the amount of conflict involving the African civilization drops significantly.

When combined with the results regarding the proportion of ethnic conflict which is civilizational, these results describe an interesting pattern of behavior for the Islamic civilization. The extent of ethnic conflict involving the Islamic civilization increased with the end of the Cold War but this increase was mostly in noncivilizational conflict. The combined results also show little change in the patterns of ethnic conflict with the end of the Cold War. This directly contradicts Huntington's predictions.

Another interesting finding is that, except for the African civilization, the majority of ethnic conflict involving all of the specific civilizations examined here is civilizational during the Cold War era and the same is true in the post-Cold War era except that the majority of conflicts involving the Islamic civilization are not civilizational. The reason a majority of conflicts overall are not civilizational is that about one-fifth of them involve mixed or indigenous groups and, therefore, can not

Table 7.3: Opponents of the Western Civilization Controlling for Civilization

Civilization in Conflict With	Minorities at Risk			State Failure	
	Cold War	Early 1990s	2000	1948 to 1989	1990 to 2001
Western	34.38%	30.99%	30.56%	46.97%	17.95%
Sino-Confucian	3.13%	2.82%	2.78%	0.00%	0.00%
Slavic-Orthodox	15.63%	14.08%	13.89%	0.00%	8.97%
Latin American	3.13%	1.41%	2.78%	0.00%	0.00%
Hindu	0.00%	0.00%	0.00%	0.00%	0.00%
Islamic	20.31%	23.94%	23.61%	41.67%	60.26%
Japanese	0.00%	0.00%	0.00%	0.00%	0.00%
African	7.81%	7.04%	6.94%	10.61%	2.56%
Indigenous	9.38%	9.86%	9.72%	0.76%	10.26%
Mixed	6.25%	9.86%	9.72%	0.00%	0.00%
No. of Cases	64	71	72	132	78

be classified as civilizational.

A similar examination of the SF data, presented in Table 7.2, shows more shifts in the patterns of conflict. With the end of the Cold War, the proportion of conflict which is civilizational increases dramatically for the Western and Sino-Confucian civilizations and less dramatically for the Slavic-Orthodox and Islamic civilizations. However, the proportion of conflict which is civilizational drops dramatically for the Hindu civilization and less dramatically for the African and Latin American civilizations. Overall the proportion of conflict which is civilizational after the Cold War is about 169 percent of what it was during the Cold War. Nevertheless, it still remains a minority of all conflict.

The extent to which each civilization engages in conflict in the SF data changes less dramatically. Five categories engage in a higher proportion of conflict and five engage is a lower proportion. The most dramatic increase is by the Islamic civilization. Thus, in the SF data the Islamic civilization engages in more conflict and a slightly higher proportion of that conflict is civilizational. However, even in the post-Cold War era, nearly two-thirds of the conflict involving Islamic groups is not civilizational.

In all, when examining the overall patterns of conflict by specific civilizations, there is little support for Huntington's predictions. According to both datasets, there is not sufficient change in the patterns of conflict to support the CoC theory. Also, in both datasets, Islamic groups fight noncivilizational conflicts more often than civilizational ones.

An analysis of the conflict patterns of each individual civilization produces similar results. The analysis of the conflict patterns of the Western civilization,

Table 7.4: Opponents of the Sino-Confucian Civilization Controlling for Civilization

Civilization in Conflict With	Minorities at Risk			State Failure	
	Cold War	Early 1990s	2000	1948 to 1989	1990 to 2001
Western	5.41%	4.76%	4.76%	0.00%	0.00%
Sino-Confucian	37.84%	38.10%	38.10%	88.52%	57.24%
Slavic-Orthodox	0.00%	4.76%	4.76%	0.00%	0.00%
Latin American	0.00%	2.38%	2.38%	0.00%	0.00%
Hindu	5.41%	9.52%	9.52%	2.87%	24.49%
Islamic	27.03%	19.05%	19.05%	0.82%	18.37%
Japanese	2.70%	2.38%	2.38%	0.00%	0.00%
African	0.00%	2.38%	2.38%	0.00%	0.00%
Indigenous	18.92%	14.29%	14.29%	7.79%	0.00%
Mixed	2.70%	2.38%	2.38%	0.00%	0.00%
No. of Cases	37	42	42	244	49

Table 7.5: Opponents of the Slavic-Orthodox Civilization Controlling for Civilization

Civilization in Conflict With	Minorities at Risk			State Failure	
	Cold War	Early 1990s	2000	1948 to 1989	1990 to 2001
Western	27.78%	15.63%	15.63%	0.00%	19.44%
Sino-Confucian	0.00%	3.13%	3.13%	0.00%	0.00%
Slavic-Orthodox	33.33%	34.38%	34.38%	40.00%	30.33%
Latin American	0.00%	0.00%	0.00%	0.00%	0.00%
Hindu	0.00%	0.00%	0.00%	0.00%	0.00%
Islamic	33.33%	34.38%	34.38%	60.00%	47.22%
Japanese	0.00%	0.00%	0.00%	0.00%	0.00%
African	0.00%	0.00%	0.00%	0.00%	0.00%
Indigenous	0.00%	0.00%	0.00%	0.00%	0.00%
Mixed	5.56%	12.50%	12.50%	0.00%	0.00%
No. of Cases	36	64	64	5	36

presented in Table 7.3, has mixed results. The analysis of the MAR data shows little change in the patterns of ethnic conflict with the end of the Cold War. Except for conflicts with other Western groups, Islamic groups, and mixed groups, the proportion of conflict with groups from a particular category does not change by more than 2 percent. Even ethnic conflicts with other Western and mixed groups do not change by more than 4 percent. However, in the SF data the extent of conflict with other Western groups decreases dramatically and conflicts with Islamic groups increases dramatically. The small changes in the MAR data also follow this trend. Thus, from the Western perspective, the data, shows an increase in West vs. Islam conflict, as predicted by Huntington. It also shows an increase in conflict involving the West which is consistent with Huntington's predictions of challenges to Western power by other civilizations. However, as this and the results regarding Islam are reflected only weakly in the MAR data, these results are not conclusive.

The analysis of the conflict patterns of the Sino-Confucian civilization, presented in Table 7.4, provides mixed support for Huntington's predictions. The only drastic change in the MAR data is a large drop in conflict with the Islamic civilization. While this is consistent with an alliance between the Sino-Confucian and Islamic civilizations against the West, there is also a slight drop in Sino-Confucian conflict with the West, which is inconsistent with this prediction. All other shifts in the MAR data are of less than 5 percent. The SF data shows that while civilizational conflict involving the Sino-Confucian civilization increased, conflict with the Islamic civilization is responsible for most of this increase. This and the fact that the SF data shows no conflict at all with the West directly contradicts Huntington's prediction of an Islamic-Sino-Confucian alliance against the West.

The analysis of the conflict patterns of the Slavic-Orthodox civilization, presented in Table 7.5, provides mixed support for the CoC theory. The MAR data shows little change in the patterns of conflict except a drop in conflict with Western groups and a rise in conflict with mixed groups. The SF data shows a drop in internal Slavic-Orthodox conflict as well as a drop in conflict with Islamic groups and an increase in conflict with Western groups. The drop in conflict with Islamic groups contradicts Huntington's predictions of an increasingly violent Islamic civilization but the rise in conflict with the West supports his predictions of an increasingly belligerent West.

The analysis of the conflict patterns of the Latin American civilization, presented in Table 7.6, provides no support for Huntington's theory. There is little change in either the MAR or SF data with the end of the Cold War. Interestingly, while the MAR data shows no conflict within the Latin American civilization, about 90 percent of the conflict in the SF dataset is within the Latin American civilization. This is because the majority of the conflict in Latin America is political and not ethnic. Furthermore, even in the MAR dataset the majority of conflict by Latin Americans is with indigenous groups and is, therefore, not civilizational.

The analysis of the conflict patterns of the Hindu civilization, presented in Table 7.7, provides little support for the CoC theory. In the MAR data there is some change in conflict patterns with the end of the Cold War but none that support the

Table 7.6: Opponents of the Latin American Civilization Controlling for Civilization

Civilization in Conflict With	Minorities at Risk			State Failure	
	Cold War	Early 1990s	2000	1948 to 1989	1990 to 2001
Western	6.67%	3.03%	5.88%	0.00%	0.00%
Sino-Confucian	0.00%	3.03%	2.94%	0.00%	0.00%
Slavic-Orthodox	0.00%	0.00%	0.00%	0.00%	0.00%
Latin American	0.00%	0.00%	0.00%	89.50%	90.91%
Hindu	0.00%	3.03%	2.94%	0.00%	0.00%
Islamic	0.00%	0.00%	0.00%	0.00%	0.00%
Japanese	0.00%	0.00%	0.00%	0.00%	0.00%
African	30.00%	30.30%	29.41%	0.00%	0.00%
Indigenous	63.33%	60.61%	58.82%	10.50%	9.09%
Mixed	0.00%	0.00%	0.00%	0.00%	0.00%
No. of Cases	30	33	34	181	55

Table 7.7: Opponents of the Hindu Civilization Controlling for Civilization

Civilization in Conflict With	Minorities at Risk			State Failure	
	Cold War	Early 1990s	2000	1948 to 1989	1990 to 2001
Western	0.00%	0.00%	0.00%	0.00%	0.00%
Sino-Confucian	13.33%	19.05%	19.05%	31.82%	30.00%
Slavic-Orthodox	0.00%	0.00%	0.00%	0.00%	0.00%
Latin American	0.00%	4.76%	4.76%	0.00%	0.00%
Hindu	26.67%	28.57%	28.57%	0.00%	30.00%
Islamic	40.00%	33.33%	33.33%	31.82%	40.00%
Japanese	0.00%	0.00%	0.00%	0.00%	0.00%
African	0.00%	0.00%	0.00%	0.00%	0.00%
Indigenous	20.00%	14.29%	14.29%	36.36%	0.00%
Mixed	0.00%	0.00%	0.00%	0.00%	0.00%
No. of Cases	15	21	21	22	40

Table 7.8: Opponents of the Islamic Civilization Controlling for Civilization

Civilization in Conflict With	Minorities at Risk			State Failure	
	Cold War	Early 1990s	2000	1948 to 1989	1990 to 2001
Western	11.61%	11.41%	10.83%	12.88%	14.46%
Sino-Confucian	8.93%	5.37%	5.10%	0.47%	2.77%
Slavic-Orthodox	10.71%	14.77%	8.92%	0.70%	5.23%
Latin American	0.00%	0.00%	5.10%	0.00%	0.00%
Hindu	5.36%	4.70%	4.46%	1.64%	4.92%
Islamic	48.21%	53.69%	53.50%	66.04%	62.77%
Japanese	0.00%	0.67%	0.64%	0.00%	0.00%
African	11.61%	7.38%	9.55%	13.82%	9.23%
Indigenous	2.68%	2.01%	1.91%	1.17%	0.00%
Mixed	0.89%	0.00%	0.00%	3.28%	0.62%
No. of Cases	112	149	157	427	325

Table 7.9: Opponents of the African Civilization Controlling for Civilization

Civilization in Conflict With	Minorities at Risk			State Failure	
	Cold War	Early 1990s	2000	1948 to 1989	1990 to 2001
Western	4.03%	4.50%	4.13%	4.36%	0.93%
Sino-Confucian	0.00%	0.90%	0.83%	0.00%	0.00%
Slavic-Orthodox	0.00%	0.00%	0.00%	0.00%	0.00%
Latin American	7.26%	9.01%	8.26%	0.00%	0.00%
Hindu	0.00%	0.00%	0.00%	0.00%	0.00%
Islamic	10.48%	9.91%	12.40%	18.38%	13.89%
Japanese	0.00%	0.00%	0.00%	0.00%	0.00%
African	77.42%	73.87%	72.73%	77.26%	85.19%
Indigenous	0.81%	1.80%	1.65%	0.00%	0.00%
Mixed	0.00%	0.00%	0.00%	0.00%	0.00%
No. of Cases	124	111	121	321	216

CoC theory. While there is a significant increase in conflict with the Sino-Confucian civilization, there are also significant drops in conflict with the Islamic civilization and indigenous groups. This finding contradicts Huntington's predictions of an increase in civilizational conflict by Islamic groups. However, the SF data shows an increase in conflict with Islamic groups. The SF data also shows an increase in conflicts within the Hindu civilization from 0 percent to 30 percent with the end of the Cold War. As this is matched by a drop in conflict with indigenous groups from 36.36 percent to 0 percent, this actually represents a slight rise in civilizational conflict in the SF data.

The analysis of the conflict patterns of the Islamic civilization, presented in Table 7.8, in no way reflects Huntington's predicted dramatic increase in civilizational violence by that civilization. The most dramatic change in the MAR data in an increase in conflict within the Islamic civilization with the end of the Cold War to a slight majority of 53.5 percent of all conflict involving Islamic groups. Also, conflict between Islam and the West decreased slightly. The SF data shows a slight decrease in internal Islamic conflict and a slight rise in Islamic-Western conflict, but nowhere near the dramatic changes one would expect if Huntington's predictions were correct. Furthermore, even in the post-Cold War era, a majority of 62.77 percent of conflict involving Muslims in the SF data is with other Muslim groups.

The analysis of the conflict patterns of the African civilization, presented in Table 7.9, provides no support for Huntington's theory. In the MAR data, the vast majority of conflict involving the African civilization is with other African groups, though this percentage drops from 77.42 percent to 73.87 percent with the end of the Cold War. Conflict with Islamic groups increases by less than 2 percent, which is very low considering that sub-Saharan Africa's biggest civilizational border is with the Islamic states in the northern part of the continent. The SF data also shows internal conflicts being by far the most common form of conflict involving the African civilization, with internal conflicts becoming even more common in the post-Cold War era. The SF data also shows a drop in conflict between the African and Islamic civilizations with the end of the Cold War.

The analysis of the conflict patterns of indigenous groups, presented in Table 7.10, while not directly relevant to the CoC theory, also shows limited change with the end of the Cold War. In the MAR data, the conflict patterns during and after the Cold War are nearly identical. In the SF data, there is a dramatic increase in conflict with Western groups, but this is more due to a drop in the overall amount of conflict involving indigenous groups with the end of the Cold War than a real increase in conflict with Western groups.

Due to the small number of conflicts involving these categories, there is no analysis of the conflict patterns of the Japanese civilization and mixed groups.

Overall, the analysis of the behavior of specific civilizations does not support the predictions of Huntington's CoC theory. While there are some specific trends that are consistent with Huntington's predictions, for each of these there is at least one which runs counter to these predictions. There is no consistent rise in

Table 7.10: Opponents of Indigenous Peoples Controlling for Civilization

Civilization in Conflict With	Minorities at Risk			State Failure	
	Cold War	Early 1990s	2000	1948 to 1989	1990 to 2001
Western	15.38%	17.07%	17.07%	1.92%	61.54%
Sino-Confucian	17.95%	14.63%	14.63%	36.54%	0.00%
Slavic-Orthodox	0.00%	0.00%	0.00%	0.00%	0.00%
Latin American	48.72%	48.78%	48.78%	36.54%	38.46%
Hindu	7.69%	7.32%	7.32%	15.38%	0.00%
Islamic	7.69%	7.32%	7.32%	19.62%	0.00%
Japanese	0.00%	0.00%	0.00%	0.00%	0.00%
African	2.56%	4.88%	4.88%	0.00%	0.00%
Indigenous	0.00%	0.00%	0.00%	0.00%	0.00%
Mixed	0.00%	0.00%	0.00%	0.00%	0.00%
No. of Cases	39	41	41	52	13

civilizational conflict involving the Islamic civilization. These results are clearly not the type of results we would have expected if there was a paradigmatical shift in conflict to civilizational conflict. They are, rather, more consistent with the random changes one would expect in conflict over time as some conflicts wane and end others begin and intensify.

One result, however, does stand out. While there is no consistent increase in conflict between the West and the predicted Islamic-Sino-Confucian alliance, from the Western perspective, there is significantly more conflict with the Islamic civilization. This result is strong in the SF data but weak in the MAR data. In contrast, from the perspective of the Islamic civilization this increase in conflict with the West is a very slight one and exists only in the SF data.

This result provides some insight into the debate over Huntington's CoC argument. Huntington is from the West and, presumably, this has influenced his perspective of the events that have transpired since the end of the Cold War. Looking at the SF data strictly from the perspective of the West, the proportion of conflicts that are with Islamic groups have increased since the end of the Cold War. However, from the perspective of the Islamic civilization, there has been little change since the end of the Cold War. In the context of all conflict, this shift is also minor. Thus, while the small increase in ethnic conflict between the Western and Islamic civilizations can seem very important to Western eyes, such as those of Huntington, from the global and Islamic perspectives it is merely a minor shift in conflict patterns.

This, perhaps, explains the intensity of the debate over whether there is an Islamic threat to the West. On one hand, this clearly seems to be the case from a

Western perspective. This explains why even some of Huntington's critics believe that there may be something to Huntington's arguments with regard to clashes between the Western and Islamic civilizations. On the other hand, looking at the overall picture shows that these conflicts are a minority of the conflicts in which Islamic groups are involved, with the majority of conflicts in the post-Cold War era which involve the Islamic civilization being internal ones.

Civilizational Conflict and Violence

Until this point, the analysis has focused on the amount of conflict. This section and the following one examine the levels of violence in conflicts. In short, we ask, has civilizational conflict become more violent in the post-Cold War era, especially in comparison to noncivilizational conflict?

The analysis of ethnic rebellion in the MAR data from 1945 to 2000, presented in Figure 7.7, shows that except for 1945 to 1949, noncivilizational minorities engaged in higher levels of rebellion than civilizational minorities. However, in the early 1990s the level of rebellion by civilizational minorities jumped to nearly the level of rebellion by noncivilizational minorities. The analysis of the yearly levels of ethnic rebellion between 1985 and 2000, presented in Figure 7.8, shows that this jump in the early 1990s is representative of the fact that in 1993 and 1995 the level of rebellion for civilizational minorities was higher than the level of rebellion for noncivilizational minorities. Thus, just after the end of the Cold War, there was a jump in the comparative level of rebellion by civilizational minorities, but it was not a consistent one. Also, from 1996 onward the level of rebellion for civilizational minorities was consistently lower than that of noncivilizational minorities. Thus, with regard to ethnic rebellion, the permanent shift in conflict patterns to more violent civilizational conflicts predicted by Huntington did not occur.

The analysis of ethnic protest in the MAR data from 1945 to 2000, presented in Figure 7.9, shows that for most of the period there was no large difference in the levels of protest by civilizational and noncivilizational minorities. Though civilizational minorities tend to engage in higher levels of protest and this trend became more pronounced, but not statistically significant, during the 1990s. The analysis of the yearly levels of ethnic protest between 1985 and 2000, presented in Figure 7.10, shows that protest by civilizational minorities became comparatively more intense beginning in 1990, with the differences being statistically significant in 1993 and 1995. However this gap closes somewhat by the late 1990s.

While this finding is consistent with Huntington's predictions, the overall evidence from the MAR data provide at best mixed support for his theory. This is due to a combination of three factors. First, the results for ethnic rebellion showed only a temporary rise in violence by civilizational minorities, not the permanent rise predicted by Huntington. Second, while the patterns of ethnic protest are not inconsistent with the CoC theory, they are not definitively consistent with the

Figure 7.7: Mean Level of Ethnic Rebellion Controlling for Civilization, 1945-2000

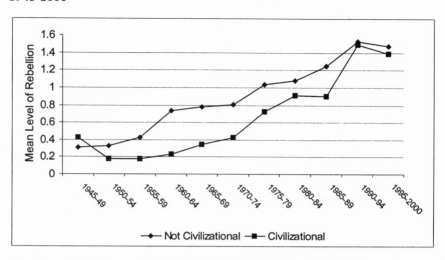

-Significance (t-test) between Civilizational and Not Civilizational < .1 in 1955-59
-Significance (t-test) between Civilizational and Not Civilizational < .05 in 1965-74
-Significance (t-test) between Civilizational and Not Civilizational < .01 in 1960-69

Figure 7.8: Mean Level of Ethnic Rebellion Controlling for Civilization, 1985-2000

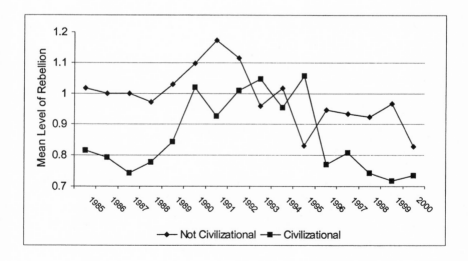

Figure 7.9: Mean Level of Ethnic Protest Controlling for Civilization, 1945-2000

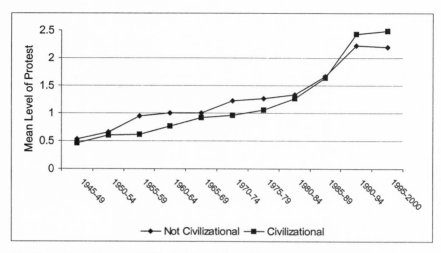

-Significance (t-test) between Civilizational and Not Civilizational < .05 in 1955-59

Figure 7.10: Mean Level of Ethnic Protest Controlling for Civilization, 1985-2000

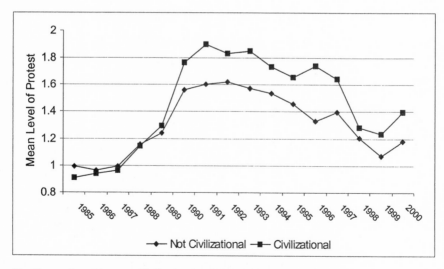

-Significance (t-test) between Civilizational and Not Civilizational < .1 in 1993
-Significance (t-test) between Civilizational and Not Civilizational < .05 in 1995

Figure 7.11: Mean Level of Fatalities in Ethnic State Failures Controlling for Civilization, 1955-2001

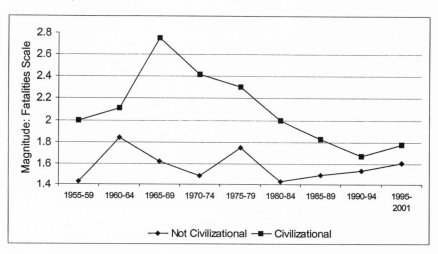

-Significance (t-test) between Civilizational and Not Civilizational < .1 in 1985-89
-Significance (t-test) between Civilizational and Not Civilizational < .05 in 1955-59 & 1975-84
-Significance (t-test) between Civilizational and Not Civilizational < .01 in 1970-74
-Significance (t-test) between Civilizational and Not Civilizational < .001 in 1965-69

theory. This is because civilizational groups engaged in higher levels of protest during the entire Cold War period and there are indications that the rise in civilizational protest during the early 1990s may be a temporary one as the gap between civilizational and noncivilizational protest began to close by the end of the 1990s. Third, as Huntington's predictions were specifically addressed at violent conflict, the results of the analysis of ethnic rebellion should be given greater weight.

The analysis of the SF data also provides, at best, mixed support for Huntington's prediction that civilizational conflict will become disproportionately violent after the end of the Cold War. The analysis of ethnic wars, presented in Figure 7.11, shows that civilizational ethnic wars were more violent that noncivilizational ones for the entire 1955 to 2001 period. On its face, this seems consistent with Huntington's predictions. However, the gap in violence between civilizational and noncivilizational ethnic wars narrows continuously from the early 1970s to the early 1990s, then rises slightly in the 1995 to 2001 period. In fact, while the gap between the two categories is statistically significant in every period from 1955 to 1989, it is not statistically significant from 1990 to 2001. Thus, civilizational ethnic wars became less violent after the end of the Cold War both in absolute terms and in comparison to non-civilizational ethnic wars. This is the opposite of what Huntington predicted.

Figure 7.12: Mean Level of Fatalities in Mass Killing State Failures Controlling for Civilization, 1960-2001

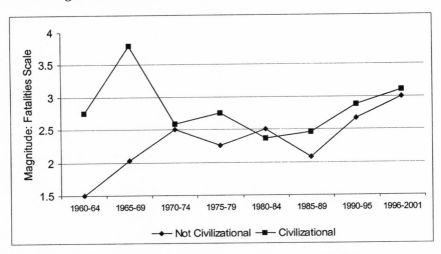

-Significance (t-test) between Civilizational and Not Civilizational < .1 in 1960-64
-Significance (t-test) between Civilizational and Not Civilizational < .001 in 1965-69

Figure 7.13: Mean Level of Fatalities in Revolutionary War State Failures Controlling for Civilization, 1948-2001

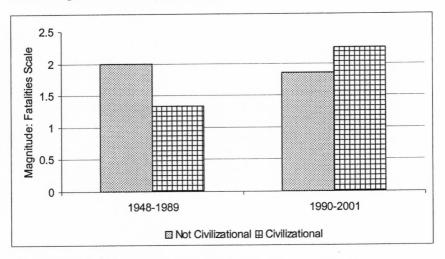

-Significance (t-test) between Civilizational and Not Civilizational < .05 in 1948-89

The analysis of mass killing state failures, presented in Figure 7.12, does not support the CoC theory. While civilizational mass killings are more violent than noncivilizational mass killings for most of the period covered in the analysis, from 1970 onward, the difference in violence between the two categories is minimal. Also, this gap narrows during the 1990 to 2001 period. Thus, civilizational mass killings did not conform to Huntington's prediction that they would become more violent relative to noncivilizational mass killings.

The analysis of revolutionary war state failures, presented in Figure 7.13, does conform to Huntington's predictions. While during the 1948 to 1989 period civilizational revolutionary wars were less violent than noncivilizational ones, during the 1990 to 2001 period they were more violent. However, less than 7 percent of all revolutionary wars were civilizational. Thus, this category of state failure includes a small minority of all state failures. Accordingly, this finding has less weight than do the other findings based on the SF dataset.

The overall analysis of the SF and MAR data does not support Huntington's prediction that civilizational conflict will become more violent relative to non-civilizational in the post-Cold War era. While some elements of the analysis are consistent with the CoC theory, most of these elements of the analysis provide only qualified support for the theory. Furthermore, the majority of the evidence runs counter to the CoC theory. In fact, the evidence supports the argument that there has been little change or even a decline in the levels of violence since the end of the Cold War at least as strongly as it supports Huntington's theory.

Specific Civilizations and Violence

This section analyzes the levels of violence exhibited by specific civilizations over time. While Huntington only made specific predictions about the Islamic civilization, we evaluate the extent of violence by all of his civilizations, as well as for indigenous and mixed groups. Huntington predicted that the Islamic civilization would become disproportionately violent after the end of the Cold War. He also predicted a general rise in conflict after the Cold War. We, therefore, assess whether this occurred for each civilization. As there are ten categories analyzed here, we divided them into two groups of five for each figure in order to enhance the readability of the figure and also included the average level of conflict in each figure for purposes of comparison. In general, when dividing the groups for purposes of presentation, we placed those groups engaging in the lowest levels of conflict in the first figure and the others in the second.

The analysis of rebellion from 1945 to 2000 in the MAR data, presented in Figures 7.14 and 7.15, shows that most of the civilizations do not become more violent, relative to the average level of conflict, after the end of the Cold War. Of course there are exceptions. The Hindu civilization becomes more violent, but the steady increase in violence by this civilization began in the 1975 to 1979 period,

Figure 7.14: Mean Level of Rebellion, Controlling for Civilizations, 1945-2000, Part I

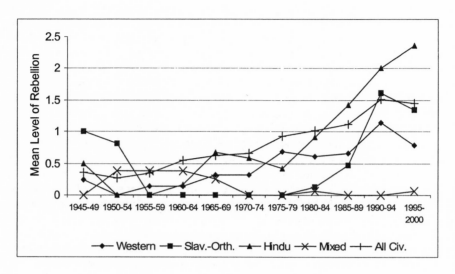

Figure 7.15: Mean Level of Rebellion, Controlling for Civilizations, 1945-2000, Part II

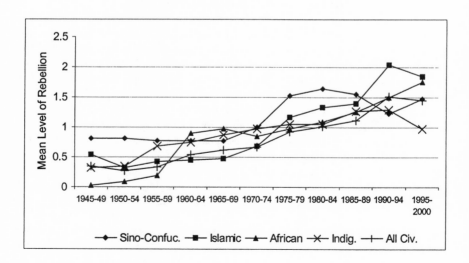

Figure 7.16: Mean Level of Rebellion, Controlling for Civilizations, 1985-2000, Part I

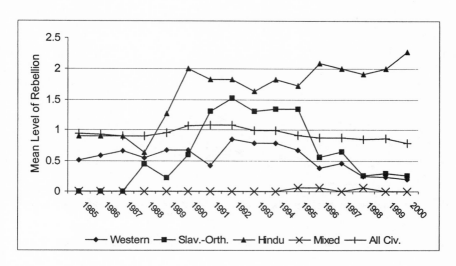

Figure 7.17: Mean Level of Rebellion, Controlling for Civilizations, 1985-2000, Part II

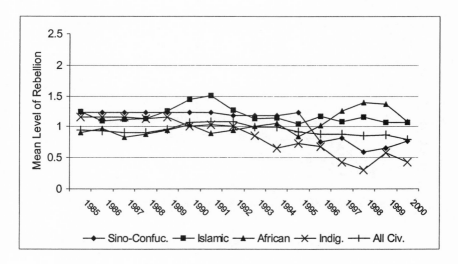

Figure 7.18: Mean Level of Protest, Controlling for Civilizations, 1945-2000, Part I

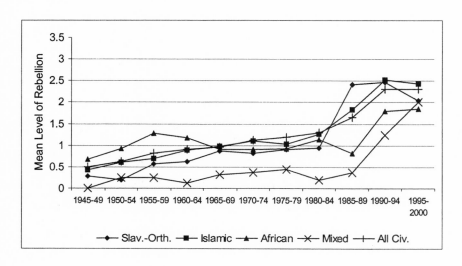

Figure 7.19: Mean Level of Protest, Controlling for Civilizations, 1945-2000, Part II

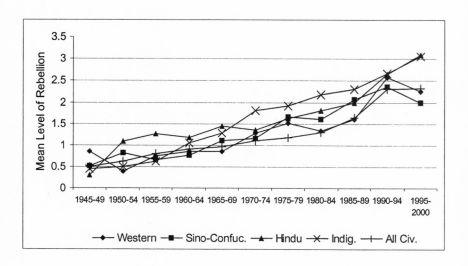

Figure 7.20: Mean Level of Protest, Controlling for Civilizations, 1985-2000, Part I

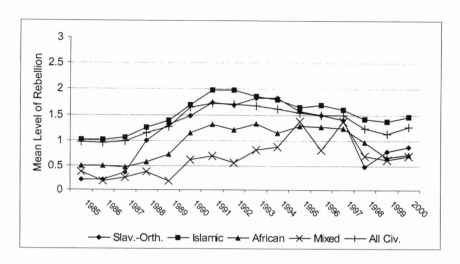

Figure 7.21: Mean Level of Protest, Controlling for Civilizations, 1985-2000, Part II

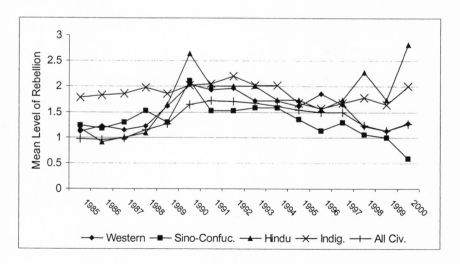

Table 7.11: Mean Level of State Failures for Minority Groups, Controlling for Cold War, 1948-2001

Civilization	Ethnic Wars 1948-89	Ethnic Wars 1990-2001	Mass Killings 1948-89	Mass Killings 1990-2001	Revolutionary Wars 1948-89	Revolutionary Wars 1990-2001
Western	1.04	1.64**	2.33	0.67**	2.08	1.14**
Sino-Confucian	1.70	1.33**	3.65	–	1.88	1.50
Slavic-Orthodox	–	1.85	–	–	–	–
Latin American	–	–	1.45	–	2.08	1.74*
Hindu	2.14	2.00	–	–	–	1.17
Islamic	1.75	1.57	2.04	2.41	1.92	2.04
African	2.19	1.84***	2.56	3.61****	1.88	2.05
Indigenous	1.17	0.85***	1.17	–	–	–
Mixed	1.21	0.50	–	–	1.00	–
Average	1.75	1.63	2.36	2.85**	1.96	1.88

* = Significance (t-test) with mean in same row and category < .1
** = Significance (t-test) with mean in same row and category < .05
*** = Significance (t-test) with mean in same row and category < .01
**** = Significance (t-test) with mean in same row and category < .001

Table 7.12: Mean Level of State Failures for Majority Groups, Controlling for Cold War, 1948-2001

Civilization	Ethnic Wars 1948-89	Ethnic Wars 1990-2001	Mass Killings 1948-89	Mass Killings 1990-2001	Revolutionary Wars 1948-89	Revolutionary Wars 1990-2001
Western	1.96	1.15***	–	–	1.63	1.11
Sino-Confucian	1.59	1.64	3.60	–	1.85	1.50
Slavic-Orthodox	2.00	2.12	–	2.83	–	–
Latin American	1.16	1.00	1.34	–	2.08	1.74*
Hindu	1.27	1.81****	–	–	–	1.17
Islamic	1.72	1.58	2.39	2.76	1.94	1.92
African	2.04	1.90	2.31	3.41****	2.04	2.24
Average	1.75	1.63	2.36	2.85**	1.96	1.88

* = Significance (t-test) with mean in same row and category < .1
** = Significance (t-test) with mean in same row and category < .05
*** = Significance (t-test) with mean in same row and category < .01
**** = Significance (t-test) with mean in same row and category < .001

well before the end of the Cold War. The Slavic-Orthodox civilization also becomes more violent, but its peak level of violence is only slightly higher than the average level of rebellion. Islamic groups also become more violent in the early 1990s but their level of rebellion is not drastically higher than the average level and drops in the 1995 to 2000 period.

The yearly results on rebellion from 1985 to 2000, presented in Figures 7.16 and 7.17, provide even less support for Huntington's theory. Only the Hindu civilization shows a dramatic and permanent increase in rebellion which coincides with the end of the Cold War. The level of rebellion for the Slavic-Orthodox civilization increases dramatically in 1991 but drops back to previous levels in 1996. The temporary instability in Eastern Europe due to regime changes there provides a better explanation for this pattern of conflict than does the CoC theory. All of the other civilizations remain below or near the average levels of conflict throughout this period.

The results for ethnic protest from 1945 to 2000, presented in Figures 7.18 and 7.19, are not consistent with Huntington's predictions. When examining these results it is important to recall that, as shown earlier in Figure 7.9, protest by both civilizational and noncivilizational minorities rose considerably in the early 1990s. The results of this analysis show that protest by no civilization rose out of proportion with this general rise in protest. The results for the yearly levels of protest between 1985 and 2000, presented in Figures 7.20 and 7.21, similarly show no dramatic rise in protest by any civilization relative to the overall level of protest.

The analysis of the SF data also does not support the CoC theory. As the violence tends to be two-sided in this data, we examine the levels of violence controlling for the civilization of the minority and majority groups in the conflict. The analysis of state failures based on the civilization of the minority group, presented in Table 7.11, shows no civilization becoming consistently more violent in the post-Cold War era. Ethnic wars by Western groups rise in violence, but mass killings and revolutionary wars drop in violence. Mass killings and revolutionary wars involving African minorities rise in violence but ethnic wars involving them drop in violence. All of the other results are either not statistically significant or represent drops in violence with the end of the Cold War.

The analysis of majority groups in the SF dataset, presented in Table 7.12, also provides scant support for Huntington's theory. Ethnic wars in Hindu states and mass killings in African ones increase in violence significantly. However, ethnic wars in Western states and revolutionary wars in Latin American states drop significantly. Thus, there is no overall pattern of a rise in violence.

In all, with one exception, the results of this analysis do not show specific civilizations engaging in higher levels of violence. This one exception is the Hindu civilization which on several of the tests did engage in higher levels of violence in the post-Cold War era. As the other civilizations did not, this is likely the exception that proves the rule. It is also important to note that the Islamic civilization, the one civilization Huntington expected to be particularly more violent in the post-Cold War era, did not conform to this prediction.

Islam vs. the West

This section examines Huntington's claim that the Islamic civilization will be a particular threat to the West in the post-Cold War era. It is important to recall that earlier in this chapter we examined the changes in the number of conflicts between specific civilizations. This included conflict between the Islamic and Western civilizations. The results of this analysis showed that while there is no consistent increase in conflict between the West and Islam, from the Western perspective in the SF data, there is significantly more conflict with the Islamic civilization. This dynamic is reflected weakly in the MAR data. In contrast, from the perspective of the Islamic civilization this increase in conflict with the West is a very slight one in the SF data and does not exist in the MAR data.

The analysis of rebellion in the MAR data does not provide support for an increase in violence between the two civilizations. The results for 1945 to 2000, presented in Figure 7.22, show that Islam-West conflicts were never statistically significantly more violent than other ethnic conflicts, especially since 1990 when the two categories engaged in nearly the same levels of rebellion. The yearly analysis of 1985 to 2000, presented in Figure 7.23, shows no consistent pattern of Islamic-West conflict being more violent. While the violence of Islamic-West conflicts spiked in 1992, 1995, and 1997, even in these years the increase was not statistically significant.

The results for ethnic protest do provide some support for Huntington's predictions. The analysis of ethnic protest between 1945 and 2000, presented in Figure 7.24, shows that Islam-West conflicts generally involved higher levels of protest, though the gap between the two categories was about the same both during and after the Cold War. This means that the fact that civilizational groups engage in more protest is not new to the post-Cold War era. Also, these differences were not statistically significant in the 1990 to 2000 period. However, the yearly results for 1985 to 2000, presented in Figure 7.25, show Islam-West conflicts involving more protest for the entire period with the results being statistically significant for seven of the eleven years between 1990 and 2000.

The results for the SF dataset, presented in Table 7.13 and Figure 7.26, provide no support for the CoC theory. Islam-West conflicts drop in violence for both ethnic wars and mass killings. Also, Islam-West conflicts are less violent than other conflicts in the post-Cold War era. There are not enough cases of revolutionary wars between Islam and the West for analysis. Finally, while there is a rise in the percentage of conflicts which are between Islamic and Western groups during the period analyzed, this rise occurs during the 1970s, not after the end of the Cold War.

In all, with the exceptions of the number of conflicts involving the Western civilization and the results for ethnic protest, the results of this analysis do not confirm Huntington's prediction of increased Islam versus West conflict in the post-Cold War era.

Figure 7.22: Mean Level of Rebellion Controlling for Islam vs. West Conflicts, 1945-2000

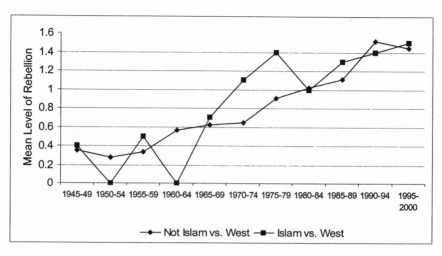

-Significance (t-test) between Not Islam vs. West and Islam vs. West < .001 in 1960-64

Figure 7.23: Mean Level of Rebellion Controlling for Islam vs. West Conflicts, 1985-2000

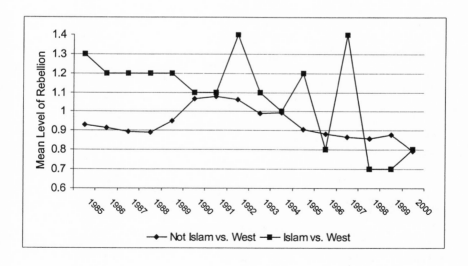

Figure 7.24: Mean Level of Protest Controlling for Islam vs. West Conflicts, 1945-2000

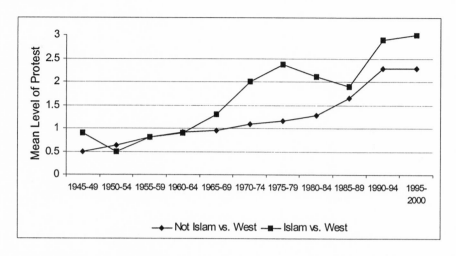

-Significance (t-test) between Not Islam vs. West and Islam vs. West < .1 in 1970-74 & 1980-84

Figure 7.25: Mean Level of Protest Controlling for Islam vs. West Conflicts, 1985-2000

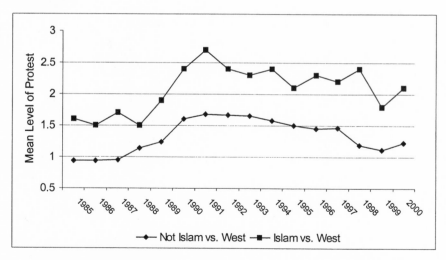

-Significance (t-test) between Not Islam vs. West and Islam vs. West < .1 in 1985, 1987, 1990, 1994, 1997, 1998, & 2000
-Significance (t-test) between Not Islam vs. West and Islam vs. West < .05 in 1991 & 1996

Table 7.13: Mean Levels of Fatalities Controlling for Islam vs. West Conflicts, 1948-2001

	Ethnic Wars		Mass Killings	
	1948-89	1990-2001	1948-89	1990-2001
Not Islam vs. West	1.70	1.68	2.38	3.01[b]
Islam vs. West	2.06[c]	1.41[bc]	2.33	0.67[ad]
Average	1.75	1.63	2.36	2.85[a]

a = Significance (t-test) with mean in same row and category < .05
b = Significance (t-test) with mean in same row and category < .01
c = Significance (t-test) with mean in same column and category < .1
d = Significance (t-test) with mean in same column and category < . 01

Figure 7.26: Percentage of State Failures which are West vs. Islam, 1948-2001

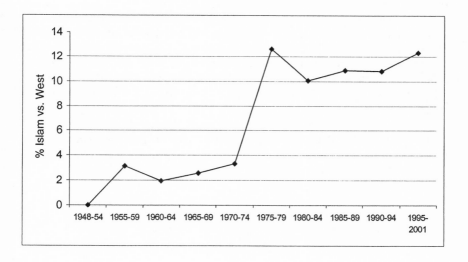

Conclusions

The results of this analysis show little support for any of Huntington's predictions. While there are a few trends that are consistent with his CoC theory, for each of these there are several which are not consistent. Thus, the preponderance of the evidence contradicts the theory.

These results, combined with those presented in Chapters 3, 4, and 5, bring up an interesting question. How is it that religion influences conflict but Huntington's civilizations, which are largely based on religion, do not? The best answer to this question is that the claims made with regard to religion's influence on conflict by me are considerably less ambitious than are Huntington's claims.

Huntington predicts a paradigmatic shift in conflict. More specifically, he claims that his concept of civilizations will be the defining factor in conflict in the post-Cold War era. Proving this prediction to be true requires dramatic and uniform changes in conflict patterns that are consistent with the theory. That is, a theory like the CoC theory which aspires to be a paradigm needs to be correct most of the time. It clearly was not.

In contrast, the claims made in this book with regard to religion are not paradigmatic claims. Rather, it is claimed that religion is one influence among many and that the influence of religion has increased since the 1980s. The evidence provided in this book is sufficient to support this less ambitious claim.

If one reexamines the analysis in this chapter, the evidence supports this less ambitious claim for three general reasons. First, the claims of the rise in religious conflict is not as time dependent as are the claims of the CoC theory. A rise at any time is sufficient to support the claims regarding religion while the claims regarding the CoC theory need to be around or after 1990. Second, since the claim is that religion influences conflict, if it influences some categories of conflict but not others, this is consistent with these claims. In contrast, the predictions of the CoC theory need to be true for most or all categories of conflict to fully support the theory. Finally, the claims regarding religion are not made in regard to any specific religions while the CoC theory does make claims with regard to specific civilizations.

Given this, it is possible that Huntington's concept of civilizations is an influence on conflict, though not as strong an influence as Huntington predicts. The next chapter examines whether this is the case through an analysis of the comparative impact of religion and civilization on conflict.

Chapter 8

Is Religion or Civilization a Better Explanation?

This chapter examines the comparative impact of religion and Huntington's concept of civilization on domestic conflict. This is done primarily with multivariate examinations of the causes of conflict including religion variables, civilization variables, and the control variables used in Chapters 4 and 5. Accordingly, in this chapter we test whether civilizations have any causal impact on conflict and if so, whether or not this impact is stronger than that of religion.

Thus, the question asked here is substantively different from the question asked in the previous chapter where we asked whether Huntington's paradigmatic claims that civilizations would be the defining influence on post-Cold War conflict were correct. Here we ask whether civilizations have any influence at all. This is a much lower hurdle for the CoC theory to overcome. However, as there is a considerable overlap between religion and civilizations, in order to jump this hurdle, the civilizations variables must not only have a significant impact, their impact must be consistently more important than the impact of religion. Otherwise there would be little evidence that the civilization variables are anything more than a surrogate variable for religion. Also, even if some civilizational variables prove to be significant, this does not prove the paradigmatic claims of Huntington's CoC theory. Rather, it would show that civilizations are one among several influences on conflict.

The majority of the tests performed in this chapter follow the pattern of those performed in Chapters 4 and 5. Thus, they use the same control variables as those in Chapters 4 and 5. Accordingly, the reasoning for the inclusion of these control variables is not discussed a second time in this chapter. Similarly, the tests for the general causes of conflict without religion or civilization variables are not repeated here. Rather, this chapter focuses only on tests which measure the impact of

Chapter 8

Table 8.1: Cross Tabulation of Civilizational and Religious Conflicts

Time Period	Civilizational Differences	Religious Differences		
		Same Religion	Different Denom.	Different Rel. or Rel. Clash
Minorities at Risk Data				
Cold War**	Not Civ.	48.9%	8.6%	5.6%
	Civilizational	7.3%	4.3%	25.3%
Early 1990**	Not Civ.	45.1%	6.1%	9.8%
	Civilizational	6.9%	4.0%	27.3%
2000**	Not Civ.	45.3%	6.7%	9.5%
	Civilizational	6.7%	3.9%	28.1%
State Failure Data, All Conflict				
1948 to 1989**	Not Civ.	64.7%	2.4%	11.9%
	Civilizational	2.0%	0.0%	19.0%
1990 to 2001**	Not Civ.	53.1%	2.0%	10.1
	Civilizational	1.0%	1.7%	32.2%
State Failure Data, Ethnic Wars				
1948 to 1989**	Not Civ.	55.0%	4.3%	7.9%
	Civilizational	0.0%	0.0%	32.7%
1990 to 2001**	Not Civ.	49.7%	2.7%	3.4%
	Civilizational	0.0%	2.4%	41.8%
State Failure Data, Mass Killings				
1948 to 1989**	Not Civ.	64.4%	0.5%	11.2%
	Civilizational	0.0%	0.0%	11.9%
1990 to 2001**	Not Civ.	36.4%	0.0%	13.6%
	Civilizational	0.0%	0.0%	50.0%
State Failure Data, Revolutionary Wars				
1948 to 1989*	Not Civ.	75.2%	0.0%	19.0%
	Civilizational	4.6%	0.0%	1.3%
1990 to 2001	Not Civ.	65.7%	0.0%	27.3%
	Civilizational	2.8%	0.0%	4.2%

* = Significance of Crosstab (Chi-Squared) < .05
** = Significance of Crosstab (Chi-Squared) < .001
Percentages represent percentage of all conflict in a given dataset and time period.

Table 8.2: Overlap between Civilizational and Religious Conflict

Category	Time Period	Measurement of Overlap		
		% If Different Denom. Is Different Religion	% If Only Different Religion Is Included	Correlation
Minorities at Risk	Cold War	78.5%	82.8%	.631**
	Early 1990s	77.2%	79.1%	.575**
	2000	76.8%	79.9%	.592**
State Failure, All Cases	1948 to 1989	85.7%	87.7%	.654**
	1990 to 2001	86.9%	87.2%	.761**
State Failure, Ethnic Wars	1948 to 1989	87.8%	92.1%	.824**
	1990 to 2001	95.9%	96.2%	.905**
State Failure, Mass Kill.	1948 to 1989	88.3%	88.8%	.760**
	1990 to 2001	86.4%	86.4%	.756**
State Failure, Rev. Wars	1948 to 1989	76.4%	76.4%	.012
	1990 to 2001	69.9%	69.9%	.168*

* = Significance (p-values) < .05,   ** = Significance (p-values) < .001

civilization on conflict. Also, as the civilizational variables are restricted to measuring identity, only the religious identity variables are used here for purposes of comparison and not the religious causes of conflict variables.

The chapter proceeds in the following stages. First, we examine the overlap between religion and Huntington's civilizations. Second, we examine the comparative impact of religion and civilization on levels of conflict. Third, we examine the comparative impact of religion and civilizations on discrimination against ethnic minorities. Finally, we examine the comparative impact of religion and civilization on intervention in ethnic conflicts.

The Overlap between Religion and Civilization

As discussed in Chapter 6, Huntington, to a large extent, bases his civilizations on religion. However, religion and civilization are not exactly the same thing. Accordingly, before comparing the impact of religion and civilization on conflict, it is necessary to establish to what extent the two overlap.

The analysis in Table 8.1 cross tabulates the religion and civilization variables used in this study for both the MAR and SF datasets. This analysis clearly shows

Figure 8.1: Mean Level of Rebellion, Controlling for Religion and Civilization, 1945-2000

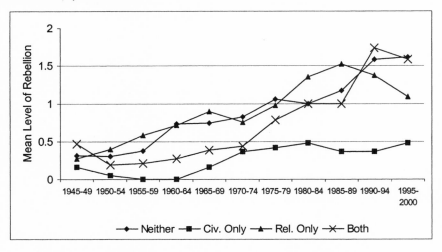

-Significance (t-test) between Neither and Civ. Only < .05 in 1950-54 & 1985-89
-Significance (t-test) between Neither and Civ. Only < .01 in 1965-69, 1975-79, & 195-2000
-Significance (t-test) between Neither and Civ. Only < .001 in 1955-64 & 1990-94
-Significance (t-test) between Neither and Both < .1 in 1965-74
-Significance (t-test) between Civ. Only and Rel. Only < .1 in 1980-84
-Significance (t-test) between Civ. Only and Rel. Only < .05 in 1955-59, 1965-69, & 1985-94
-Significance (t-test) between Civ. Only and Rel. Only < .01in 1960-64
-Significance (t-test) between Civ. Only and Both < .1 in 1985-89
-Significance (t-test) between Civ. Only and Both < .05 in 1955-64
-Significance (t-test) between Civ. Only and Both < .01 in 1995-2000
-Significance (t-test) between Civ. Only and Both < .001 in 1990-94

that while there is considerable overlap between religion and civilization, the two are not the same thing. The analysis in Table 8.2 shows more clearly the extent of this overlap. Depending on which category of conflict is examined and whether denominational differences are considered religious differences, the overlap between religion and civilization is between 69.9 percent and 96.2 percent. This measure of overlap represents the proportion of cases where whether conflicts are civilizational and whether conflicts are religious match up.

There is little change over time in the extent of this overlap. The overlap for the MAR dataset ranges between 76.8 percent and 82.8 percent in all of the time periods and categories examined. The range for the entire SF dataset is even narrower with the changes being less than 2 percent. Ethnic wars in the SF dataset have the highest level of overlap at between 87.8 percent and 96.2 percent. The lowest overlap is revolutionary wars in the SF dataset for which the overlap ranges between 69.9 percent and 76.4 percent. Overall, these measures of overlap, almost

Figure 8.2: Mean Level of Rebellion, Controlling for Religion and Civilization, 1985-2000

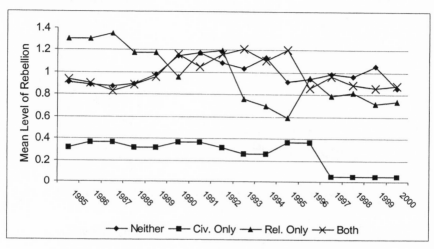

-Significance (t-test) between Neither and Civ. Only < .1 in 1985, 1988, 1995, & 1996
-Significance (t-test) between Neither and Civ. Only < .05 in 1989-91
-Significance (t-test) between Civ. Only and Rel. Only < .1 in 1991
-Significance (t-test) between Civ. Only and Rel. Only < .05 in 1985-89, 1992, & 1997-2000
-Significance (t-test) between Civ. Only and Both < .1 in 1985, 1989, & 1991
-Significance (t-test) between Civ. Only and Both < .05 in 1990, 1992, & 1995
-Significance (t-test) between Civ. Only and Both < .01 in 1993-94
-Significance (t-test) between Civ. Only and Both < .001 in 1997-2000
-Significance (t-test) between Rel. Only and Both < .1 in 1995

all of which prove to be statistically significant when doing a correlation test, are high but are by no means 100 percent. This means that the overall impression that there is a strong overlap between religion and civilization but the two are not the same thing is accurate with respect to domestic conflict. It also means that there is a possibility that a comparison between the two will show that the two influence conflict differently.

Religion, Civilization, and Levels of Conflict

This section analyzes the impact of religion and civilization on the various types of conflict examined in this study. With the exception of the level of violence in mass killings, this means measuring the extent to which minorities are violent. In many of the tests performed here, conflicts are divided into four categories: conflicts which are neither civilizational nor religious; conflicts which are civilizational but

Figure: 8.3 Mean Level of Protest Controlling for Religion and Civilization, 1945-2000

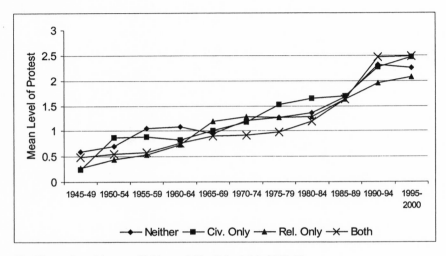

-Significance (t-test) between Neither and Civ. Only < .1 in 1945-49
-Significance (t-test) between Neither and Rel. Only < .1 in 1960-64
-Significance (t-test) between Neither and Rel. Only < .05 in 1945-49 & 1955-59
-Significance (t-test) between Neither and Both < .1 in 1960-64
-Significance (t-test) between Neither and Both < .01 in 1955-59
-Significance (t-test) between Rel. Only and Both < .1 in 1990-94

not religious; conflicts which are religious but not civilizational; and conflicts which are both civilizational and religious. In the multiple regression analyses religion and civilization are generally measured by separate variables.

The examination of ethnic rebellion between 1945 and 2000 in the MAR data, presented in Figure 8.1, provides mixed results. Conflicts which are civilizational but not religious are consistently the least violent throughout this period. Conflicts which are religious but not civilizational are the most violent for most of the Cold War era, but become comparatively less violent during the 1990s. Conflicts which are both civilizational and religious are the second least violent until 1990 when they rise sharply. However, the violence of no category of conflict is ever statistically significantly higher than the level of violence in conflicts which are neither civilizational nor religious.

The examination of ethnic rebellion between 1985 and 2000 in the MAR data, presented in Figure 8.2, does little to clarify these results. Conflicts which are civilizational but not religious remain the least violent. Other than this, there are nearly no statistically significant differences between the other categories of conflict. The only consistent result in the analysis of ethnic rebellion is that conflicts which are civilizational but not religious have the lowest levels of conflict. Thus,

Figure 8.4: Mean Level of Protest Controlling for Religion and Civilization, 1985-2000

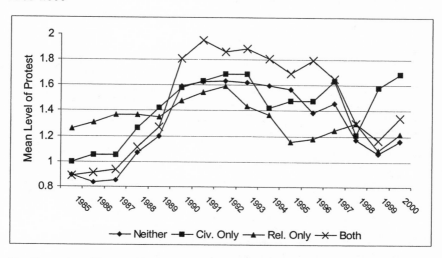

-Significance (t-test) between Civ. Only and Rel. Only < .1 in 1985
-Significance (t-test) between Civ. Only and Rel. Only < .05 in 1986-87 & 1995
-Significance (t-test) between Rel. Only and Both < .1 in 1985-87, 1991, 1993-94, & 1997
-Significance (t-test) between Rel. Only and Both < .05 in 1995-96

while there is little conclusive evidence that religion causes more conflict, there is conclusive evidence that some types of civilizational conflict are the least violent.

Overall, the results of the analysis of ethnic protest in the MAR data show even less difference between the categories but they do show some indication of civilizational conflicts exhibiting more protest in the post-Cold War era. The analysis of the 1945 to 2000 period, presented in Figure 8.3, shows all four categories of conflict exhibiting nearly the same level of conflict for the entire period. The yearly analysis of the 1985 to 2000 period, presented in Figure 8.4, shows some evidence of change over time. Conflicts which are both civilizational and religious exhibited the highest levels of protest between 1990 and 1996. Also, at the end of the period, there was a steep increase in the level of protest in conflicts which were civilizational but not religious. While this evidence is by no means conclusive, it does show a trend: protest becoming more common in civilizational conflicts in the post-Cold War era.

The analysis in Chapter 4 shows that ethnic conflicts tend to be more violent if they are separatist conflicts. Accordingly, this analysis reexamines the comparative impact of religion and civilization on conflict in the MAR data looking only at separatist conflicts. Before we begin the analysis, there is one general result which needs to be emphasized: that no conflicts which were civilizational but not religious

Figure 8.5: Mean Level of Rebellion among Separatist Groups, Controlling for Religion and Civilization, 1945-2000

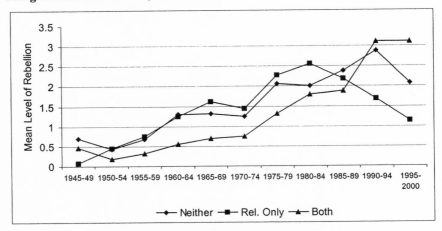

-Significance (t-test) between Neither and Rel. Only < .05 in 1945-49
-Significance (t-test) between Neither and Both < .1 in 1995-2000
-Significance (t-test) between Rel. Only and Both < .1 in 1945-49 & 1990-94
-Significance (t-test) between Rel. Only and Both < .01 in 1995-2000

Figure 8.6: Mean Level of Rebellion among Separatist Groups, Controlling for Religion and Civilization, 1985-2000

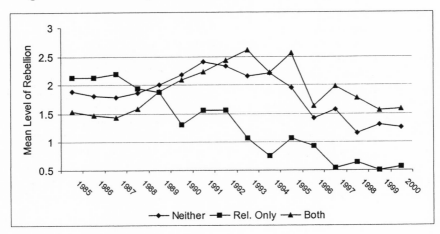

-Significance (t-test) between Neither and Rel. Only < .1 in 1993 & 1999
-Significance (t-test) between Neither and Rel. Only < .05 in 1997
-Significance (t-test) between Neither and Rel. Only < .01 in 1994
-Significance (t-test) between Rel. Only and Both < .1 in 1998 & 2000
-Significance (t-test) between Rel. Only and Both < .05 in 1993-95, 1997, & 1999

Figure 8.7: Mean Level of Protest among Separatist Groups, Controlling for Religion and Civilization, 1945-2000

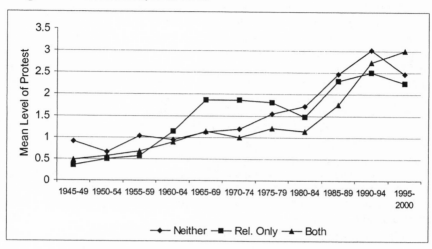

-Significance (t-test) between Neither and Rel. Only < .1 in 1945-59 & 1965-74
-Significance (t-test) between Neither and Both < .1 in 1980-89 & 1995-2000
-Significance (t-test) between Rel. Only and Both < .1 in 1995-2000
-Significance (t-test) between Rel. Only and Both < .05 in 1970-74

Figure 8.8: Mean Level of Protest among Separatist Groups, Controlling for Religion and Civilization, 1985-2000

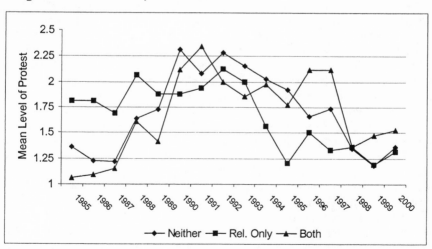

-Significance (t-test) between Neither and Rel. Only < .05 in 1995
-Significance (t-test) between Rel. Only and Both < .1 in 1985-86 & 1997

involved separatism. This alone can be taken as an indicator that civilizational differences by themselves are not a major explanation for ethnic violence.

The analysis of rebellion among separatist groups, presented in Figures 8.5 and 8.6, shows conflicts that are both religious and civilizational becoming comparatively more violent in the post-Cold War era. While conflicts in this category are the least violent for most of the pre-1990 period, they are consistently more violent than conflicts which are religious but not civilizational from 1990 onward and more violent than all other categories from 1992. Furthermore, the difference between conflicts which are both religious and civilizational and conflicts which are religious but not civilizational is statistically significant for much of the 1992 to 2000 period. Thus, there is evidence that civilization has an impact on ethnic rebellion, but only when civilizational differences and religious differences coincide. However, religion also seems to have little impact on rebellion unless the conflict is also civilizational. It also needs to be emphasized that these results must be taken in light of the fact that in the post-Cold War era those conflicts which are both civilizational and religious are only slightly more violent than those conflicts which are neither civilizational nor religious.

The analysis of protest among separatist groups, presented in Figures 8.7 and 8.8, shows few consistent differences in the levels of protest. The only exception to this is the 1960 to 1979 period where protest was consistently higher in conflicts which were religious but not civilizational. While religion, for a time, did impact on ethnic protest, it was before the end of the Cold War.

The analysis of the levels of violence in the SF data are presented in Table 8.3. In the post-Cold War era neither religion nor civilization has a significant impact on violence. During the Cold War era, however, there are some differences. Ethnic wars which are religious but not civilizational are less violent than conflicts which are neither civilizational nor religious and conflicts which are both religious and civilizational are the most violent. This is consistent with the results from the MAR data. Both categories of religious mass killings are more violent than conflicts which are neither civilizational nor religious but this result is only statistically significant for mass killings which are both religious and civilizational. Revolutionary wars which are civilizational but not religious are the least violent and those which are religious but not civilizational are the most violent.

In all, the simple analysis of the comparative impact of religion and civilization on violence does not provide any conclusive results. However, it does produce two general trends. First, religion is associated with higher levels of conflict more often than is Huntington's concept of civilizations. Second, when religion is associated with higher levels of violence it is more often than not the case that it does so in combination with civilizational differences.

The multivariate analysis of the civilizational and religious causes of ethnic rebellion, presented in Table 8.4, shows that religion variables are more often significant than are civilizational variables. In this analysis, civilization and religion are examined both individually and in combination with separatism variables because the analysis in Chapter 4 shows such variables to be important predictors

Table 8.3: Mean Level of Violence of State Failures, Controlling for Civilization and Religion

Type of Conflict	Category	Mean Level of Violence in	
		1948 to 1989	1990 to 2001
Ethnic Wars	Neither	1.65	1.53
	Civilizational Only	–	–
	Religious Only	1.19[c]	1.89
	Both	2.13[ce]	1.73
Mass Killings	Neither	2.21	2.97
	Civilizational Only	–	–
	Religious Only	2.60	–
	Both	2.71[b]	2.98
Revolutionary Wars	Neither	2.12	1.84
	Civilizational Only	1.21[a]	–
	Religious Only	1.88[d]	1.90
	Both	–	–

a = Significance (t-test) between this category and neither in the same type of conflict < .05
b = Significance (t-test) between this category and neither in the same type of conflict < .01
c = Significance (t-test) between this category and neither in the same type of conflict < .001
d = Significance (t-test) between this category and Civ. Only in the same type of conflict < .05
e = Significance (t-test) between this category and Rel. Only in the same type of conflict < .001

of rebellion. The regressions also include whether the minority and majority groups involved in the conflict are Muslim in order to account for Huntington's predictions regarding Muslims. At least one of the combined religion and separatism variables is significant in each regression. In the 1996 and 2000 regressions the simple religion variable is negative. This means that it is specifically the combination of religion and separatism which leads to rebellion.

In contrast, the only civilizational variable which proves to be significant is a combined civilization and separatism variable in the 1993 regression. Also, the only Muslim variable which is significant is whether the minority group is Muslim in 1993 and this variable has a negative impact on rebellion. Thus, there is little support for the CoC theory when controlling for other factors including religion and, if anything, conflicts involving the Islamic civilization are less violent. Also, as is the case with the previous analyses in Chapter 4, nonreligious factors including repression, the spread of conflict across borders, international support, and mobilization have a greater impact on rebellion than do religious factors.

Table 8.4: Multiple Regression for Causes of Rebellion for All Minorities, Including Civilizational and Religious Identity Variables

Independent Variables	Regressions for Rebellion in			
	1990	1993	1996	2000
Civilizational Clash	(-.021)	(-.029)	(-.027)	(.024)
Minority Group Muslim	(-.037)	-.115***	(-.032)	(-.042)
Majority Group Muslim	(-.025)	(.022)	(.005)	(-.021)
Different Religions	(-.029)	(-.027)	-.166***	-.092**
Separatism	(.070)	(.022)	-.237*	(.019)
Separatism * Civ. Clash	(.032)	.217****	(-.015)	(.027)
Separatism * Diff. Religion	.170***	(-.019)	.291**	(.027)
Autonomy Grievances	(-.005)	(-.035)	(.018)	(.094)
Aut. Griev. * Civ. Clash	(-.014)	(-.031)	(.019)	(-.086)
Aut. Griev. * Diff. Relig.	(-.013)	.087*	(.033)	.087*
Cultural Grievances	(.001)	(-.007)	(.023)	-.112***
Economic Grievances	(-.008)	(-.021)	-.140***	(.034)
Political Grievances	(-.026)	(-.001)	.086*	(-.012)
Cultural Differences	(.049)	(.028)	(.058)	(-.039)
Polity	(.031)	(-.032)	(.074)	(.049)
Repression	–	–	.298****	.577****
Int. Military Support	.115**	.228****	.282****	.141***
Contagion of Reb. 1980s	.198****	(.007)	(-.063)	-.165**
Contagion of Reb. 1990s	–	.092**	.144***	.174**
Diffusion of Reb. 1980s	(-.011)	(.014)	(-.088)	(-.016)
Diffusion of Reb. 1990s	–	(.070)	.092*	(.023)
# of Militant Orgs. 1990s	(.098)	(-.022)	(.050)	.160***
Support, Mil. Orgs. 1990s	.403****	.449****	.143**	(.059)
ΔMil. Org. to Year of Regr.	–	–	(-.056)	(-.010)
df	284	284	284	284
Adjusted R²	.377	.532	.421	.552

* = Significance < .1, ** = Significance < .05, *** = Significance < .01, **** = Significance < .001
All values in table are beta values. Means are substituted for missing data. Values in parentheses were excluded from the regression due to the fact they proved to be insignificant. The values in the parentheses are what the beta of the variable would have been if it were included in the regression. Religious conflicts are those where the two groups belong to different religions.

In contrast, civilizational variables do seem to have an impact on ethnic protest. The analysis, presented in Table 8.5, shows a complex interaction between the civilizational and religion variables. The simple civilizational clash variable is positive in three of the regressions. The simple separatism variable is positive in two of the regressions and the autonomy grievance variable is significant in three of the regressions. The first combined separatism and civilizational clash variable is negative in two of the regressions but the second is positive in one of the regressions. The first combined religion and separatism variable is positive in one regres-

Table 8.5: Multiple Regression for Causes of Protest, Including Religious and Civilizational Identity Variables

Independent Variables	Regressions for Protest in			
	1990	1993	1996	2000
Civilizational Clash	(.065)	.200***	.198****	.119**
Minority Group Muslim	(.004)	.119**	(.060)	(.021)
Majority Group Muslim	-.116**	(-.043)	(.018)	(-.002)
Different Religions	(.069)	(-.086)	(-.005)	(.013)
Separatism	.404***	.516****	(-.007)	(-.081)
Separatism * Civ. Clash	-.322**	-.893****	(.003)	(-.090)
Separatism * Diff. Religion	(.099)	.328*	(.005)	(.009)
Autonomy Grievances	(.031)	.196****	.513****	.487****
Aut. Griev. * Civ. Clash	.553****	(-.135)	(.253)	(-.174)
Aut. Griev. * Diff. Relig.	-.367**	(-.246)	-.320**	-.300**
Cultural Grievances	(.054)	(-.024)	(-.071)	(.015)
Economic Grievances	(.011)	(-.002)	(.023)	.148***
Political Grievances	.216****	.158***	(.061)	(.061)
Cultural Differences	(.017)	(-.085)	(-.006)	(.056)
Polity	.146***	.128**	.095*	.201****
Repression	–	–	.283****	.226****
Int. Political Support	.179****	.120**	(-.002)	(-.024)
Contagion of Prot. 1980s	(.024)	(.013)	(-.074)	(.065)
Contagion of Prot. 1990s	–	(-.042)	(-.067)	(-.001)
Diffusion of Prot. 1980s	(.069)	(.031)	.104**	.241****
Diffusion of Prot. 1990s	–	(-.028)	(-.028)	(-.045)
Contagion of Reb. 1980s	.169***	(-.082)	(.040)	(.012)
Contagion of Reb. 1990s	–	(-.062)	(.056)	.170***
Diffusion of Reb. 1980s	(.031)	(-.018)	(-.066)	(-.041)
Diffusion of Reb. 1990s	–	(.046)	(-.029)	(.001)
# of Political Orgs. 1990s	(.049)	.175**	.117*	.126**
Support, Pol. Orgs. 1990s	.229****	.197***	.147**	(-.076)
df	284	284	284	284
Adjusted R^2	.285	.318	.269	.315

* = Significance < .1, ** = Significance < .05, *** = Significance < .01, **** = Significance < .001
All values in table are beta values. Means are substituted for missing data. Values in parentheses were excluded from the regression due to the fact they proved to be insignificant. The values in the parentheses are what the beta of the variable would have been if it were included in the regression. Religious conflicts are those where the two groups belong to different religions.

sion but the second is negative in three of the regressions. In all four of the regressions, the weight of the negative religion or civilization related variables is stronger than the weight of the positive ones. However, separatist groups consistently protest more. Thus, the overall influence of this complex interaction is that religious and civilizational minorities protest less and separatist minorities protest more.

Another major difference between the analysis of the causes of protest and

Figure 8.9: Cultural Discrimination Controlling for Religious and Civilizational Identity, 1990 to 2000

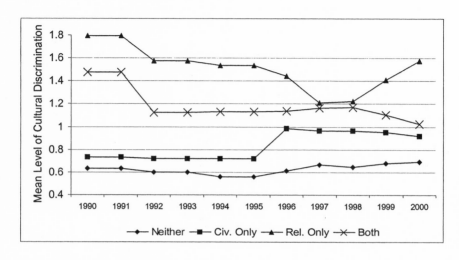

-Significance (t-test) between Neither and Civ. Only < .1 in 1996
-Significance (t-test) between Neither and Rel. Only < .1 in 1997-98
-Significance (t-test) between Neither and Rel. Only < .05 in 1996 & 1999
-Significance (t-test) between Neither and Rel. Only < .01 in 1990-95 & 2000
-Significance (t-test) between Neither and Both < .05 in 1992-93 & 1996-99
-Significance (t-test) between Neither and Both < .01 in 1994-95
-Significance (t-test) between Neither and Both < .001 in 1990-91
-Significance (t-test) between Civ. Only and Rel. Only < .1 in 2000
-Significance (t-test) between Civ. Only and Rel. Only < .05 in 1990-95
-Significance (t-test) between Civ. Only and Both < .01 in 1990-91

rebellion is that the religion, civilization, and separatism variables combined influence the regressions more than do the other variables. Thus, these factors are the primary factors in determining the amount of protest.

There is also little evidence supporting Huntington's contention that Muslims are more conflictive from this analysis. Two of the Muslim variables prove to be significant, one positive and one negative.

In all, religion seems to have a greater impact on ethnic conflict, as well as on conflict in general, than does Huntington's concept of civilizations. Religion variables impact on conflict more often than do civilizational variables. This is especially true when focusing on violent conflict. The results for ethnic protest are more mixed, but there is no clear evidence that civilizations impact on protest more than religion. These results, combined with the significant overlap between the two concepts, indicate that any impact civilizations have on conflict is likely because it is a surrogate variable for religion.

Figure 8.10: Economic Discrimination Controlling for Religious and Civilizational Identity, 1990-2000

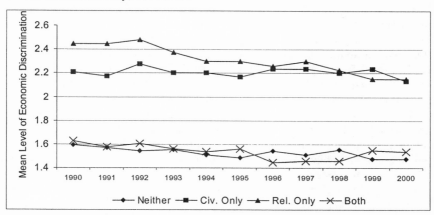

-Significance (t-test) between Neither and Civ. Only < .1 in 1990-91
-Significance (t-test) between Neither and Civ. Only < .05 in 1992-98 & 2000
-Significance (t-test) between Neither and Civ. Only < .01 in 1999
-Significance (t-test) between Neither and Rel. Only < .05 in 1998-2000
-Significance (t-test) between Neither and Rel. Only < .01 in 1993-97
-Significance (t-test) between Neither and Rel. Only < .001 in 1990-92
-Significance (t-test) between Civ. Only and Both < .1 in 1990-91, 1993, 1995, & 2000
-Significance (t-test) between Civ. Only and Both < .05 in 1992, 1994, & 1996-99
-Significance (t-test) between Rel. Only and Both < .05 in 1999-2000
-Significance (t-test) between Rel. Only and Both < .01 in 1990-1998

Figure 8.11: Political Discrimination Controlling for Religious and Civilizational Identity, 1990-2000

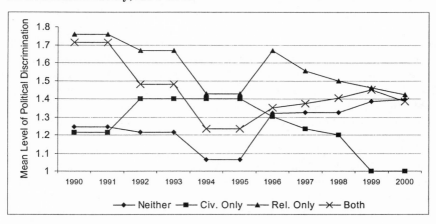

-Significance (t-test) between Neither and Both < .1 in 1990-91

Causes of Ethnic Discrimination and Repression

This section analyzes the comparative impact of religion and civilizations on discrimination and repression against ethnic minorities. The analysis of cultural discrimination, presented in Figure 8.9, shows that while both religion and civilization have an impact, the impact of religion is stronger. Conflicts which are only civilizational have marginally higher levels of discrimination than do conflicts which are neither civilizational nor religious; however, this difference is only statistically significant in 1996. In contrast, cultural discrimination in conflicts which are religious but not civilizational is consistently the highest and the difference between this category and conflicts which are neither civilizational nor religious is statistically significant for the entire period examined here. Conflicts which are both civilizational and religious have levels of cultural discrimination which fall in between the levels for those which are only civilizational and those which are only religious. The level of cultural discrimination in conflicts which are both civilizational and religious is also statistically significantly higher than that of conflicts which are neither civilizational nor religious for the entire period examined here.

As presented in Figure 8.10, both civilization and religion impact on economic discrimination about equally, with perhaps a slight tendency for religion to impact more. Both conflicts which are religious but not civilizational and civilizational but not religious have levels of economic discrimination which are statistically significantly higher than the level for conflicts which are neither religious nor civilizational for the entire period tested here. However, conflicts which are both civilizational and religious have levels of economic discrimination which are at about the same level as conflicts which are neither religious nor civilizational. While there is no statistical significance to this result, conflicts which are religious but not civilizational have higher levels of economic discrimination than do conflicts which are civilizational but not religious in nine of eleven years examined here.

The difference in the impact of religion and civilization on political discrimination, presented in Figure 8.11, is very slight and has almost no statistical significance. Nevertheless, in general, conflicts which are religious but not civilizational tend to have the highest levels of political discrimination, followed by conflicts which are both civilizational and religious, and conflicts which are civilizational but not religious. Thus, religion does have a greater impact on political discrimination than does civilization, but this difference does not rise to the level of statistical significance.

As presented in Figure 8.12, religion also has a greater impact on repression than does civilization. Those conflicts which are religious, whether in combination with civilization or not, are those with the highest levels of repression. Interestingly, conflicts which are civilizational but not religious have lower levels of repression than do conflicts which are neither religious nor civilizational. All of these relationships are statistically significant for at least some of the period examined here.

Figure 8.12: Repression Controlling for Religious and Civilizational Identity, 1996-2000

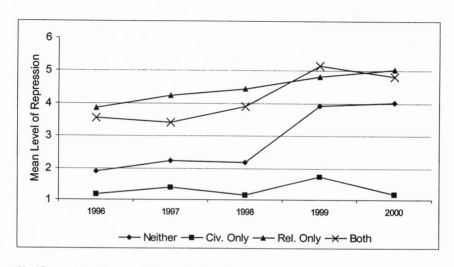

-Significance (t-test) between Neither and Civ. Only < .1 in 1999
-Significance (t-test) between Neither and Civ. Only < .001 in 2000
-Significance (t-test) between Neither and Rel. Only < .1 in 1996 & 1998
-Significance (t-test) between Neither and Rel. Only < .05 in 1997
-Significance (t-test) between Neither and Both < .1 in 1997
-Significance (t-test) between Neither and Both < .05 in 1996 & 1998
-Significance (t-test) between Civ. Only and Rel. Only < .05 in 1996-97 & 1999
-Significance (t-test) between Civ. Only and Rel. Only < .01 in 1998 & 2000
-Significance (t-test) between Civ. Only and Both < .05 in 1997
-Significance (t-test) between Civ. Only and Both < .01 in 1996 & 1999
-Significance (t-test) between Civ. Only and Both < .001 in 1998 & 2000

Overall, religion has a greater impact on discrimination and repression than does civilization. An interesting dynamic is that adding civilization to a religious conflict generally results in lower levels of discrimination. This indicates that conflicts in which the two groups are differentiated primarily by religion are those that are most likely to have the highest levels of discrimination. This is because civilizational differences indicate a wide range of cultural differences between two groups, even if a large portion of those differences are religious ones. Thus, if two groups have different religions but not different civilizations, it is likely that religion is the only difference or at last one of very few cultural differences between the two groups.

Figure 8.13: Intervention in Ethnic Conflicts Controlling for Religion and Civilization, 1990-1995.

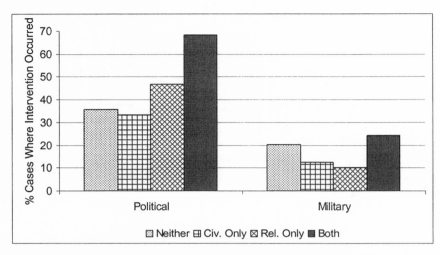

-Significance (Chi-squared) for table including pol. intervention and no pol. intervention < .001

Figure 8.14: Religious and Civilizational Affinities between Interveners and Intervenees, 1990-1995

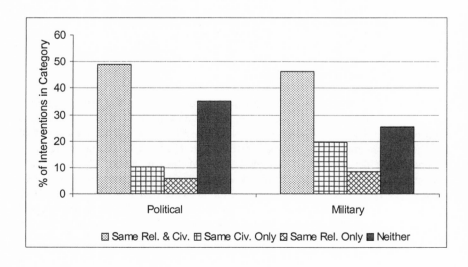

Table 8.6: Logistic Regression of Multiple Factors That Influence the Decision to Intervene

Variables	Intervention by Foreign Government 1990-1995	
	Political	Military
Civilizational Clash	(1.8798)	(1.0609)
Religious Differences	(0.5752)	(0.0595)
Separatism	-1.8982**	(0.0595)
(Civ. Clash +1) * Separatism	(0.0004)	(0.0414)
(Religious Differences + 1) * Separatism	1.0672**	(0.0014)
Cultural Differences	(0.3957)	(0.0333)
Protest 1990-1995	0.1748*	(0.0698)
Rebellion 1990-1995	0.1368*	0.6732****
Contagion Protest 1980s	-1.4300****	(1.6154)
Contagion Protest 1990s	2.8499****	(0.6515)
Diffusion Protest 1980s	(1.0873)	0.3608***
Diffusion Protest 1990s	(0.9051)	(0.0470)
Contagion Rebellion 1980s	(0.8663)	(0.0101)
Contagion Rebellion 1990s	1.4980****	(0.0925)
Diffusion Rebellion 1980s	(0.1019)	(0.1228)
Diffusion Rebellion 1990s	(0.5241)	(0.0374)
N	262	262
% Correctly Predicted, Overall	68.32%	86.26%
Simulated R^2 (Nagelkerke)	.192	.446

* = Significance < .1, ** = Significance < .05, *** = Significance < .01, **** = Significance < .001
All values in table are real values. Values in parentheses were excluded from the regression due to the fact they proved to be insignificant. The values in the parentheses are what the value of the variable would have been if it were included in the regression.

Religion, Civilization, and International Intervention

This section examines the combined impact of religion and civilization on international intervention in ethnic conflicts. As is the case with the analysis in Chapter 4, this analysis includes an examination of political and military intervention looking both at what types of conflicts attract intervention and at who intervenes.

The bivariate analysis of which conflicts attract intervention, presented in Figure 8.13, shows that religion has a stronger impact. Conflicts which are civilizational but not religious attract less political intervention than do conflicts which are neither civilizational nor religious. Conflicts which are religious but not civilizational attract more political intervention than do conflicts which are neither civilizational but not religious. However, the type of conflict which attracts the most political intervention is those that are both religious and civilizational. The results of this entire analysis are statistically significant.

The results for military intervention are less dramatic. The only category of conflict which attracts more military intervention than does conflicts which are neither religious nor civilizational is those that are both religious and civilizational. Thus, in the bivariate analysis, only conflicts which have a religious component attract a disproportionate level of intervention, though often these religious conflicts are also civilizational. However, the presence of civilizational differences alone is associated with lower levels of intervention.

The multivariate analysis, presented in Table 8.6, confirms that religion has a greater impact on intervention than does civilization. For political intervention, one of the religion variables and none of the civilizational variables are significant. For military intervention neither the civilizational nor the religion variables were significant.

In contrast, the analysis of who intervenes, presented in Figure 8.14, shows that civilization has a greater impact. Nearly half of interveners share both civilizational and religious affinities with those on whose behalf they intervene. However, the proportion of interveners which are civilizationally similar but religiously dissimilar to those on whose behalf they intervene is about double that of those who are religiously similar but civilizationally dissimilar to the intervenees.

In all, the results for international intervention are mixed. Religion has a greater impact on which conflicts attract intervention, but civilization has a greater impact on who intervenes in ethnic conflicts.

Conclusions

The overall result of the analysis presented in this chapter is that religion has a greater impact on conflict than does civilization. However, this is not to say that this was found to be true in every aspect of the analysis. Rather, when comparing the impact of the two, religion's impact is stronger more often than is the impact of civilization.

Given the overlap between the two variables, this has two implications. First, it is likely that much of the impact civilization has on conflict is as a surrogate variable for religion. Second, and in contrast, as civilization and religion are not the same thing and as civilization includes aspects of culture other than religion, it is likely that culture has an impact on conflict independent of religion. However, this impact is less than that of religion.

Chapter 9

Conclusions

The analysis presented here was intended to answer a few simple questions: What influence, if any, does religion have on domestic conflict? Is Samuel Huntington's Clash of Civilizations (CoC) theory correct? Does his concept of civilizations truly define the nature of conflict in the post-Cold War era? Implicit in these questions is another set of questions: What is the overlap between religion and Huntington's civilizations? Assuming that either has an impact on domestic conflict, which one has a greater impact? Is civilization a surrogate variable for religion or does it have an independent influence?

The discussion in this chapter proceeds in two stages. First, we try to provide some basic answers to the above questions. Second, we discuss some more specific trends found in the data analysis.

Some Answers

The answers to these questions are both simple and not so simple. In short, religion has an impact on domestic conflict but it is not the primary cause. That is, while other factors like the desire for self-determination seem to be the primary motivation for ethnic conflict, religion still has an impact in a number of ways. However, as discussed below, our information on ethnic conflict is more complete than it is for other types of civil wars so the possibility that religion is a fundamental cause of nonethnic civil wars remains open.

In contrast, Huntington's CoC theory is not supported by the data. His concept of civilizations is simply not sufficient to explain domestic conflict in the post-Cold War era. Yet civilizations have a strong overlap with religion in that the vast majority of civilizational conflicts are religious ones and the vast majority of non-civilizational conflicts are not religious ones.

This opens the question of why religion is found to have an influence but Huntington's concept of civilizations does not have the impact that he predicts. There are two answers to this question. First, the standards of proof for our propositions regarding religion and Huntington's propositions regarding his concept of civilizations are different. Huntington's theory requires that civilization be the defining factor of conflict in the post-Cold War era. For this to be correct, two findings are necessary. First, civilizational identity must have a strong and uniform impact on conflict to the extent that it provides the dominant explanation for all post-Cold War conflict. Second, there must be a consistent and dramatic shift in conflict patterns during or after 1990, the end of the Cold War, to patterns more consistent with the CoC theory. Neither of these occur.

In contrast, the standard of proof for religion as an influence on conflict is lower. The argument made here with regard to religion is not that it is the basic driving force behind all domestic conflict. Rather, we make the less ambitious argument that religion influences conflict. This type of argument needs to meet a much lower threshold of proof than do the paradigmatic claims made by Huntington. We simply need to show that in some situations religion has a clear and statistically significant influence on domestic conflict. The data analysis here shows that this burden is easily met and that religion, in fact, does influence conflict but is not the primary cause.

Furthermore, in head-to-head comparisons between religion and civilization variables, the religion variables prove to have a stronger influence on conflict than do the civilization variables. Given the overlap between religion and civilization, this can be interpreted as meaning that civilization is little more than a surrogate variable for religion. However, this is likely not the case. In some instances the civilization variables seem to have an independent influence on domestic conflict. Thus, the nonreligious cultural aspects of Huntington's concept of civilization may have an independent influence on domestic conflict, though this influence is clearly much weaker than the influence of religion. Thus, while civilization may have a small impact on domestic conflict, this impact clearly does not reach the level of the paradigmatic claims made by Huntington.

The second reason why religion is found to have a strong influence on domestic conflict but Huntington's concept of civilizations does not is the difference between identity and more specific influences. When examining the impact of religion, two types of variables were analyzed. The first is identity variables. These variables analyze only whether the religious identities of two groups were different. For example, using the prism of identity, conflicts between Muslims and Christians are considered religious conflicts and conflicts between Protestant Christians and other Protestant Christians are not. The second type of variable is those that look at more specific influences. These include whether a minority expresses complaints over religious discrimination and whether a minority expresses a desire for more religious rights. These two variables measure whether religious issues were involved in a conflict. Unless the religious identities of the two groups involved in a conflict are different, religious issues are unlikely to be relevant, but they are not relevant in all conflicts in which religious identity is involved. Other more specific factors like religious legitimacy and the impact of religious institutions were also examined.

A basic analysis showed that religious identity has an impact on domestic conflict. However, a deeper analysis shows that, for ethnic conflict at least, most of the seeming impact of identity was really due to the presence of religious issues in the conflict. The reason identity appeared to have an impact was because religious issues did not come into play except in conflicts involving religious identities. What happened was that when comparing broad identity categories, some of the religious conflicts, as defined by identity, involved religious issues. This influenced the average level of conflict for the entire category. However, when comparing the impact of religious issues within the category of religious identity conflict, it became clear that most of this impact was due to religious issues.

In contrast, Huntington's concept of civilizations includes only identity. There is no provision for more specific factors. In fact, his theory is precisely that civilizations are a new form of identity group which will dominate conflict in the post-Cold War era. While it is possible to define religious discrimination and grievances over that discrimination, there is no such thing as civilizational discrimination.

Specific types of religious discrimination include:

- Restrictions on the public observance of religious services, festivals, and/or holidays.
- Restrictions on the building, repairing, and/or maintaining of places of worship.
- Forced observance of religious laws of another religion.
- Restrictions on formal religious organizations.
- Restrictions on the running of religious schools and/or religious education in general.
- Restrictions on the observance of religious laws concerning personal status, including marriage and divorce.
- Restrictions on the ordination of and/or access to clergy.

However, there is no analogous list of restrictions on civilizational rights. Certainly, minorities defined by any form of identity can be the target of discrimination. This discrimination can be political, economic, cultural, or religious. However, unlike religion, there is no type of discrimination that is unique to civilizational minorities. Similarly, there are no issues that are uniquely civilizational.

Does this mean that identity does not influence conflict at all? Probably not. Identity is important, if for no other reason, because it defines who is on what side of a conflict. Furthermore, other types of identity have been shown in this study and others to influence conflict. For example, national or ethnic identity is one of the driving forces behind ethnic conflict. However, in this study, the strength of national identities is measured through a group's desire for self-determination. Thus, it is arguable that it is the issue of self-determination rather than national identity which is the cause of ethnic conflict.

Be that as it may, it is still arguable that it is identity which is the cause of conflict. This is because, while a basic motivation for conflict may be identity, this identity, whether it be religious, ethnic, national, or civilizational, is not a very tangible concept. In essence it provides some way to differentiate between groups, between "us" and "them." However, for conflict to manifest, there must be some form of issue between groups. This issue can be competition for resources, desire for self-rule, competition for ideological or religious hegemony or freedom, or any number of other issues. What differentiates sources of identity like ethnicity, nationality, and religion from Huntington's civilizational identities is that there are specific issues unique to religious, ethnic, and national identities, but there are none unique to civilizational identities. Thus, all of these forms of conflict, other than civilization, have a vehicle to manifest themselves.

From this perspective, the proper question is not whether religion or other forms of identity are more influential than civilizational identity, but rather whether civilizational identity is at all relevant to conflict. This is because if identity needs some form of issue to manifest itself in conflict, and there is no type of issue associated with civilizations, there is no way civilization can have an impact. All of the impacts that Huntington describes are more appropriate to categories of identity like religion, nation, and ethnicity. In this light, Huntington's concept of civilization seems like an artificial construct for phenomena better explained by more traditional bases of identity.

Major Findings and Trends

This section reviews the major findings and trends found in the data analysis. As noted above, the most basic finding is that religion is found to have an impact on domestic conflict, but this impact is as an important intervening variable and not as a primary cause of conflict. Also, Huntington's CoC theory falls short of his ambitious goals, but the cultural aspects of civilization may have some minor impact on domestic conflict.

The basic goal of this section is not to provide a comprehensive listing of all of the specific findings in this study. Rather, it is to look at some of the larger issues and trends uncovered by the analysis.

Ethnic vs. Nonethnic Conflict

While the differences between ethnic and nonethnic conflict are not strictly a trend, the nature of these differences colors the entire analysis. Accordingly, it is important to discuss them up front. There are two such differences.

First, while all ethnoreligious conflicts involve religious identity, not all revolutionary wars and mass killings which are considered religious conflicts involve religious identity. Some of them are other types of religious conflicts. For instance, some of them are challenges to the state by religiously motivated revolutionaries. In these cases all sides of the conflict belong to the same religion and what differentiates the two sides is their level of commitment to religion as a basis for running a government. Thus, the Iranian revolution of 1977 and 1978, the Afghan war against the Soviet supported government during the 1980s, and the Algerian civil war which began in the early 1990s are qualitatively different from ethnic conflicts which involve religious identity. In fact, these nonethnic religious revolutions can be said, by definition, to involve religious issues as important and even primary elements of the conflict. Certainly most nonethnic religious revolutions involve other issues, but they would not be religious revolutions if they did not also involve religious issues.

In addition, there is one instance of an ethnic conflict which is classified as a religious war in the SF data for reasons other than identity. The conflict in Afghanistan from 1992 onward, while still ethnic in nature, also involved separate religious issues. This is because, while the wars in Afghanistan were to a great extent between the country's four major ethnic groups, the Pashtuns, Uzbeks, Tajiks, and Hazaras, there were separate religious issues. All of these ethnic groups are Muslims and all except the Hazaras are Sunni Muslims. In addition to the ethnic fighting, there was also fighting between factions who supported a religious state and those that did not. A large part of this fighting occurred within the Pashtuns, who constitute the largest ethnic group in Afghanistan. Elements among the Pashtuns were the major backers of the now infamous Taliban government and other elements among the Pashtuns, along with most Hazaras, Tajiks, and Uzbeks, opposed this movement. Thus, the ten years of conflict between 1992 and 2001 coded in Afghanistan included both ethnic and nonethnic elements and can be classified, at least in part, as a nonethnic religious revolutionary war. This constitutes a small minority of 1.5 percent of all ethnic conflict in the SF dataset.

This type of conflict constitutes 80 of 449 (17.8 percent) conflict years in the revolutionary war section and 29 of 249 (11.6 percent) conflict years of mass killings in the SF dataset. When taking overlapping cases into account, nonethnic religious wars constitute 93 of 1,106 (8.4 percent) years of conflict in the SF dataset as opposed to 327 conflict years (35.1 percent of all conflict) of religious identity conflict. Thus, although identity-based religious conflict constitutes a majority of 77.9 percent of all religious conflict, a substantial minority of 22.1 percent is not identity based.

This means that a minority of the religious conflicts examined in the SF data involved religious issues but not religious identity. As discussed in the previous section, the multivariate analysis of the MAR data showed that it was religious issues which most often influenced conflicts and not identity. This implies that those conflicts which are religious solely because of the religious issues involved in the conflict may be substantively different from the religious identity conflicts.

The second important difference between ethnoreligious and other religious conflicts is that the multivariate analyses were only carried out for ethnic conflict.

This is not because the other types of conflict are not worthy of multivariate analysis. Rather, it is because the MAR data on ethnic conflict had enough depth for this type of analysis and the SF data, our only source of data on nonethnic conflict, did not have this level of depth. While this limitation is unavoidable due to the nature of the available data, it nevertheless has implications for the findings of this study.

The most important of these implications is that the causal findings of this study only apply to ethnic conflict. That is, while we can show that nonethnic religious conflicts exist and have properties that are different from nonreligious, nonethnic conflicts, we cannot show that these differences are because of religion. Thus, our conclusions regarding the impact of religion on nonethnic conflict are based on inference. This is because, in order to fully test causality, it is necessary to control for other factors. This can only be done with multivariate analysis. In other words, the findings from the multivariate analysis, like the finding that religion is an influence on conflict but not the primary influence, only apply to ethnic conflict. While these findings have implications for nonethnic conflict, these implications are based on induction rather than deduction.

When these two differences between the analyses of ethnic and nonethnic conflicts are combined, this results in an interesting dynamic. We established that when looking at religion's influence on conflict, it is religious issues which have the primary impact on ethnic conflict rather than religious identity. We furthermore established that this impact of religion is secondary to other factors. However, we were only able to establish this for ethnic conflicts because multivariate analyses were not possible on other types of conflict. Yet, we established that there are a minority of religious conflicts which involve religious issues but not religious identity. In fact, they tend to take place within national and ethnic groups rather than between them.

This means that not only do these conflicts involve religious issues, but also that they do not involve religious, national, or ethnic identity. Thus, it is logical to assume that at least some of these conflicts are primarily about religion. In other words, a small minority of 8.4 percent of all conflict and 22.1 percent of religious conflict may fit into the category of conflicts which are primarily about religion. Since a multi-variate analysis is not possible, we cannot at this time establish definitively whether this is true for all or any portion of these conflicts in the SF dataset, but the implication that this is true is a strong one.

Accordingly, all of the results discussed below are shadowed by this. That is, while the results discussed below are valid for the populations in which they were tested, the incomplete nature of the data makes all of these results incomplete. Nevertheless, the results of this study do constitute the most comprehensive quantitative study of the impact of religion on conflict to date of which I am aware. Thus, even with these flaws, they are valid and are a significant advancement of our knowledge on the topic.

Religion as an Intervening Variable

Religion impacts on conflict in a number of ways. However, before we discuss this impact it is important to emphasize that this impact tends to be secondary to other factors. Religious conflict is, overall, less common than nonreligious conflict. This remains true even when taking the limitations of the data discussed in the previous section into account. In addition, when looking at the conflict patterns of individual religions, most conflicts are with members of the same religion. These results are consistent for the entire period of 1945 to 2001 analyzed here in the combined data of both datasets. Despite this, it is important to remember that while less common than other types of conflict, religious conflicts existed throughout the entire period analyzed here.

In addition, in the multivariate analyses of ethnic conflict, the impact of religion is generally secondary to other influences on ethnic conflict. The most striking of these other factors is the desire for self-determination. Among religious minorities, rebellion is extremely rare in the absence of a desire for self-determination. Religion, when combined with self-determination, can significantly increase the level of violence, but religion without self-determination has little impact on rebellion. This is demonstrated by the fact that when religion is significant in the multiple regressions, it is nearly always in the form of a combined religion and self-determination variable.

Other factors like the spread of conflict across borders, international intervention, ethnic grievances, repression, international support for the minority group, and the political organizations of the minority group also had an impact. Thus, religion's secondary influence occurs in a context where there are a number of other secondary influences. It is arguable that religion is the most important of the nonprimary influences on ethnic rebellion, but it is nevertheless not the primary influence. It is, rather, a very important intervening variable.

Nevertheless, the influences of religion on various forms of conflict are important and multiple. As noted above, religion exacerbates ethnic rebellion. These factors include religious grievances, demands for more religious rights, and religious institutions. All of these factors, along with religious legitimacy, also impact on discrimination against ethnoreligious minorities. Religion also impacts on international intervention in ethnic conflicts. Ethnoreligious conflicts are more likely to attract intervention than are other ethnic conflicts, and interveners in ethnic conflicts are most often religiously similar to the minorities on whose behalf they intervene.

The Changing and Increasing Impact of Religion on Violence

One of the most striking findings of this study is that the impact of religion on violence has changed. These results are consistent across the MAR and SF datasets.

The MAR data shows that beginning in the early 1980s religion began to exacerbate separatist conflicts (Figure 4.3). Before then, there was little difference between religious separatist conflicts and nonreligious separatist conflicts. Since the early 1980s this exacerbation has increased to the point where by the late 1990s only religious-separatist conflicts were more violent than other types of conflicts. That is, those separatist conflicts that were more violent than other ones were religious separatist conflicts. The SF data similarly show an increasing gap between the level of violence in religious and nonreligious ethnic conflicts beginning in the early 1980s which increases over time (Figure 3.18).

This has important implications for the theoretical work on religion and conflict. As will be recalled from Chapter 2, there are three views of what will be the nature of religious conflict in the modern era. First, modernization and secularization theory posits that religion will become a primordial thing of the past, having no real impact on conflict in the modern era. Second, many posit that religion always has and always will be important. Finally, many posit that processes inherent within modernization will cause a revitalization or resurgence of religion in the modern era.

The first of these predictions has been clearly proven false, at least with regard to domestic conflict from 1945 through the twenty-first century. When choosing between the second two predictions, the results described above provide evidence that the third of these predictions is most correct. We see that religion has had an increasing impact on conflict since 1980.

Some might argue that this provides evidence that Huntington's CoC theory is correct but I contend that it does not for the following reasons. First, the increase in the importance of religion began around 1980, well before the end of the Cold War. In short, the timing is off. Second, while there was an increase in the impact of religion on ethnic violence starting in 1980 which increased in strength over the next two decades, the nature of this change is not what one would expect if Huntington were correct. This is because it is the combination of religion and self-determination which leads to greater ethnic violence. Without self-determination, religion has little impact on ethnic violence. Thus, as noted above, religion is an intervening variable, not the primary cause. Huntington, in contrast, predicts that his religious-based civilizations will, in fact, be the primary cause of conflict in the post-Cold War era. Thus, the findings presented here, while important, are not of the nature that Huntington predicted.

Third, in more direct tests of Huntington's CoC theory using the same data, the results did not support Huntington's contentions. Finally, in head-to-head comparisons between the impact of religion and Huntington's concept of civilizations, the religion variables proved to be better explanations for ethnic conflict than did the civilization variables.

To be fair to Huntington, as shown in Figures 3.8 and 3.9, in the SF data, there was a sharp increase in the number of religious conflicts around 1990. However, even with this sharp increase, the number of religious conflicts overall never outnumbered the number of nonreligious conflicts, though the number of ethnoreligious conflicts in some years during the 1990s slightly outnumbered the number of other ethnic conflicts. However, if Huntington's predictions were correct, we would have expected religious conflicts to consistently and significantly outnumber nonreligious from the early 1990s onward, which did not happen. Also, when using Huntington's civilizational categories, rather than religion, civilizational conflict remains less common than noncivilizational conflict throughout the entire period examined here both in the MAR data and in the SF data for conflict in general and for ethnic conflict (Figures 7.3 and 7.4).

Religion and Ethnic Protest

The impact of religion on ethnic protest is very different from its impact on ethnic rebellion. In short, if anything, the various religious factors tested here often cause *less* ethnic protest. This counterintuitive result is found throughout the data analysis. While the findings of the bivariate analysis are inconsistent, in the multivariate analysis religious identity had a consistently negative impact on protest.

The impact of the more specific religion variables is mixed. In the bivariate analysis only religious institutions had a statistically significant impact on protest with ecclesiastical networks, the most developed religious institutions, being associated with the lowest levels of protest. However, formal houses of worship, the next highest level of institution, were associated with the highest level of protest.

The multivariate analysis also shows that the impact of these factors is mixed. Religious grievances and religious institutions are associated with lower levels of protest. However, religious demands and religious legitimacy are associated with higher levels of protest.

It is important to emphasize that, as is the case with ethnic rebellion, factors other than religion have a greater impact. Thus, religion is not the primary influence on ethnic protest.

Be that as it may, the finding that religion often has a negative impact on protest is extremely counterintuitive. In short, the presence of religious identity and complaints over religious issues in an ethnic conflict make protest less likely. This is exactly the opposite of what we would expect. That this relationship remains consistent even when controlling for a number of factors shows that those things which we can measure cannot explain this phenomenon. We must, therefore, examine less tangible explanations.

One potential explanation is that violence is inherent in religion. That is, at some basic level, religion is violent. Girard (1977) makes such an argument. He argues that one of the origins of religion is to limit violence and keep it out of the community. It does so by including within it violent imagery and symbolic violence. Thus, people can satisfy their emotional need for violence through symbolic religious practices. Juergensmeyer (1991: 102) similarly argues that

> The altar–symbol of a sacred chopping block–and the priest, originally a sacred
> executioner, remain today at the focal point of worship throughout the world in
> a surprising variety of religious contexts. They, and the notions of sacrifice and
> martyrdom that lie behind them, are so integral to religion that without them many
> religious concepts would be almost unthinkable.

Sacrifice symbolically portrays the hidden desire to destroy someone or something similar to oneself. Furthermore, the rhetoric of war is "prominent in modern religious vocabulary" and "virtually all cultural traditions are filled with martial metaphors." (Juergensmeyer, 1991: 104-108)

This notion that some primordial aspect of religion is violent can explain our findings regarding protest. Simply put, some religious issues are beyond peaceful resolution and call for violence. The findings here show that this appears to be true of religious identity, religious institutions, and religious grievances. If this is true, why are religious demands and religious legitimacy associated with higher levels of protest? One possible answer is that religious identity, grievances, and institutions are more primordial or at least closer to core irrational aspects of religion than religious demands and legitimacy.

That identity is a core aspect of human psychology and that it is not a fully rational concept is not in dispute. Religious grievances represent anger at restrictions on one's religion. This too is not a fully rational phenomenon. While, clearly, there are rational aspects to the desire to stop discrimination there are also irrational aspects to religious grievances. Since religion is at the core of many people's identity, attacks on religion are also attacks on that identity. In other words, "Religion deals with the constitution of being as such. Hence, one can not be pragmatic on concerns challenging this being." (Laustsen and Waever, 2000: 719) Finally, religious institutions are the very establishments which, according to Girard (1977), were created to regulate violence. Thus, that they are associated with violence is not surprising.

Religious demands, in contrast, represent the desire to improve the legal status of one's religion within a state. By definition, any group willing to express such a demand openly is a group that feels that there exists a chance that this goal can be met within the existing political system. Thus, if more peaceful actions like protest can help to achieve this goal, they are likely to be used.

Religious legitimacy also is connected with nonviolence. The concept of legitimacy is linked to the idea that the ruled accept the right of the rulers to rule. In the context of this study it also means that religion is a legitimate topic for public discourse. Both of these factors lend themselves to peaceful activities like protest.

Conclusions

This study constitutes the most thorough quantitative analysis of the impact of religion and civilization on domestic conflict of which I am aware. It provides definitive answers in two related debates that have taken place within the social sciences during the late twentieth century.

For much of the twentieth century, the first debate, which was over the importance of religion in the modern era, was less of a debate than dogma. Until the 1980s, nearly all social scientists assumed that religion's influence on politics, society, and conflict was diminishing, if it existed at all. Only in the late twentieth century did some social scientists begin to argue that religion was important.[1] The results here show definitively that religion does impact on conflict in a variety of ways and that religious conflict has existed throughout the 1945 to 2001 period analyzed here. Furthermore, rather than diminishing in impact, the impact of religion on conflict has been increasing since around 1980.

Thus, the academic trends in the debate over religion's importance and the impact of religion on domestic conflict coincide. Around 1980, when religion's impact on conflict began to increase, social scientists began to argue that religion is important. Over the next two decades the increase in the impact of religion on domestic conflict and the academic attention to religion as a cause of domestic conflict increased roughly simultaneously.

The second debate examined here is the "Clash of Civilizations" debate. Huntington posited that in the post-Cold War era civilizational conflicts would be more common and that the Islamic civilization would become more violent.[2] Neither of these predictions was found to be true of domestic conflict in the analysis presented here. That this is so, despite the overlap between civilizations and religion, is the result of two factors. First, the claims made here with regard to religion are less ambitious than the paradigmatic claims made by Huntington. Huntington claims that civilization will be the primary explanation for post-Cold War conflict, which is simply not the case for domestic conflict through 2001. In contrast, we claim here only that religion will have an impact, which it does. However, to be clear, while religion has an impact on domestic conflict, it is as an intervening variable. Other factors like self-determination have a greater impact.

Second, Huntington's CoC theory is an artificial construct that distorts factors like religion, nationalism, and culture. All three of these factors do impact on domestic conflict and the CoC theory only succeeds in obfuscating their impact. They are, therefore, more productively studied in their more traditional forms.

Based on the results presented here, there is a strong need to develop data on religion and conflict as well as on religion and other aspects of politics. The dominance of the dogma that religion is not important to politics, society, and conflict for much of the twentieth century has left this field of study mostly barren of quantitative research, though there are some notable exceptions. Data on basic issues like separation of religion and state, religious aspects of political party platforms, and religious influences on international relations are very primitive, if they exist at all. The study presented here demonstrates that, at least for domestic conflict, religion is becoming increasingly important. This implies that this may be true of other aspects of society, politics, and conflict.

The comparative literature on these topics has been developing over the past few decades. It has made significant contributions to our knowledge of the impact of religion on conflict. It is important that the empirical branch of the social sciences catch up in order for both branches to advance. This is because the interaction between the comparative and empirical branches provides the most fruitful results. The comparative branch provides a source of theories and the many details which the empirical branch lacks. The empirical branch provides a more objective testing ground for theories and a tool for unearthing general trends for which no one would have looked. For example, this study proved that religion has an impact on domestic conflict but that Huntington's CoC theory is not supported by the evidence. It also unearthed counterintuitive trends like the negative impact of some aspects of religion on protest. Thus, this study provides both a good start and evidence that similar inquiries into other potential influences of religion on society, politics, and conflict are warranted.

Notes

1. For more details on this debate, see Chapter 2.
2. For more details on this debate, see Chapter 6.

Appendix A

Cases Included in the Study

This analysis is limited to those cases included in the MAR and SF datasets. This appendix lists those cases included in the study.

Minorities at Risk

There are 337 cases included in the MAR dataset. The unit of analysis in this dataset is the minority group within a state. For each of the 337 cases there is a minority and a majority group. Thus, the same majority group and the same minority may appear several times in the dataset. What is unique to each case is that the same pair of majority and minority groups do not appear more than once. As there have been political changes in the 1945 to 2000 period covered by the MAR dataset, some minorities appear more than once. For example, the former USSR and Russia are listed separately. Some of the minorities in the former USSR became majority groups in their own state after the breakup of the former USSR. Others remained minorities within Russia.

Below in Table A.1 is a listing of all 337 cases along with the religions and civilizations of the majority and minority groups for each case. The religions of majority and minority groups are coded on the following scale:

1. Christian, Catholic
2. Christian, Protestant
3. Christian, Other or Mixed
4. Islam, Sunni
5. Islam, Shi'i
6. Islam, Other or Mixed
7. Buddhist

8. Animist
9. Other, Mixed, or Undetermined

The civilizations of the majority and minority groups are coded on the following scale:

0. Western
1. Sino-Confucian
2. Slavic-Orthodox
3. Latin American
4. Hindu
5. Islamic
6. Japanese
7. African
8. Indigenous Minority
9. Mixed

Table A.1: Groups in the Minorities at Risk Dataset

		Religion		Civilization	
Country	Group	Min.	Maj.	Min.	Maj.
Western Democracies					
Australia	Aborigines	3	3	8	0
Canada	French Canadians	1	2	0	0
	Indigenous Peoples	3	2	8	0
	Quebecois	1	2	0	0
France	Basques	1	1	0	0
	Bretons	1	1	0	0
	Corsicans	1	1	0	0
	Muslim (Noncitizens)	4	1	5	0
	Roma	3	1	9	0
Germany	Turks	4	2	5	0
Greece	Muslims	4	3	5	6
	Roma	3	3	9	0
Italy	Roma	3	1	9	0
	Sardinians	1	1	0	0
	South Tyrolians	1	1	0	0
Japan	Koreans	9	9	1	6
New Zealand	Maori	3	3	8	0
Nordic Countries	Saami	3	2	8	0
Spain	Basques	1	1	0	0
	Catalans	1	1	0	0
	Roma	3	1	9	0

Continued on next page

Table A.1—Continued

Country	Group	Religion Min.	Religion Maj.	Civilization Min.	Civilization Maj.
Switzerland	Foreign Workers	3	2	9	0
	Jurassians	1	2	0	0
United Kingdom	Afro-Caribbeans	2	2	7	0
	Asians	1	1	1	0
	Catholics in N. Ireland	1	2	0	0
	Scots	1	2	0	0
United States	African Americans	2	2	7	0
	Hispanics	1	2	3	0
	Native Americans	2	2	8	0
	Native Hawaiians	2	2	8	0

Former Soviet Bloc

Country	Group	Religion Min.	Religion Maj.	Civilization Min.	Civilization Maj.
Albania	Greeks	3	4	2	5
Azerbaijan	Armenians	3	5	2	5
	Lezgins	4	5	5	5
	Russians	3	5	2	5
Belarus	Poles	1	3	0	2
	Russians	3	3	2	2
Bosnia	Croats	1	6	0	2
	Muslims	4	6	5	2
	Serbs	3	6	2	0
Bulgaria	Roma	3	3	9	2
	Turks	4	3	5	2
Croatia	Roma	3	1	9	0
	Serbs	3	1	2	0
Czech Rep.	Roma	3	3	9	2
	Slovaks	3	3	2	2
Czechoslovakia	Hungarians	1	3	0	2
	Slovaks	3	3	2	2
Estonia	Russians	3	2	2	0
Georgia	Abkhazians	4	3	5	2
	Adzhars	9	9	5	4
	Ossetians (South)	3	3	2	2
	Russians	3	3	2	2
Hungary	Roma	3	2	9	0
Kazakhstan	Germans	2	4	0	5
	Russians	3	4	2	5
Kyrgyzstan	Russians	3	4	2	5
	Uzbeks	4	4	5	5
Latvia	Russians	3	2	2	0
Lithuania	Poles	1	3	0	2
	Russians	3	3	2	2
Macedonia	Albanians	4	3	5	2
	Roma	3	3	9	2
	Serbs	3	3	2	2

Continued on next page

Table A.1—Continued

Country	Group	Religion Min.	Religion Maj.	Civilization Min.	Civilization Maj.
Moldova	Gagauz	3	3	2	2
	Slavs	3	3	2	2
Romania	Germans	2	3	0	2
	Magyars (Hungarians)	3	3	0	2
	Roma	3	3	9	2
Russia	Avars	4	3	5	2
	Buryat	7	3	1	2
	Chechens	4	3	5	2
	Ingush	4	3	5	2
	Karachay	4	3	5	2
	Kumyks	4	3	5	2
	Lezgins	4	3	5	2
	Roma	4	3	9	2
	Tatars	4	3	5	2
	Tuvinians	7	3	1	2
	Yakut	3	3	2	2
Slovakia	Hungarians	1	3	0	2
	Roma	3	3	9	2
Tajikistan	Russians	3	4	2	5
	Uzbeks	4	4	5	5
Turkmenistan	Russians	3	4	2	5
Ukraine	Crimean Russians	3	3	2	2
	Crimean Tatars	4	3	5	2
	Russians	3	3	2	2
USSR	Armenians	3	3	2	2
	Azerbaijanis	5	3	5	2
	Chechen/Ingush	4	3	5	2
	Estonians	3	3	2	2
	Georgians	3	3	2	2
	Germans	2	3	0	2
	Jews	9	3	0	2
	Kazakhs	4	3	5	2
	Kirghiz	4	3	5	2
	Kurds	4	3	5	2
	Letts/Latvians	2	3	0	2
	Lithuanians	3	3	2	2
	Moldavians	3	3	2	2
	Tadzhiks	4	3	5	2
	Tatars	4	3	5	2
	Turkmens	4	3	5	2
	Ukrainians	3	3	2	2
	Uzbeks	4	3	2	2
Uzbekistan	Russians	3	4	2	5
	Tajiks	4	4	5	5
Yugoslavia	Croats	1	3	0	2
	Hungarians	1	3	0	2
	Kosovo Albanians	4	3	5	2

Continued on next page

Table A.1—Continued

Country	Group	Religion Min.	Religion Maj.	Civilization Min.	Civilization Maj.
Yugoslavia	Roma	3	3	9	2
	Sandzak Muslims	4	3	5	2

Asia

Country	Group	Religion Min.	Religion Maj.	Civilization Min.	Civilization Maj.
Afghanistan	Hazaras	5	4	5	5
	Pashtuns	4	4	5	5
	Tajiks	4	4	5	5
	Uzbeks	4	4	5	5
Bangladesh	Biharis	5	5	5	5
	Chittagong Hill Tribes	7	5	1	5
	Hindus	9	5	4	5
Bhutan	Lhotshampas	9	7	4	1
Burma	Kachins	8	7	8	1
	Karens	7	7	1	1
	Mons	7	7	1	1
	Rohingya (Arakanese)	4	7	5	1
	Shans	7	7	1	1
	Zomis (Chins)	3	7	8	1
Cambodia	Chams	6	7	5	1
	Vietnamese	7	7	1	1
China	Hui Muslims	4	9	5	1
	Tibetans	3	9	9	2
	Turkmen	6	9	5	1
Fiji	East Indians	3	3	4	1
	Fijians	1	3	1	1
India	Assamese	9	9	4	4
	Bodos	9	9	4	4
	Kashmiris	5	9	5	4
	Mizos	3	9	8	4
	Muslims	4	9	5	4
	Nagas	3	9	8	4
	Santals	9	9	4	4
	Scheduled Tribes	9	9	4	4
	Sikhs	9	9	5	4
	Tripuras	3	9	8	4
Indonesia	Acehnese	4	4	5	5
	Chinese	7	4	1	5
	East Timorese	1	4	0	5
	Papuans	3	4	8	5
Laos	Hmong	8	7	8	1
Malaysia	Chinese	7	4	1	5
	Dayaks	3	4	8	5
	East Indians	9	4	4	5
	Kadazans	1	4	8	5
Myanmar	Hill Tribals	7	7	1	1

Continued on next page

Table A.1—Continued

Country	Group	Religion Min.	Religion Maj.	Civilization Min.	Civilization Maj.
Pakistan	Ahmadis	6	4	5	5
	Baluchis	4	4	5	5
	Hindus	9	4	4	5
	Mohajirs	4	4	5	5
	Pashtuns (Pushtuns)	4	4	5	5
	Sindhis	5	5	5	5
Papua New Guinea	Bouganvilleans	3	3	8	7
Philippines	Igorots	3	3	8	0
	Moros	6	3	5	0
Singapore	Malays	6	7	5	1
South Korea	Honamese	9	7	1	1
Sri Lanka	Indian Tamils	9	7	4	1
	Sri Lankan Tamils	9	7	4	1
Taiwan	Aboriginal Taiwanese	3	3	8	1
	Mainland Chinese	9	3	9	1
	Taiwanese	9	3	0	1
Thailand	Chinese	7	7	1	1
	Malay Muslims	4	7	5	1
	Northern Hill Tribes	8	7	8	1
Vietnam	Chinese	7	7	1	1
	Montagnards	8	7	8	1

North Africa and the Middle East

Country	Group	Religion Min.	Religion Maj.	Civilization Min.	Civilization Maj.
Algeria	Berbers	4	4	5	5
Bahrain	Shi'i	5	4	5	5
Cyprus	Turkish Cypriots	4	3	5	2
Egypt	Copts	3	4	0	5
Iran	Arabs	4	5	5	5
	Azerbaijanis	5	5	5	5
	Baha'i	9	5	5	5
	Bakhtiari	5	5	5	5
	Baluchis	4	5	5	5
	Christians	3	5	0	5
	Kurds	6	5	5	5
	Turkmen	4	5	5	5
Iraq	Kurds	4	4	5	5
	Shi'i	5	4	5	5
	Sunnis	4	4	5	5
Israel	Arabs	4	9	5	0
	Palestinians	4	9	5	0
Jordan	Palestinians	4	4	5	5
Lebanon	Druze	9	3	5	0
	Maronite Christians	3	4	0	5
	Palestinians	4	3	5	0
	Shi'i	5	3	5	0

Continued on next page

Table A.1—Continued

Country	Group	Religion Min.	Religion Maj.	Civilization Min.	Civilization Maj.
Lebanon	Sunnis	4	3	5	0
Morocco	Berbers	4	4	5	5
	Saharawis	4	4	5	5
Saudi Arabia	Shi'i	5	4	5	5
Syria	Alawi	9	4	5	5
Turkey	Kurds	4	4	5	5
	Roma	9	4	5	9

Sub-Saharan Africa

Country	Group	Religion Min.	Religion Maj.	Civilization Min.	Civilization Maj.
Angola	Bakongo	3	3	7	7
	Cabinda	3	3	7	7
	Ovimbundu	3	3	7	7
Botswana	San Bushmen	8	3	7	7
Burundi	Hutus	1	1	7	7
	Tutsis	1	1	7	7
Cameroon	Bamileke	8	4	7	5
	Kirdis	8	4	7	8
	Westerners	3	4	0	5
Chad	Northerners	4	4	5	5
	Southerners	8	4	7	5
Congo	Lari	3	3	7	7
	M'boshi	9	3	7	7
Djibouti	Afars	4	4	5	5
Dem. Rep. Congo	Hutus	1	3	7	7
	Luba	3	3	7	7
	Lunda, Yeke	3	3	7	7
	Ngbandi	3	3	7	7
	Tutsis	1	3	7	7
Eritrea	Afars	4	3	5	7
Ethiopia	Afars	4	3	5	7
	Amhara	3	3	7	7
	Eritreans	3	3	7	7
	Nilo-Saharans	3	3	7	7
	Oromo	6	3	7	7
	Somalis	4	3	5	7
	Tigreans	3	3	7	7
Ghana	Ashanti	3	3	7	7
	Ewe	3	3	7	7
	Mossi-Dagomba	6	3	5	7
Guinea	Fulani	6	6	5	5
	Malinka	6	6	5	5
	Susu	6	6	5	5
Ivory Coast	Lebanese	1	8	0	7
Kenya	Kalenjins	3	3	7	7
	Kikuyu	3	3	7	7

Continued on next page

Table A.1—Continued

Country	Group	Religion Min.	Religion Maj.	Civilization Min.	Civilization Maj.
Kenya	Kisii	3	3	7	7
	Luhya	3	3	7	7
	Luo	9	3	7	7
	Maasais	8	3	7	7
	Rendille/Borana	8	3	7	7
	Somalis	4	3	5	7
	Turkana/Pokot	8	3	7	7
Liberia	Americo-Liberian	2	3	0	7
Madagascar	Merina	3	3	7	7
Mali	Mande	4	4	5	5
	Tuareg	4	4	5	5
Mauritania	Black Moors	4	4	5	5
	Kewri	4	4	5	5
Namibia	Basters	3	3	7	7
	East Caprivians	9	9	7	7
	Europeans	3	3	0	7
	San Bushmen	8	3	7	7
Niger	Djerema-Songhai	4	4	5	5
	Hausa	4	4	5	5
	Tuareg	4	4	5	5
Nigeria	Hausa-Fulani	4	6	5	5
	Ibo	3	6	7	5
	Ijaw	4	9	7	5
	Ogani	3	6	7	5
	Yoruba	9	6	5	5
Rwanda	Hutus	1	1	7	7
	Tutsis	1	1	7	7
Senegal	Diolas in Casamance	1	4	7	5
Sierra Leone	Creoles	9	9	7	7
	Limba	9	9	7	7
	Mende	9	9	7	7
	Temne	9	9	7	7
Somalia	Issaq	9	4	7	5
South Africa	Asians	9	3	1	7
	Black Africans	3	3	7	7
	Coloreds	3	3	7	7
	Europeans	3	3	0	7
	Xhosa	3	3	7	7
	Zulus	3	3	7	7
Sudan	Nuba	9	4	7	5
	Southerners	3	4	7	5
Tanzania	Zanzibaris	4	3	5	7
Togo	Ewe	9	9	7	7
	Kabre	8	9	7	7
Uganda	Acholi	3	3	7	7
	Ankole	3	3	7	7
	Baganda	3	3	7	7

Continued on next page

Table A.1—Continued

Country	Group	Religion Min.	Religion Maj.	Civilization Min.	Civilization Maj.
Uganda	Kakwa	3	3	7	7
	Karamojong	3	3	7	7
	Konjo/Amba	3	3	7	7
	Langi	3	3	7	7
	Lugbara/Madi	3	3	7	7
	Nyarwanda	3	3	7	7
Zaire	Bakongo	3	3	7	7
	Kivu Region	3	3	7	7
	Lingala	3	3	7	7
Zambia	Bemebe	3	3	7	7
	Lozi	3	3	7	7
	Tonga	3	3	7	7
Zimbabwe	Europeans	3	3	0	7
	Ndebele	3	3	7	7

Latin America

Country	Group	Religion Min.	Religion Maj.	Civilization Min.	Civilization Maj.
Argentina	Indigenous Peoples	8	1	8	3
	Jews	9	1	0	3
Bolivia	Indig. Highland Peoples	8	1	8	3
	Indig. Lowland Peoples	8	1	8	3
Brazil	Afro-Brazilians	1	1	7	3
	Amazonian Indians	1	1	8	3
Chile	Indigenous Peoples	8	2	8	3
Colombia	Blacks	1	1	7	3
	Indigenous Peoples	1	1	8	3
Costa Rica	Antillean Blacks	2	1	7	3
Dominican Rep.	Haitian Blacks	1	1	7	3
Ecuador	Blacks	1	1	7	3
	Indig. Highland Peoples	1	1	8	3
	Indig. Lowland Peoples	8	1	8	3
El Salvador	Indigenous Peoples	1	1	8	3
Guatemala	Indigenous Peoples	1	1	8	3
Guyana	Africans	1	3	7	3
	East Indians	9	3	4	3
Honduras	Black Caribs	1	1	7	3
	Indigenous Peoples	1	1	8	3
Mexico	Mayans	1	1	8	3
	Other Indigenous Peoples	1	1	8	3
	Zapotecs	8	1	8	3
Nicaragua	Indigenous Peoples	2	1	8	3
Panama	Blacks	2	1	7	3
	Chinese	7	1	1	3
	Indigenous Peoples	1	1	8	3
Paraguay	Indigenous Peoples	8	1	8	3
Peru	Blacks (Afro-Peruvians)	1	1	7	3

Continued on next page

Table A.1—Continued

Country	Group	Religion Min.	Maj.	Civilization Min.	Maj.
Peru	Indig. Highland Peoples	1	1	8	3
	Indig. Lowland Peoples	1	1	8	3
Venezuela	Blacks	1	1	7	3
	Indigenous Peoples	8	1	8	3

Several of the tests performed on the MAR data used a subset of ethnoreligious minorities for which data was collected on religious discrimination, religious grievances, demands for more religious rights, religious legitimacy, and religious institutions. These 105 cases are listed below in Table A.2.

Table A.2: Subset of 105 Ethnoreligious Minorities

Country	Group	Country	Group
		Russia	Ingush
Western Democracies			Karachay
			Kumyks
Canada	French Canadians		Lezgins
	Quebecois		Tatars
France	Muslim (Noncitizens)		Tuvinians
Germany	Turks	Tajikistan	Russians
Greece	Muslims	Turkmenistan	Russians
Switzerland	Jurassians	Ukraine	Crimean Tatars
United Kingdom	Catholics in N. Ireland	Uzbekistan	Russians
	Scots	Yugoslavia	Kosovo Albanians
			Sandzak Muslims
Former Soviet Bloc			
Albania	Greeks	**Asia**	
Azerbaijan	Armenians	Bangladesh	Hindus
	Lezgins	Bhutan	Lhotshampas
	Russians	Burma	Kachins
Bulgaria	Turks		Rohingya (Arakanese)
Georgia	Abkhazians		Zomis (Chins)
	Adzhars	China	Hui Muslims
Kazakhstan	Germans		Tibetans
	Russians		Turkmen
Kyrgyzstan	Russians	India	Kashmiris
Macedonia	Albanians		Mizos
Russia	Avars		Muslims
	Buryat		Nagas
	Chechens		Sikhs

Continued on next page

Table A.2—Continued

Country	Group	Country	Group
India	Tripuras		
Indonesia	Chinese	**Sub-Saharan Africa**	
	East Timorese	Botswana	San Bushmen
	Papuans	Cameroon	Bamileke
Laos	Hmong		Kirdis
Malaysia	Chinese	Chad	Southerners
	Dayaks	Ethiopia	Afars
	East Indians		Somalis
	Kadazans	Ghana	Mossi-Dagomba
Pakistan	Ahmadis	Kenya	Maasais
	Hindus	Namibia	San Bushmen
Philippines	Moros	Nigeria	Ibo
Singapore	Malays		Ogani
Sri Lanka	Indian Tamils	Senegal	Diolas in Casamance
	Sri Lankan Tamils	South Africa	Asians
Thailand	Malay-Muslims	Sudan	Southerners
	Northern Hill Tribes		
Vietnam	Montagnards		
		Latin America	
		Argentina	Indigenous Peoples
		Bolivia	Indig. Highland Peoples
North Africa and the Middle East			Indig. Lowland Peoples
Egypt	Copts	Chile	Indigenous Peoples
Iran	Baha'is	Costa Rica	Antillean Blacks
	Baluchis	Ecuador	Indig. Lowland Peoples
	Christians	Mexico	Zapotecs
	Turkmen	Nicaragua	Indigenous Peoples
Iraq	Shi'i	Panama	Blacks
Israel	Arabs		Chinese
	Palestinians	Paraguay	Indigenous Peoples
Lebanon	Druze	Venezuela	Indigenous Peoples
	Maronite Christians		
	Palestinians		
	Shi'i		
	Sunnis		
Saudi Arabia	Shi'i		

State Failure

Unlike the MAR dataset, the SF dataset uses a year of conflict as the unit of analysis. This means that only when conflicts are sufficiently violent to meet the criteria of the SF project were they included. This study uses data from three sections of the state failure dataset, those concerning revolution, ethnic war, and mass killings. Revolutionary wars are defined as "episodes of violent conflict between governments and politically organized groups (political challengers) that seek to overthrow the central government, to replace its leaders, or to seize power in one region.

Conflicts must include substantial use of violence by one or both parties to qualify as wars." (Gurr, Harff, and Marshall 1997) Ethnic wars are defined as "episodes of violent conflict between governments and national, ethnic, religious, or other communal minorities (ethnic challengers) in which the challengers seek major changes in their status." (Gurr, Harff, and Marshall 1997) Mass killings are defined as

> the promotion, execution, and/or implied consent of sustained policies by governing elites or their agents–or in the case of civil war, either of the contending authorities–that result in the deaths of a substantial portion of a communal group or politicized non-communal group. In genocides the victimized groups are defined primarily in terms of their communal (ethnolinguistic, religious) characteristics. In politicides, by contrast, groups are defined primarily in terms of their political opposition to the regime and dominant groups. Geno/politicide is distinguished from state repression and terror. In cases of state terror authorities arrest, persecute or execute a few members of a group in ways designed to terrorize the majority of the group into passivity or acquiesence. In the case of geno/politicide authorities physically exterminate enough (not necessarily all) members of a target group so that it can no longer pose any conceivable threat to their rule or interests. (Gurr, Harff and Marshall 1997)

The unit of analysis for the State Failure dataset is a conflict year. Each year during which a particular type of conflict was occurring in a particular state is coded separately, including partial years in which the conflict began or ended. The cases included in the study are shown in Tables A.3 and A.4 below. Table A.3 shows the civilizational and religious identity codings for the cases and Table A.4 shows the descriptions of the conflicts provided with the SF dataset.

Table A.3: Groups in the State Failure Dataset

Country	Time Span		Religion		Civilization	
	Began	Ended	Min.	Maj.	Min.	Maj.
Ethnic Wars						
Afghanistan	1992	ongoing	6	4	5	5
Algeria	1962	1962	1	4	0	5
Angola	1975	ongoing	3	3	7	7
Bangladesh	1976	1991	9	6	9	5
Bosnia	1992	1995	3	4	2	5
	1992	1995	1	4	0	5
Burundi	1972	1972	1	1	7	7
	1988	ongoing	1	1	7	7
Chad	1965	1994	8	4	7	5
China	1956	1959	7	9	1	1

Continued on next page

Table A.3—Continued

Country	Time Span Began	Time Span Ended	Religion Min.	Religion Maj.	Civilization Min.	Civilization Maj.
China	1988	1998	6	9	5	1
Congo-Kinshasa	1960	1965	3	3	7	7
	1977	1978	3	3	7	7
	1992	ongoing	3	3	7	7
Croatia	1991	1995	3	1	2	0
Cyprus	1963	1964	4	5	5	2
	1974	1974	4	5	5	2
Ethiopia	1961	1991	3	3	7	7
	1963	1964	3	3	7	7
	1977	1978	3	3	7	7
	1999	2000	3	3	7	7
Georgia	1991	1993	4	3	5	2
	1991	1993	3	3	2	2
Guatemala	1975	1994	1	1	8	3
India	1956	1958	3	9	8	4
	1967	1971	9	9	8	4
	1983	1993	9	9	5	4
	1990	ongoing	6	9	5	4
Indonesia	1967	1971	3	4	8	5
	1975	1991	1	4	0	5
	1981	1984	4	4	5	5
	1997	1999	1	4	0	5
	1998	ongoing	1	4	0	5
Iran	1979	1985	6	5	5	5
Iraq	1961	1970	4	4	5	5
	1974	1975	4	4	5	5
	1980	1988	4	4	5	5
	1991	1998	4	4	5	5
	1991	1998	5	4	5	5
Israel	1987	ongoing	4	9	5	0
Kenya	1964	1966	4	3	5	7
	1991	1993	3	3	7	7
Laos	1961	1979	8	7	8	1
Lebanon	1975	1991	6	3	5	0
Mali	1990	1995	4	4	5	5
Moldova	1992	1992	3	3	2	2
Morocco	1975	1989	4	4	5	5
Myanmar	1961	ongoing	7	7	1	1
Nicaragua	1981	1984	2	1	8	3
Nigeria	1966	1970	3	6	7	5
Pakistan	1971	1971	5	4	5	5
	1973	1977	4	4	5	5
	1983	1998	4	4	5	5
Papua New Guin.	1989	1997	3	3	8	0
Philippines	1972	ongoing	6	3	5	0
Russia	1994	1996	4	3	5	2
	1999	ongoing	4	3	5	2

Continued on next page

Table A.3—Continued

Country	Time Span Began	Time Span Ended	Religion Min.	Religion Maj.	Civilization Min.	Civilization Maj.
Rwanda	1963	1966	1	1	7	7
	1990	1998	1	1	7	7
	2001	2001	1	1	7	7
Senegal	1992	1999	1	4	7	5
Somalia	1988	ongoing	4	4	5	5
South Africa	1987	1986	3	3	7	7
Sri Lanka	1983	ongoing	9	7	4	1
Sudan	1956	1972	3	4	7	5
	1983	ongoing	3	4	7	5
Turkey	1984	2000	4	4	5	5
Uganda	1966	1966	3	3	7	7
	1980	1999	3	3	7	7
United Kingdom	1971	1982	1	2	0	0
Yugoslavia	1991	1992	1	3	0	2
	1998	1999	4	3	5	2
Zimbabwe	1981	1987	3	3	7	7

Mass Killings

Country	Time Span Began	Time Span Ended	Religion Min.	Religion Maj.	Civilization Min.	Civilization Maj.
Afghanistan	1978	1992	6	4	5	5
Algeria	1962	1962	1	4	0	5
Angola	1975	1994	3	3	7	7
	1998	ongoing	3	3	7	7
Argentina	1976	1980	1	1	3	3
Bosnia	1992	1995	4	3	5	2
Burundi	1965	1973	1	1	7	7
	1988	1988	1	1	7	7
	1993	1993	1	1	7	7
Cambodia	1975	1979	7	9	1	1
Chile	1973	1976	1	1	3	3
China	1959	1959	7	9	1	1
	1966	1975	3	3	1	1
Congo-Kinshasa	1964	1965	3	3	7	7
	1977	1979	3	3	7	7
El Salvador	1980	1989	1	1	3	3
Ethiopia	1976	1979	3	3	7	7
Guatemala	1978	1990	1	1	8	3
Indonesia	1965	1966	1	4	0	5
	1975	1992	1	4	0	5
Iran	1981	1992	6	5	5	5
Iraq	1963	1975	4	4	5	5
	1988	1991	4	4	5	5
Myanmar	1978	1978	9	7	9	1
Pakistan	1971	1971	5	4	5	5
	1973	1977	4	4	5	5
Philippines	1972	1976	3	6	0	5

Continued on next page

Table A.3—Continued

Country	Time Span Began	Ended	Religion Min.	Maj.	Civilization Min.	Maj.
Rwanda	1963	1964	1	1	7	7
	1994	1994	1	1	7	7
Somalia	1988	1991	4	4	5	5
Sri Lanka	1989	1990	9	7	4	1
Sudan	1956	1972	3	4	7	5
	1983	ongoing	3	4	7	5
Syria	1981	1982	4	4	5	5
Uganda	1971	1979	3	3	7	7
	1980	1986	3	3	7	7
Vietnam South	1965	1975	7	7	1	1
Yugoslavia	1998	1999	4	3	5	2

Revolutionary Wars

Country	Began	Ended	Min.	Maj.	Min.	Maj.
Afghanistan	1978	1992	6	4	5	5
	1992	ongoing	6	4	5	5
Albania	1997	1997	4	4	5	5
Algeria	1962	1962	1	4	0	5
	1991	ongoing	4	4	5	5
Angola	1975	ongoing	3	3	7	7
Cambodia	1970	1975	7	9	1	1
	1979	1991	7	9	1	1
China	1966	1969	9	9	1	1
	1989	1989	9	9	1	1
Colombia	1948	1960	1	1	3	3
	1984	ongoing	1	1	3	3
Congo-Brazzav.	1997	1999	3	3	7	7
Congo-Kinshasa	1960	1965	3	3	7	7
	1996	ongoing	1	1	7	7
Cuba	1956	1959	1	1	3	3
Dominican Rep.	1965	1965	1	1	3	3
Egypt	1992	1999	4	4	5	5
El Salvador	1979	1992	1	1	3	3
Ethiopia	1975	1991	3	3	7	7
Georgia	1992	1993	3	3	2	2
Guatemala	1966	1996	1	1	3	3
Guinea-Bissau	1998	1999	6	6	5	5
Hungary	1956	1956	2	2	0	0
Indonesia	1949	1961	4	4	5	5
	1958	1961	4	4	5	5
	1998	1999	4	4	5	5
Iran	1977	1979	5	5	5	5
	1981	1983	5	5	5	5
Iraq	1959	1959	4	4	5	5
Jordan	1970	1971	4	4	5	5

Continued on next page

Table A.3—Continued

| Country | Time Span | | Religion | | Civilization | |
	Began	Ended	Min.	Maj.	Min.	Maj.
Laos	1960	1962	7	7	1	1
	1963	1979	8	7	8	1
Lebanon	1958	1958	6	3	5	0
Lesotho	1998	1998	3	3	7	7
Liberia	1985	1985	6	3	5	7
	1989	1993	6	3	5	7
	2000	ongoing	6	3	5	7
Mozambique	1976	1992	3	3	7	7
Myanmar	1988	1989	9	7	9	1
Nepal	1996	ongoing	9	9	4	4
Nicaragua	1978	1979	1	1	3	3
	1981	1988	1	1	3	3
Nigeria	1980	1985	6	6	5	5
Oman	1970	1976	4	4	5	5
Peru	1982	1997	1	1	3	3
Philippines	1972	1996	3	3	0	0
Romania	1989	1989	3	3	2	2
Sierra Leone	1991	ongoing	3	3	7	7
Somalia	1988	1994	4	4	5	5
South Africa	1984	1990	2	2	7	0
Sri Lanka	1987	1989	7	7	1	1
Tajikistan	1992	1998	4	4	5	5
Thailand	1965	1983	7	7	1	1
Uganda	1983	1985	3	3	7	7
Vietnam South	1958	1965	9	7	1	1
Yemen	1994	1994	4	4	5	5
Yemen North	1962	1970	4	4	5	5
Yemen South	1986	1986	4	4	5	5
Zambia	1964	1964	3	3	7	7
Zimbabwe	1972	1979	3	3	7	0

Table A.4: Descriptions of State Failures[1]

Country	Time Span	Description
Ethnic Wars		
Afghanistan	1992 ongoing	Civil war for control of government among factions based on Pashtuns, Tajiks, Uzbeks, Hazaris. Alliance between Tajiks, Uzbeks, Hazaris unable to stop Taliban (Pashtuns); by September 1998, Taliban controls 90 percent of country.
Algeria	1962 to 1962	In the wake of independence from France, Algerian militants attack Europeans and Muslim civilians who collaborated with French colonial authorities.

Continued on next page

Table A.4—Continued

Country	Time Span	Description
Angola	1975 ongoing	Postindependence civil war has ethnic base, as Ovimbundu, Bakongo, and Cabindan rebels battle Mbundu-dominated central government. Breakdown in peace talks leads to renewed fighting in September 1998.
Bangladesh	1976 to 1991	Separatist war waged by the Shanti Bahini resisting encroachments by Bengali settlers in the Chittagong Hills breaks out in August 1976 and eventually leads to legislation for greater local autonomy for indigenous peoples in June 1991.
Bosnia	1992 to 1995	Ethnic Serbs fight newly independent Bosnian government troops to partition Bosnia into autonomous regions or unite with Serbia.
	1992 to 1995	Ethnic Croats fight newly independent Bosnian government troops to partition Bosnia into autonomous regions or unite with Croatia.
Burundi	1972 to 1972	Hutu insurgents launch a coordinated attack against government authorities in the south and east, indiscriminately attacking Tutsis and Hutus who refuse to join the rebellion. The rebellion is brutally repressed by Tutsi-dominated armed forces.
	1988 ongoing	Attempted democratic reforms prompt violence between historically dominant Tutsi government and Party for the Liberation of Hutu Peoples (Palipehutu) challengers.
Chad	1965 to 1994	Recurring civil wars among Chad's many communal groups with shifting alliances, but mainly along north-south lines. Fighting mostly ends with formal peace accords signed in August and October 1994.
China	1956 to 1959	Armed resistance to Chinese occupation of Tibet breaks out in February 1956 and spreads throughout the region. Rebellion is suppressed by Chinese forces in April 1959.
	1988 to 1998	Episodic violent protests by Uighers in Xinjiang province against Han Chinese control escalate into terror campaign by 1996.
Congo-Kinshasa	1960 to 1965	Katanga and South Kasai secede from newly independent Congo (1960) followed by secession of Orientale and Kivu (1961) and rebellions in Stanleyville and Kwilu (1964).
	1977 to 1978	Independence movement of Lunda/Yeke (FNLA) invades Shaba (Katanga) province, their traditional homeland.
	1992 ongoing	After Pres. Mobutu is pressured into appointing a new prime minister, communal violence erupts in Shaba (Katanga) between Luba-Kasai minority and the dominant Lunda. Communal rebellions subsequently erupt elsewhere in eastern Zaire.
Croatia	1991 to 1995	Serbs in eastern Croatia and Krajina fight newly independent Croat government for autonomy; fighting checked in 1992 by UN peacekeeping force.
Cyprus	1963 to 1964	Constitutional amendments proposed by President Makarios are unacceptable to the Turkish-Cypriots. This leads to communal fighting from 1963-1964, with a brief flare-up in 1967. UN peacekeepers intervene.

Continued on next page

Table A.4—Continued

Country	Time Span	Description
Cyprus	1974 to 1974	A July 15 military coup removes Pres. Makarios and installs Greek-Cypriot nationalist Nicos Sampsom. Ethnic clashes lead to invasion by forces from Turkey and the establishment of separate Turkish-Cypriot state in the north.
Ethiopia	1961 to 1991	Eritrean secessionists led by Eritrean Liberation Front and Eritrean People's Liberation Front fight for independence from successive imperial and Marxist regimes in Addis Ababa. War ends in May 1991 with the capture of the Ethiopian capital, Addis Ababa, by combined secessionist and revolutionary forces.
	1963 to 1964	Ethnic-Somalis forming the Ogaden Liberation Front
	1977 to 1978	Somali separatists of the Western Somali Liberation Front launch systematic attacks in the Ogaden region and are joined by forces from Somalia. The rebellion is quickly repressed following the withdrawal of Somalian troops in March 1978.
	1999 to 2000	Ethiopia's border war with Eritrea provides an opportunity for Oromo rebels to press separatist goals from bases in Somalia and with backing from Eritrea. Fighting becomes sporadic with the negotiated ending of the greater war with Eritrea in June 2000.
Georgia	1991 to 1993	Abkhaz regional governments fight for independence with backing from Russian military and political elements. Effective autonomy secured in both regions by 1993; Commonwealth of Independent States peacekeepers control conflicts.
	1991 to 1993	South Ossetian regional governments fight for independence with backing from Russian military and political elements. Effective autonomy secured in both regions by 1993; Commonwealth of Independent States peacekeepers control conflicts.
Guatemala	1975 to 1994	Indigenous Mayans, some of whom support populist and revolutionary causes, are targets of severe government repression.
India	1956 to 1958	The Naga separatist movement began resisting incorporation of tribal lands in the Union of India in 1949. In May 1956, separatist militants began an armed rebellion that was brutally repressed by Indian troops. The rebels' main forces were subdued in 1958.
	1967 to 1971	The Jharkhand separatist movement, otherwise known as the Naxalite rebellion, involved mainly Santal tribes in eastern Bihar and West Bengal; issues centered on land reform. The rebellion was largely contained by intense repression.
	1983 to 1993	Sikh militants declare a "War of Independence" for Khalistan (Punjab and Haryana) in April 1983. Violence continues through the early 1990s until it is finally contained through concessions, elections, and repression.
	1990 ongoing	Mass protests against Indian rule erupt in violence in January 1990 as protesters clash with Indian troops. Militants of the Jammu and Kashmir Liberation Front (JKLF) escalate attacks on Indian authorities in April 1990.

Table A.4—Continued

Country	Time Span	Description
Indonesia	1967 to 1971	Indonesian authorities use indiscriminate force to subdue the Free Papua Movement (OPM) prior to the 1969 popular referendum on incorporation of the former Dutch territory in Indonesia. OPM resistance is then driven into the interior of the island.
	1975 to 1991	Revolutionary Front for an Independent East Timor (Fretilin) rebels fight to regain autonomy lost when Indonesia invaded the former Portuguese colony in November 1975. The Fretilin leader is captured and the movement is brutally repressed by 1991.
	1981 to 1984	Indonesia's "Transmigrasi" policy of resettling people from overcrowded Java to West Papua leads to an escalation of OPM resistance. Indonesia's indiscriminate use of force in repressing OPM resistance succeeds in driving the OPM out of West Papua.
	1997 to 1999	East Timor (Fretilin) rebels resume autonomy fight in 1997; a popular referendum for the independence of East Timor in 1999 triggers intense violence and the introduction of international peacekeepers in September 1999.
	1998 ongoing	Following the withdrawal of Indonesia armed forces from Aceh in August 1998, a repressed rebellion by the Free Aceh Movement (GAM) flares into open violence.
Iran	1979 to 1985	Rebellion by Kurds against the new Khomeini government to establish regional autonomy. Iran actively pursues Kurd support in its war with Iraq; resistance declines after 1985.
Iraq	1961 to 1970	Barzani's Kurdish Democratic Party revolts against General Qassim's regime and its successors in a quest for regional autonomy.
	1974 to 1975	Kurds rebel in response to a government autonomy plan that falls short of their demands.
	1980 to 1988	Some Iraqi Kurds take advantage of Iran-Iraq war and Iranian support to mount a new rebellion for autonomy.
	1991 to 1998	Kurdish rebels take advantage of Iraq's defeat in the Gulf War to establish a Kurdish state, protected by coalition forces led by the U.S.
	1991 to 1998	Shi'i rebellion in south is crushed by Iraqi forces and Shi'i targeted for repression by government forces.
Israel	1987 ongoing	Palestinians in the "occupied territories" of the West Bank and Gaza Strip initiate a concerted civil disobedience campaign ("Intifada") in December 1987 against Israeli authorities with the professed goal of establishing an independent Palestinian state.
Kenya	1964 to 1966	Independence of Kenya ignites ethnic-Somali separatism in the Northern Frontier District.
	1991 to 1993	Kalenjin and Masai supporters of the government are encouraged in attacks aimed at driving Kikuyu, Luo, and other rival groups from their villages in the highlands.

Continued on next page

Table A.4—Continued

Country	Time Span	Description
Laos	1961 to 1979	Hmong (Meo) rebels encouraged by U.S., fight the Pathet Lao; rebellion was suppressed after Pathet Lao takeover in 1975; only sporadic guerrilla activity after 1979.
Lebanon	1975 to 1991	Christian-dominated government collapses in civil war among Druze, Shi'i, Maronite, and Sunni forces.
Mali	1990 to 1995	Rebellion by nomadic Tuaregs seeking regional autonomy.
Moldova	1992 to 1992	President Snegur declares a state of emergency in March 1992 and attempts to forcibly disarm Gagauz and Russian (Trans-Dniester) ethnic militias. A more conciliatory strategy is adopted in December and violence subsides in stalemate.
Morocco	1975 to 1989	Saharawis seek independence in southwestern part of the country annexed by Morocco after Spanish colonial rule.
Myanmar	1961 ongoing	Karens, Kachins, Shan, Mons, Chin and other non-Burman peoples fight for greater regional autonomy.
Nicaragua	1981 to 1984	Indigenous Miskitos of Atlantic coast region rebel against Sandinista government. Rebellion subsides with government's offer of amnesty and greater autonomy in 1984. Formal autonomy agreement is concluded in September 1987.
Nigeria	1966 to 1970	Military coup and retaliatory massacres of Ibos in north precipitate secessionist civil war by Biafra, based on Ibos of eastern region.
Pakistan	1971 to 1971	Postelection tensions between East and West Pakistan erupt into full-scale civil war; Indian intervention leads to establishment of independent Bangladesh.
	1973 to 1977	Baluchi rebel against central authority, backed by opposition National Awami Party.
	1983 to 1998	Antigovernment violence by Sindhis seeking autonomy, along with attacks on Muhajirs.
Papua New Guin.	1989 to 1997	Bougainvillean Revolutionary Army fights PNG forces to end large-scale mining and gain independence for the island of Bougainville. New government takes a more conciliatory stance that leads to a cessation of fighting in May 1997 and a permanent cease-fire agreement in January 1998.
Philippines	1972 ongoing	Muslim Moros led by the Moro National Liberation Front mount a guerrilla war for independence that declines after the mid-1970s into sporadic insurgency.
Russia	1994 to 1996	In August 1994, the Provisional Council of Chechnya attempts a coup to oust nationalist leader of Chechnya, President Dudayev. Civil war ensues and Russian troops are called in to restore order. Intense fighting results in military stalemate; truce agreement is reached in August 1996.
	1999 ongoing	Attempts by Chechen fighters to extend control to neighboring Dagestan in August 1999 triggers new war in Chechnya as Russian forces impose central authority.
Rwanda	1963 to 1966	Attacks by Tutsi rebels prompt attacks and massacres by Hutus, and flight of 200,000 Tutsi refugees.
	1990 to 1998	Tutsi exiles of Rwanda Patriotic Front launch successive invasions from Uganda, prompting sporadic ethnic violence between Hutu army and Tutsi civilians.

Continued on next page

Table A.4—Continued

Country	Time Span	Description
Rwanda	2001 to 2001	Hutu fighters launch a major attack in northwestern Rwanda from bases in the Dem. Rep. of Congo in May 2001 but the attack is quickly crushed by the Rwandan Patriotic Army.
Senegal	1992 to 1999	An August 1992 split in the Movement of Democratic Forces in the Casamance (MDFC) over the issue of independence leads to an outbreak of armed attacks in September 1992. Violence continues until a newly elected government initiates a new peace agreement.
Somalia	1988 ongoing	United Somali Congress, based on southern Hawiye clan, overthrows Siad Barre regime; chronic violence among clan-based warlords prevents establishment of effective central government.
South Africa	1987 to 1986	Zulu Inkatha movement wars with African National Congress supporters for political control in Natal, initially with clandestine support from government security forces.
Sri Lanka	1983 ongoing	Tamil grievances against pro-Sinhalese governmental policies erupt into secessionist civil war.
Sudan	1956 to 1972	Anyanya rebellion by non-Muslim population of southern Sudan against Muslim-dominated government ended with 1972 autonomy agreement.
	1983 ongoing	Southern rebellion resumes under Susan People's Liberation Army leadership after Muslim government violates autonomy agreement; breakup of SPLA in 1991 leads to new inter-communal violence within the south.
Turkey	1984 to 2000	In August 1984, Kurds of militant Kurdistan Workers Party (PKK) engage in protracted conflict with Turkish authorities in quest for independence. Capture of Ocalan, the PKK leader, by Turkish authorities leads to PKK renunciation of armed struggle in February 2000.
Uganda	1966 to 1966	A rebellion by followers of the Kabaka of Buganda breaks out in May 1966 over loss of regional autonomy and tribal prerogatives. The rebellion is quickly suppressed by forces loyal to Obote; Buganda loses its administrative status.
	1980 to 1999	From 1980, banditry, rebellion, and repression involving tribal supporters of ousted dictator Amin. From 1986, Langi and Acholi peoples at war with government forces dominated by Bagandans.
United Kingdom	1971 to 1982	Catholic IRA (Irish Republican Army) uses terror against British forces and militant Protestants in quest for union with Republic of Ireland. Violence begins to subside in late 1970s and early 1980s as all sides search for alternatives to violence, eventually culminating in October 1994 peace agreement.
Yugoslavia	1991 to 1992	Slovenes and Croats fight wars of independence against Yugoslav federal troops.
	1998 to 1999	President Milosevic rescinds Kosovar autonomy (1989), leading to declaration of independence by ethnic Albanians (1990), who establish shadow government and form Kosovo Liberation Army-KLA (1996). Serbian crackdown in 1998 leads to open warfare.

Continued on next page

Table A.4—Continued

Country	Time Span	Description
Zimbabwe	1981 to 1987	Ndebele people initiate rioting and local rebellions against the Shona-dominated Zimbabwe African National Union governing coalition.

Mass Killings

Country	Time Span	Description
Afghanistan	1978 to 1992	Communist coup results in political purges of ruling circles followed by Soviet invasion. Widespread Mujahedin rural insurgency provokes systematic terror, destruction of villages, and execution of prisoners by Soviet and Afghan government
Algeria	1962 to 1962	In the wake of independence from France, Algerian militants attack Europeans and Muslim civilians who collaborated with French colonial authorities.
Angola	1975 to 1994	Both National Union for the Total Independence of Angola (UNITA) rebels and government forces perpetrate destructive campaigns and atrocities against civilians throughout conflict.
	1998 ongoing	Reconciliation between UNITA fighters and government forces breaks down in December 1998 and civil war resumes. Contending forces target civilian populations in their attempts to gain tactical advantages.
Argentina	1976 to 1980	Military stages coup and declares state of siege. Death squads target subversives for disappearances, kidnappings, torture, and murder.
Bosnia	1992 to 1995	Muslim residents of Bosnia are subject to "ethnic cleansing" measures including destruction of property, forced resettlement, execution, and massacres by Serb and Croat forces seeking union with Serbia and Croatia.
Burundi	1965 to 1973	Attempted coup by Hutu units in 1965 results in massacres of Tutsis in the countryside. Ruling Tutsis respond by unleashing Tutsi-dominated army to destroy Hutu leaders. In 1972, militant Hutus massacre Tutsis, Tutsi regime responds with massive killings.
	1988 to 1988	As a result of disorganized rural violence against local Tutsi officials, Tutsi-dominated army massacres Hutus.
	1993 to 1993	Disaffected Tutsi military forces revolt, assassinating Hutu president. Armed clashes and massacres occur in three waves: Tutsi soldiers against Hutu civilians, Hutus against Tutsis, and Tutsis against Hutus.
Cambodia	1975 to 1979	Khmer Rouge initiate restructuring of society with massive deaths by starvation, deprivation, executions, and massacres of supporters of the old regime, city dwellers, and ethnic and religious minorities (particularly Muslim Chams).
Chile	1973 to 1976	In wake of military coup, supporters of former regime and other leftists are arrested, tortured, disappeared, exiled, and summarily executed.
China	1959 to 1959	Army and security forces suppress counterrevolutionary elements of society, including Tibetan Buddhists, landowners, and supporters of former Chiang Kai-shek regime.

Continued on next page

Table A.4—Continued

Country	Time Span	Description
China	1966 to 1975	With support of military and with the consent of the Party faction, Red Guard youth gangs target a wide spectrum of society for arrest, harassment, reeducation, torture, and execution.
Congo-Kinshasa	1964 to 1965	To consolidate control, rebels massacre counterrevolutionaries, including educated Congolese, missionaries, and other Europeans.
	1977 to 1979	Episodic rebellions and agitation are countered by killings of political opponents, dissident tribesmen, and prisoners.
El Salvador	1980 to 1989	In the face of widespread insurgency, military, security units, and death squads kill, imprison, and harass suspected leftists among clergy, peasants, urban workers, and intellectuals.
Ethiopia	1976 to 1979	Army, internal security units, and civilian defense squads massacre political and military elites, workers, students, bureaucrats, and others thought to oppose the revolutionary regime.
Guatemala	1978 to 1990	Military-dominated governments initiate series of anti-subversive antiguerrilla campaigns with indiscriminate use of death squads against suspected leftists and indigenous Mayans. Killings become systematic and widespread after July 1978.
Indonesia	1965 to 1966	After attempted Communist coup, Muslim vigilantes massacre Party members and ethnic Chinese. After government formally bans Party, military eliminates suspected Communists and sympathizers.
	1975 to 1992	Indonesian backed coup plunges East Timor into civil war followed by Indonesian invasion. Resisting Timorese are killed in massacres and famine.
Iran	1981 to 1992	To consolidate Islamic revolution, government violently suppresses dissident Muslims (Mujahedeen) and rebel Kurds and selectively executes prominent Baha'i.
Iraq	1963 to 1975	To suppress repeated rebellions for independent Kurdistan in northern Iraq, government engages in large-scale massacres.
	1988 to 1991	Military and security forces launch Al-Anfal campaign of indiscriminate destruction across Iraqi Kurdistan to neutralize Kurdish guerrillas. Measures include gassing, massacres, disappearances, forced resettlement, and demolition of villages.
Myanmar	1978 to 1978	To secure border region, regular military units supported by militant Buddhist elements depopulate Arakanese Muslim communities in Western Burma by oppression, destruction, torture, and murder.
Pakistan	1971 to 1971	General strikes by Bengali nationalists are met with martial law. Military deploys in force with tanks, airpower, and artillery and indiscriminately attacks civilians.
	1973 to 1977	Baluchi rebellion suppressed by military using indiscriminate violence against civilians.

Continued on next page

Table A.4—Continued

Country	Time Span	Description
Philippines	1972 to 1976	Moro resistance to government-sponsored Christian settlement and support of guerrillas fighting for autonomy results in military and paramilitary terror tactics in which many Moros are killed in massacres and napalm bombings.
Rwanda	1963 to 1964	Local Hutu officials orchestrate vengeance attacks against Tutsis following cross-border incursions by Tutsi rebels.
	1994 to 1994	RPF insurgency leads to full-scale civil war. Hutu-dominated government deploys military and armed gangs to systematically slaughter primarily Tutsis but also Hutu moderates.
Somalia	1988 to 1991	Rebellion in the north by Somali National Movement leads to indiscriminate government anti-insurgency operations, causing many civilian deaths (particularly among Issaq clan). Actions lead to wider war that topples the Siad Barre regime in 1991.
Sri Lanka	1989 to 1990	Revolutionary campaign by Marxist Sinhalese People's Liberation Front (JVP) prompts government to unleash military and police death squads. Killings of JVP leaders, supporters, and poor Sinhalese youth in rural areas eliminates JVP.
Sudan	1956 to 1972	Government dominated by northern Muslim-Arabs uses indiscriminate violence to suppress mostly non-Muslim Africans who support a secessionist movement in the south.
	1983 ongoing	Non-Muslim supporters of secession are targeted for destruction by indiscriminate military attacks, massacres by government-supported tribal militias, and government-induced privation and population displacement.
Syria	1981 to 1982	Government military and security forces crush revolt by Muslim Brotherhood centered in cities of Hama and Aleppo.
Uganda	1971 to 1979	After General Amin seizes power, he systematically exterminates political opponents and personal enemies. Tribes closely associated with his predecessor also are targeted for destruction. Amin's regime is ousted by Tanzanian invasion in April 1979.
	1980 to 1986	After Amin is overthrown, former Prime Minister Obote takes control of government. Political and tribal rivals of Obote are targeted by army and armed bands.
Vietnam South	1965 to 1975	Government military and paramilitary forces engage in killings, reprisals, and bombardments against villagers supporting Viet Cong.
Yugoslavia	1998 to 1999	Serb militias backed by Yugoslavian armed forces target ethnic-Albanians to counterinsurgency and cleanse Kosovo of Albanians. Targeting ends with Yugoslavia's withdrawal in June 1999 following NATO air attacks.

Revolutionary Wars

Afghanistan	1978 to 1992	Regionally based Mujahedin factions battle government forces who are supported by Soviet Union.

Continued on next page

Table A.4—Continued

Country	Time Span	Description
Afghanistan	1992 ongoing	Civil war for control of government among factions based on Pashtuns, Tajkis, Uzbeks, Hazaras, and others. Alliance between Tajiks, Uzbeks, and Hazaras unable to stop Taliban (Pashtun) advance; by September 1998, Taliban controls 90 percent of country.
Albania	1997 to 1997	Collapse of pyramid investment schemes plunges country into chaos and anarchy. New elections are called.
Algeria	1962 to 1962	In the wake of independence from France, Algerian militants attack Europeans and Muslim civilians who collaborated with French colonial authorities.
	1991 ongoing	Islamic Salvation Front wins elections, but government cancels results. Islamic militants conduct an intensive terrorist campaign to overthrow the secular government.
Angola	1975 ongoing	Civil war between Mbundu-dominated central government and National Union for the Total Independence of Angola (UNITA), based on Ovimbundu people of S. Angola; peace plans and elections fail to stop renewed war in 1992 and 1998.
Cambodia	1970 to 1975	Communist insurgents, supported by North Vietnam, battle royalist government forces.
	1979 to 1991	Vietnamese forces invade Cambodia in December 1978, drive out the Khmer Rouge, and install a new government. Khmer Rouge continues armed resistance, eventually joining forces with other opposition groups. Resistance continues until a cease-fire is brokered in May 1991, followed by a peace settlement in October.
China	1966 to 1969	Red Army suppresses Red Guards in an attempt to control the Cultural Revolution.
	1989 to 1989	Students occupy Tiananmen Square demanding democratic reforms. Government violently suppresses their activities.
Colombia	1948 to 1960	A protracted civil war breaks out between the Conservative and Liberal parties vying for state power. The period known as "la violencia" begins in earnest with riots in Bogota following the assassination of Liberal leader Gaitan in April 1948. The violence begins to decrease with the election of a moderate Liberal-Conservative coalition, the National Front, in 1958 and continues to diminish through 1960.
	1984 ongoing	Variety of left-wing groups battle government forces. Right-wing death squads institute reign of terror against leftist and Communist political parties and their supporters.
Congo-Brazzaville	1997 to 1999	Civil war erupts amid preelection tensions when President Lissouba's army attacks the residence of former dictator Sassou-Nguesso. Rebels backed by Angolan troops, take Brazzaville; fighting continues until September 1999. Pointe Noire Peace Agreement (December 1999) ends fighting.
Congo-Kinshasa	1960 to 1965	Mutiny within ranks of military escalates into full-scale civil war. Rebels expel remnants of Belgian colonial apparatus.
	1996 ongoing	Tutsis residing in eastern Zaire form the core of a rebel army which, with substantial help from Rwanda, defeats government troops, and ousts Mobutu's regime.

Continued on next page

Table A.4—Continued

Country	Time Span	Description
Cuba	1956 to 1959	Rural-based insurgents led by Fidel Castro fight Batista regime.
Domin. Rep.	1965 to 1965	Rebel military forces battle U.S.-supported Wessin regime.
Egypt	1992 to 1999	Terror campaign by militant Islamic groups against the secular government.
El Salvador	1979 to 1992	Rightist government battles left-wing Farabundo Marti National Liberation Front (FMLN) insurgency.
Ethiopia	1975 to 1991	Tigrean Liberation Front, in coalition with regional separatists, fights a successful revolutionary war for control of the central government.
Georgia	1992 to 1993	Ousted President Gamsakhurdia fights unsuccessful civil war.
Guatemala	1966 to 1996	Communist insurgents battle military-dominated government forces in protracted conflict.
Guinea-Bissau	1998 to 1999	Brig. Asumane Mane dismissed over allegation of arms smuggling. Rebel soldiers, led by Mane, attempt coup, leading to civil war. President Vieira's government is ousted in May 1999 and a transitional government is set up, leading to January 2000 elections.
Hungary	1956 to 1956	Factionalism within the ruling Hungarian Workers Party leads to the outbreak of a popular insurrection against hardliners in late October 1956. Hardliners, backed by Warsaw Pact forces, retake the government in November and crush the insurrection.
Indonesia	1949 to 1961	Islamic rebels in West Java, Aceh, and South Sulawesi challenge the secular state of President Sukarno in an attempt to set up an Islamic regime, Darul Islam.
	1958 to 1961	Opponents to Sukarno's regime attempt to set up an alternative government, the Revolutionary Government of the Republic of Indonesia (PRRI), in February 1958. The PRRI, or "Permesta," rebellion is defeated by loyalist forces and an amnesty is declared in 1961.
	1998 to 1999	Economic decline leads to mass demonstrations, widespread protest, and rioting in Jakarta. Suharto resigns; Habibie takes over in interim, but riots and mass protests continue.
Iran	1977 to 1979	Islamic rebels overthrow Shah and establish fundamentalist state.
	1981 to 1983	Moderates (National Front) and conservatives Iranian Revolutionary Party (IRP) use terror and repression in political competition for post-Shah Iran.
Iraq	1959 to 1959	In March 1959, rebellion army units allied with members of the Shammar tribe seized the town of Mosul. Loyal forces attacked the rebels mercilessly. Subsequent violence in Kirkuk leads to repression of Kurdish elements in the Communist Party.
Jordan	1970 to 1971	Government crackdown on Palestinian guerrilla groups in February 1970 triggers intense fighting that finally ends with Jordanian military victory in July 1971.
Laos	1960 to 1962	Military coup sparks sustained conflict as rebels attempt to overthrow rightist Somsanith regime.

Continued on Next Page

Table A.4—Continued

Country	Time Span	Description
Laos	1963 to 1979	Neutralists and Conservatives join forces to oppose communist Pathet Lao insurgents. Pathet Lao gain power in 1975 but resistance by rightist forces continues.
Lebanon	1958 to 1958	Muslim opposition groups rebel against Christian-dominated government.
Lesotho	1998 to 1998	Protests against results of May elections are joined by mutiny of soldiers and shutdown of government by civil servants.
Liberia	1985 to 1985	Brig. Gen. Quiwonkpa leads the National Patriotic Front (NPF) in a failed coup against Samuel Doe following October's contested elections. Doe executes the coup leader and purges supporters of the NPF in Monrovia.
	1989 to 1993	Ethnic repression by military accelerates civil war. National Patriotic Forces of Liberia (NPFL) and militias of rival communal groups compete for control of devastated society.
	2000 ongoing	A loose coalition of rebel forces, Liberians United for Reconciliation and Democracy (LURD), initiates an armed rebellion in Liberia from bases in Guinea in November 2000 with the expressed aim of toppling Charles Taylor from power.
Mozambique	1976 to 1992	Anticommunist Mozambican National Resistance (RENAMO) rebels, supported by Rhodesia and South Africa, challenge Marxist regime, conclude 1992 peace agreement.
Myanmar	1988 to 1989	Students in Rangoon organize increasingly violent protests against military rule and attempt to form a revolutionary coalition with ethnic rebels.
Nepal	1996 ongoing	Militants associated with the Communist Party of Nepal (Maoist) initiate armed insurrection. Following the assassinations of the Nepalese royal family and the ascension of King Gyanendra, Prime Minister Deuba initiates peace talks in July 2001, but the talks fail.
Nicaragua	1978 to 1979	Sandinista communists (FSLN) battle government forces of Somoza regime.
	1981 to 1988	Anti-Sandinista forces (Contras), with substantial support from the United States, fight protracted guerrilla war. Peace negotiations result in a March 1988 cease-fire and 1990 elections; Sandinista party relinquishes power.
Nigeria	1980 to 1985	A militant Islamic cult, the Maitatsine, challenges government authority in northern cities. Although the cult's leader, Marwa, was killed in 1980 and the movement was outlawed, outbreaks of violence by followers continue until the movement is finally crushed.
Oman	1970 to 1976	A Dhofar tribal insurrection escalates in June 1970 to ideological struggle between rebels and autocratic regime. Rebels defeated by March 1976; government offers amnesty.
Peru	1982 to 1997	Maoist guerrillas of Sendero Luminoso (Shining Path) attack government troops, terrorize rural and urban supporters of government.
Philippines	1972 to 1996	Leftist New People's Army (NPA) fights protracted guerrilla war aimed at overthrowing Manila regimes of Marcos, Aquino, Ramos.

Continued on next page

Table A.4—Continued

Country	Timespan	Description
Romania	1989 to 1989	Broad anti-Ceausescu coalition (National Salvation Front) overthrows Stalinist regime.
Sierra Leone	1991 ongoing	Revolutionary United Front mobilizes rural peoples, mainly Mende of the south and east, in an armed rebellion. Major Koroma ousts elected President Kabbah in violent coup May 1997. Nigeria-led West African peacekeeping mission troops restore Kabbah regime in March 1998; rebels continue fight.
Somalia	1988 to 1994	United Somali Congress, based on southern Hawiye clan, overthrows Siad Barre regime; chronic violence among clan-based warlords prevents establishment of effective central government.
South Africa	1984 to 1990	Violent protests and armed struggle breaks out in black townships over poor economic conditions and lack of political rights under apartheid policies. Progress in negotiations leads the African National Congress (ANC) to suspend armed struggle on August 1
Sri Lanka	1987 to 1989	People's Liberation Front (JVP) challenges government forces for the second time; government utilizes death squads.
Tajikistan	1992 to 1998	Civil war by Islamic and democratic forces against a Russian-backed regime dominated by old-line communists.
Thailand	1965 to 1983	A Maoist insurgency begins in November 1965 in outlying regions and increases through the 1970s. Insurgency collapses in 1983 amid mass defections.
Uganda	1983 to 1985	Widespread corruption, repression, and ethnic conflict lead to overthrow of Obote's military-backed civilian regime by National Resistance Army.
Vietnam, South	1958 to 1965	South Vietnamese communists, supported by North Vietnam, rebel against regime; became internationalized civil war after 1965.
Yemen	1994 to 1994	Lingering tensions between north and south in the newly united Yemen erupt in April 1994. On May 21, the south declares it secession from the union, but the rebellion quickly collapses when northern forces capture Aden in July 1994.
Yemen North	1962 to 1970	Royalist and Republican forces battle for control of government. Rival tribes join opposite sides.
Yemen South	1986 to 1986	Rival factions in the Yemen Socialist Party (YSP) battle for control of government.
Zambia	1964 to 1964	Fighting breaks out in July 1964 when followers of the militant-anarchist Lumpa Church refuse to join the United National Liberation Party (UNLP) which controls the government. Clashes continue until Lumpa leaders, having voluntarily surrendered, are released in Spetember.
Zimbabwe	1972 to 1979	White-dominated government fights black nationalists of Zimbabwe African People's Union (ZAPU) and Zimbabwe African National Union (ZANU), leading to negotiated settlement and black majority government in 1979.

Note

1. The descriptions provided in this table are taken directly from the descriptions provided in the State Failure dataset with some modifications based on a similar but more detailed listing on the project's website: State Failure Task Force. Internal Wars and Failures of Governance, 1955-2002. Compiled by Monty G. Marshall, Ted Robert Gurr, and Barbara Harff. College Park, MD: Center for International Development and Conflict Management, URL: www.cidcm.umd.edu/inscr/stfail.

Appendix B

Variable Descriptions

The datasets used in this study are described in detail in Chapter 1. This Appendix describes the variables used in this study. The description is divided into two sections, one for the variables in each dataset.

The Minorities at Risk Variables

This section describes the variables used in the analysis of the MAR dataset. This includes the variables from the dataset itself and the supplemental variables on religion and civilization used in conjunction with the MAR data.

Supplemental Religion and Civilization Variables

Religious identity codes whether the two groups in a given conflict belong to different religions on the following scale:

0. Both Groups belong to the same religion.
1. The two groups belong to different denominations of the same religion.
2. The two groups belong to different religions.

The specific religions of the majority and minority groups are also coded into the following three categories: Christian, Muslim, and Other. While the supplemental data on religion contains more detailed information on the religions of the minority and majority groups, which is used to code the religious identity variable, these more general categories are used in order for there to be enough cases in each category for the purposes of comparison. Thus, this coding is not intended to deny the diversity of beliefs within Islam and Christianity, not to mention within the "other" category.

Religious affinities between interveners and intervenees was coded using the same scale as religious identity. This variable measures the religious similarities between states which intervene on behalf of ethnic minorities and the ethnic minorities on whose behalf they intervene. This study also coded the religion of the intervener using the same categories as the above variable.

The rest of the religion variables measure more specific potential religious influences on ethnic conflict. Unless otherwise noted, all of these variables are coded separately for 1990 to 1991, 1992 to 1993, and 1994 to 1995.

Religious grievances measures the level of complaints expressed by a minority group over religious discrimination against them. The component variables were coded on the following scale, based on statements and actions by group leaders, members, and outside observers: 3 = issue important for most of the group; 2 = issue is significant but its relative importance cannot be judged; 1 = issue is of lesser importance, or of major concern to only one faction of the group; 0 = issue is not judged to be of any significant importance. The following type of religious grievances are so coded:

- Diffuse religious grievances, explicit objectives not clear. (Only code if more specific category below cannot be coded.)
- Greater right to observe festivals, holidays, and/or other forms of public observance.
- Greater right to build, repair, and/or maintain places of worship.
- Freedom from imposition of religious laws of other group.
- Right to maintain formal religious organizations.
- Right to maintain religious schools and/or teach religion.
- Right to observe religious laws concerning personal status, including marriage and divorce.
- Right to ordain and/or have access to clergy.
- Right to observe other religious practices. (Specify.)

The total scores of these variables are added to create a composite variable ranging from 0 to 24.

Religious demands are defined as the demand for religious rights and/or privileges. This variable differs from religious grievances, which are complaints against religious discrimination. Thus, religious grievances are reactive, whereas religious demands are active demands for more rights and privileges. Religious demands were coded using the following scale:

0. None.
1. The group is demanding more religious rights.
2. The group is seeking a privileged status for their religion which offends the religious convictions of the dominant group.

3. The group is seeking to impose some aspects of its religious ideology on the dominant group.
4. The group is seeking a form of ideological hegemony for its framework which will affect some of the dominant group.
5. The group is seeking a form of ideological hegemony for its framework which will affect most or all of the dominant group.

Religious institutions measures the level of formal organization and centralization of the religious institutions of an ethnic minority. The presence of religious institutions was coded only once during the 1990 to 1995 period using the following scale:

0. No religious institutions exist.
1. Informal institutions exist (i.e., layperson led prayer meetings).
2. A formally ordained clergy exists but there are no established houses of worship.
3. Formal houses of worship exist but they are not organized under a formal unified ecclesiastical structure (i.e., mosques in most Muslim states).
4. Formal houses of worship organized under a formal unified ecclesiastical structure (i.e., the Catholic Church).

Religious legitimacy is defined here as the extent to which it is legitimate to invoke religion in political discourse. For the purposes of this study it is coded as 1 if the state has an official religion and 0 if it does not.

Religious relevance to the conflict measures the importance of religious issues as compared to other issues in the conflict. It was coded only once for the entire 1990 to 1995 period using these categories:

0. None.
5. Marginal relevance. Issues are basically of a nonreligious nature but religion is being used to legitimize those issues and/or mobilize the group.
6. Religious issues are significant but are less important than other non-religious issues.
7. Religion is one of several significant issues which are of roughly equal importance.
8. Religion is the primary issue of the conflict but there are other significant issues involved.
9. Religion is the only issue relevant to the conflict.

Civilizational identity measures whether the minority and majority groups belong to the same civilization. It is coded as 0 if they belong to the same civilization and as 1 if they do not.

The specific civilization of the majority and minority groups are also coded into the following categories: Western, Sino-Confucian, Islamic, Hindu,

Slavic-Orthodox, Japanese, African, Latin American, mixed, and indigenous minority. The latter two categories are not part of Huntington's list of civilizations and are included to cover minorities which do not fit into any of his classifications. For more details see Chapter 6.

General Ethnic Conflict Variables

Rebellion is coded on the following Guttman scale each year from 1985 to 2000 and for five-year blocks from 1945 to 2000:

0. None.
1. Political banditry, sporadic terrorism.
2. Campaigns of terrorism.
3. Local rebellions: armed attempts to seize power in a locale. If they prove to be the opening round in what becomes a protracted guerrilla or civil war during the year being coded, code the latter rather than local rebellion. Code declarations of independence by a minority-controlled regional government here.
4. Small-scale guerrilla activity. (Small-scale guerrilla activity has all these three traits: fewer than 1,000 armed fighters; sporadic armed attacks [less than six reported per year]; and attacks in a small part of the area occupied by the group, or in one or two other locales.)
5. Intermediate-scale guerrilla activity. (Intermediate-scale guerrilla activity has one or two of the defining traits of large-scale activity and one or two of the defining traits of small-scale activity.)
6. Large-scale guerrilla activity. (Large-scale guerrilla activity has all these traits: more than 1,000 armed fighters; frequent armed attacks [more than six reported per year]; and attacks affecting a large part of the area occupied by the group.)
7. Protracted civil war, fought by rebel military with base areas.

Protest is coded on the following Guttman scale each year from 1985 to 2000 and for five-year blocks from 1945 to 2000:

0. None reported.
1. Verbal opposition (public letters, petitions, posters, publications, agitation, etc.). Code requests by a minority-controlled regional group for independence here.
2. Scattered acts of symbolic resistance (e.g., sit-ins, blockage of traffic, sabotage, symbolic destruction of property).
3. Political organizing activity on a substantial scale. (Code mobilization for autonomy and/or secession by a minority-controlled regional government

here.)
4. A few demonstrations, rallies, strikes, and/or riots, total participation less than 10,000.
5. Demonstrations, rallies, strikes, and/or riots, total participation estimated between 10,000 and 100,000.
6. Demonstrations, rallies, strikes, and/or riots, total participation over 100,000.

This study also provides measures of *the spread of conflict across borders*. It is coded separately for protest and rebellion. This is divided into two categories. The first, diffusion, represents the highest coding for kindred groups in adjoining states with the term "adjoining" interpreted loosely "in order to account for groups that have close kindred spread across many borders." The second, contagion, measures the spread of conflict within a region. Operationally, this is the mean level of protest or rebellion in the region the group resides. All of these variables are coded separately for the 1980s and the 1990 to 1995 period.

There are three indicators each for *mobilization* for protest and rebellion. The indicators are identical except that the protest mobilization variables measure open (legal) political organizations and the mobilization for rebellion variables measure militant (illegal) organizations. The first pair of variables are tallies of the number of communal organizations during the 1990s:

0. None reported.
1. One.
2. Two.
3. Three or more.

The second pair of variables are estimates of the scope of support for those organizations during the 1990s on the following scale:

0. No political movements recorded.
1. Limited: No political movement is supported by more than a tenth of the minority. If movements are identified by name but information is not sufficient to code scope of support for any of them, also code here.
2. Medium: The largest political movement is supported by a quarter to half of the minority.
3. Large: The largest political movement is supported by more than half of the minority.

The third variable is only available for mobilization for rebellion. It measures the change in the scope of support (the second variable) between 1995 and the year which is being analyzed. In this study we use the values for 1996 and 2000.

Political discrimination is defined as restrictions on a minority's access to political power and its ability to participate in the political process. It is a composite variable created from a checklist of specific aspects of the group's political status and participation that are selectively and deliberately restricted by public policy. The scope of each type of restriction is coded on the following scale: 2 = the activity is prohibited or sharply restricted for most or all group members; 1 = the activity is slightly restricted for most or all group members or sharply restricted for some of them; 0 = not significantly restricted for any. The following activities are so coded:

- Restrictions on freedom of expression
- Restrictions on free movement, place of residence
- Restrictions on rights in judicial proceedings
- Restrictions on political organization
- Restrictions on voting
- Restrictions on recruitment to police, military
- Restrictions on access to civil service
- Restrictions on attainment of high office
- Other

The codings are summed and divided by two, creating an indicator ranging from 0 to 9. It is coded biyearly for the 1990 to 1995 period and yearly from 1996 until 2000.

Economic discrimination is defined as restrictions on a minority's ability to participate in normal economic activities. It is measured yearly from 1990 to 2000 using a Guttman scale, which codes the most severe of the categories described below which affect the group in question:

0. None.
1. The group is economically advantaged. Public policies are designed to improve the relative economic position of other groups.
2. Significant poverty and underrepresentation in desirable occupations due to historical marginality, neglect, or restrictions. Public policies are designed to improve the group's material well-being.
3. Significant poverty and underrepresentation due to historical marginality, neglect, or restrictions. No social practice of deliberate exclusion. Few or no public policies aim at improving the group's material well-being.
4. Significant poverty and underrepresentation due to prevailing social practice by dominant groups. Formal public policies toward the group are neutral or, if positive, inadequate to offset active and widespread discrimination.
5. Public policies (formal exclusion and/or recurring repression) substantially restrict the group's economic opportunities by contrast with other groups.

Cultural restrictions are defined as restrictions on a minority's ability to engage in the group's cultural practices. The cultural restrictions indicator measures the restrictions that are placed on the pursuit or expression of the group's cultural interests. However, according to the MAR coding manual,

> public restrictions that apply to all citizens because they are necessary for the common good, e.g. requirements that families have only one child, or that all children be vaccinated, are not restrictions even if they violate the cultural norms of the communal group being coded. Lack of public support for group cultural activities is not a restriction unless public support is provided to similar activities by other groups.

The indicators that are combined to form the cultural discrimination variable are coded on the following scale: 3 = the activity is prohibited or sharply restricted by public policy; 2 = the activity is somewhat restricted by public policy; 1 = the activity is restricted by widespread but informal social practice (e.g., by discrimination against people who follow group customs or use the group's language); 0 = no significant restrictions on the activity. The following restrictions are so coded:

- Restrictions on speaking and publishing in group's language or dialect
- Restrictions on instruction in group's language
- Restrictions on celebration of group holidays, ceremonies, cultural events
- Restrictions on dress, appearance, behavior
- Restrictions on marriage, family life
- Restrictions on organizations that promote the group's cultural interests
- Other

The codings are summed and divided by two, creating an indicator ranging from 0 to 10.5. It is coded biyearly for the 1990 to 1995 period and yearly from 1996 until 2000.

Repression is a composite variable combining twenty-three individual measures of repression. Each one is measured on the following scale and the resulting codes are added:

0. Tactic not used.
1. Tactic used against group members engaged in collective action.
2. Tactic used against group members in ambiguous situations.
3. Tactic used against group members not engaged in collective action.

The categories so coded are:

- Small-scale arrests of group members
- Large-scale arrests of group members
- The arrest of group leaders
- Show trials of group leaders
- Torture of group members

- Execution of group members
- Execution of group leaders
- Reprisal killings of civilians
- Killings by death squads
- Property confiscated or destroyed
- Restrictions on movement
- Forced resettlement
- Interdiction of food supplies
- Ethnic cleansing
- Systematic domestic spying
- States of emergency
- Saturation of police/military
- Limited use of force against protestors
- Unrestrained use of force against protestors
- Military campaigns against armed rebels
- Military targets and destroys rebel areas
- Military massacres of suspected rebel supporters
- Other government repression

Nonreligious grievances are defined here as complaints openly expressed by group representatives over the political, economic, or cultural status of the group. All of the grievance variables are measured using composite indicators coded separately for 1990 to 1991, 1992 to1993, and 1994 to 1995 and yearly for 1996 to 2000. Each of the categories of grievance was coded on the following scale, based on statements and actions by group leaders, members, and outside observers: 3 = issue important for most of the group; 2 = issue is significant but its relative importance cannot be judged; 1 = issue is of lesser importance, or of major concern to only one faction of the group; 0= issue is not judged to be of any significant importance. The following types of *political grievances* are so coded:

- Diffuse political grievances, explicit objectives not clear. (Code only if more specific categories, below, cannot be coded.)
- Greater political rights in own community or region (own leaders, assembly, legal system, end to military rule, etc.).
- Greater participation in politics and decision making at the central state level.
- Equal civil rights and status.
- Change in unpopular local officials or policies.
- Other.

The highest possible value of the composite indicator is 15. The following types of *economic grievances* are so coded:

- Diffuse economic grievances, explicit objectives not clear. (Code only if

more specific categories, below, cannot be coded.)
- Greater share of public funds, services.
- Greater economic opportunities (better education, access to higher status occupations, resources).
- Improved working conditions, better wages, protective regulations (if sought specifically for group members).
- Protection of land, jobs, resources being used for the advantage of other groups.
- Other.

The highest possible value of the composite indicator is 15. The following types of *cultural grievances* are so coded:

- Promotion of group culture and lifeways.
- Right to teach and publish in own language.
- Right to use own language in dealings with other groups, including government.
- Protection from threats and attacks by other communal groups.
- Other.

The highest possible value of the composite indicator is 15. The following types of *autonomy grievances* are so coded:

- General concern for autonomy.
- Desire for union with kindred groups living elsewhere.
- Desire for political independence.
- Desire for widespread regional autonomy.
- Desire for limited regional autonomy.
- Other.

The highest possible value of the composite indicator is 18.

Separatism is another variable which measures the extent to which a group is separatist. It is coded as 1 if the group is actively separatist and as 0 if it is not.

Regime type measures whether the state is democratic or autocratic on a scale of -10 through 10 with -10 being the most autocratic and 10 being the most democratic. This scale is based on the competitiveness of political participation, the competitiveness and openness of executive recruitment, and constraints on the chief executive. The variable is coded for 1990, 1995, and 2000 and was taken by the MAR dataset from the Polity dataset. For more details, see Jaggers and Gurr (1995) and the Polity website at www.cidcm.umd.edu/inscr/mar.

International support for protest and rebellion measure the extent to which foreign entities support an ethnic minority's struggle against the state. International military support is coded on the following scale:

0. None.
1. Funds for military supplies or direct grants of military equipment.
2. Military training or the provision of military advisors.
3. Rescue missions, cross-border raids, or peacekeeping.
4. Cross-border sanctuaries or in-country combat units.

Political intervention is coded on the following scale:

0. None.
1. Ideological or diffuse support.
2. Nonmilitary financial support.
3. Access to external markets and communications.
4. Peacekeeping units of instituting a blockade.

In some tests a scaled down version of both variables is used in which 0 represents no intervention and 1 represents an intervention occurred.

The State Failure Variables

The religious and civilizational identity variables used with the SF dataset are coded identically to the ones for the MAR dataset described above. This also includes the specific identities of civilizations. The specific religions, however, are coded differently for the SF data using the following categories: Christian, Muslim, Buddhist, Animist, and other.

There are two variables which measure the yearly level of violence. The first is coded for ethnic and revolutionary wars on the following scale:

0. less than 100 fatalities
1. 100 to 1,000 fatalities
2. 1,000 to 5,000 fatalities
3. 5,000 to 10,000 fatalities
4. more than 10,000 fatalities

The second is coded for mass killings on the following scale:

0   less than 300
0.5 300 - 1,000
1.0 1,000 - 2,000
1.5 2,000 - 4,000
2.0 4,000 - 8,000
2.5 8,000 - 16,000
3.0 16,000 - 32,000

3.5 32,000 - 64,000
4.0 64,000 - 128,000
4.5 128,000 - 256,000
5.0 256,000 +

While it would have been preferable for exact numbers to be used instead of the scales above, the State Failure project did not do so because in many cases it was simply not feasible to get exact numbers. In recent and well-covered conflicts on which there is no shortage of information, the numbers of combatants and casualties are often unclear or in dispute. In conflicts that occurred thirty or forty years ago, this situation is even worse. Thus, these scales are the best approximation that can be constructed given the information available. They are based on the concept of magnitude, with each category being double or more of the preceding category.

Bibliography

Ahari, M. E. "The Clash of Civilizations: An Old Story or New Truth." *New Perspectives Quarterly* 14 (2) (1997): 56-61.

Ajami, Faoud. "The Summoning." *Foreign Affairs* 72 (4) (1993): 2-9.

Alfred, Gerald R., and Franke Wilmer. "Indigenous Peoples, States, and Conflicts." in David Carment and Patrick James, eds., *Wars in the Midst of Peace*. Pittsburgh: University of Pittsburgh Press, 1997, 26-44.

Almond, Gabriel. "Introduction: A Functional Approach to Comparative Politics." in Almond and James C. Coleman, eds., *The Politics of the Developing Areas*. Princeton: Princeton University Press, 1960.

Anwar, Said Tariq. "Civilizations versus Civilizations in a New Multipolar World." *Journal of Marketing* 62 (2) (1998): 125-128.

Appleby, R. Scott. *The Ambivalence of the Sacred: Religion, Violence, and Reconciliation*. New York: Rowman & Littlefield, 2000.

Apter, David, ed. *The Politics of Modernization*. Chicago: University of Chicago Press, 1965.

Ayres, R. W., and Stephen Saideman. "Is Separatism as Contagious as the Common Cold or as Cancer? Testing International and Domestic Explanations." *Nationalism and Ethnic Politics* 6 (3) (2000): 91-113.

Aysha, Emad El Din. "Samuel Huntington and the Geopolitics of American Identity: The Function of Foreign Policy in America's Domestic Clash of Civilizations." *International Studies Perspectives* 4 (2) (2003): 113-132.

Bader, Viet. "Religious Pluralism: Secularism or Priority for Democracy." *Political Theory* 27 (5) (1999): 597-633.

Barber, Benjamin R. "Fantasy of Fear." *Harvard International Review* 20 (1) Winter 1997/(1998): 66-71.

Barret, D. B., G. T. Kurian, and T.M. Johnson. *World Christian Encyclopedia*. 2nd ed. Oxford: Oxford University Press, 2001.

Bartley, Robert L. "The Case for Optimism." *Foreign Affairs* 72 (4) (1993): 15-18.

Beckford, James A., "The Insulation and Isolation of the Sociology of Religion." *Sociological Analysis* 46 (4) 1985, 347-354.

Beedham, Brian. "The New Geopolitics: A Fading Hell." *The Economist* July 31, (1999): s10.

Beyer, Peter. "Secularization from the Perspective of Globalization: A Response to Dobbelaere." *Sociology of Religion* 60 (3) (1999): 289-301.

————. *Religion and Globalization*, London: Sage, 1994.

Borntrager, Ekkehard W. *Borders, Ethnicity, and National Self-Determination*. Austria: Braumuller, 1999.

Byman, Daniel. "The Logic of Ethnic Terrorism." *Studies in Conflict and Terrorism* 21 (2) (1998): 149-169.

Carment, David and Patrick James. "Explaining Third-Party Intervention in Ethnic Conflict: Theory and Evidence." *Nations and Nationalism* 6 (2) (2000): 173-202.

————. "Escalation of Ethnic Conflict." *International Politics* 35, (1998): 65-82.

————. "The International Politics of Ethnic Conflict: New Perspectives on Theory and Policy." *Global Society* 11 (2) 1997a: 205-232.

————. eds., *Wars in the Midst of Peace*. Pittsburgh: University of Pittsburgh Press, 1997b.

————. "Two-Level Games and Third-Party Intervention: Evidence from Ethnic Conflict in the Balkans and South Asia." *Canadian Journal of Political Science* 29 (3) (1996): 521-554.

Carment, David and Dane Rowlands. "Three's Company: Evaluating Third-Party Intervention in Intrastate Conflict." *Journal of Conflict Resolution* 42 (5) (1998): 572-599.

Chaves, Mark. "Secularization as Declining Religious Authority." *Social Forces*, 72 (3) March (1994): 749-774.

Chong, Dennis. *Collective Action and Civil Rights*. Chicago: University of Chicago Press, 1991.

Coleman, James S. "Commentary: Social Institutions and Social Theory." *American Sociological Review* 55, (1990): 333-339.

Comaroff, John L. and Paul C. Stern eds. *Perspectives on Nationalism and War*. Luxembourg, Australia: Gordon and Breach, 1995.

Connor, Walker. "Nation Building or Nation Destroying?" *World Politics* 26 (1972): 319-355.

Cooper, Robert and Mats Berdal. "Outside Intervention in Ethnic Conflicts." *Survival* 35 (1) (1993): 118-142.

Cox, Harvey. *The Secular City: Seculariztion and Urbanization in Theological Perspective*. London: SCM Press, 1965.

David, Steven R. "Internal War: Causes and Cures." *World Politics* 49, (1997): 552-576.

Davies, James C., "Toward a Theory of Revolution." *American Sociological Review* 27, (1962): 5-19.

Davis, David R. and Will H. Moore. "Ethnicity Matters: Transnational Ethnic Alliances and Foreign Policy Behavior." *International Studies Quarterly* 41 (1) March (1997): 171-184.

Davis, David R., Keith Jaggers, and Will H. Moore. "Ethnicity, Minorities, and International Conflict." in David Carment and Patrick James eds., *Wars in the Midst of Peace.* Pittsburgh: University of Pittsburgh Press, (1997): 148-163.

Deeb, Mary J. "Militant Islam and the Politics of Redemption." *Annals, American Acadamey of Political and Social Sciences* 524, (1992): 52-65.

Deihl, Paul F. Jennifer Reifschneidr, and Paul R. Hensel "United Nations Intervention in Recurring Conflict." *International Organization* 50 (4) (1996): 683-700.

Deutsch, Karl W. *Nationalism and Social Communication.* Cambridge, Mass.: MIT Press, 1953.

————. "The Limits of Common Sense." in Nelson Polsby, ed., *Politics and Social Life.* Boston: Houghton Mifflin, (1963): 51-57.

Dinstein, Yoram. "Freedom of Religion and the Protection of Religious Minorities." *Israel Yearbook on Human Rights* 20, (1991): 155-179.

Dobbelaere, Karel. "Towards an Integrated Perspective of the Processes Related to the Descriptive Concept of Secularization." *Sociology of Religion* 60 (3) (1999): 229-247.

Don-Yehiyah, Eliezer. "The Book and the Sword: The Nationalist Yeshivot and Political Radicalism in Israel." in Martin E. Marty and R. Scott Appleby eds., *Accounting for Fundamentalisms: The Dynamic Character of Movements.* Chicago: University of Chicago Press, (1994): 264-302.

Drake, C. J. M. "The Role of Ideology in Terrorists' Target Selection." *Terrorism and Political Violence* 10 (2) (1998): 53-85.

Eisenstadt, S. N. "The Reconstruction of Religious Arenas in the Framework of 'Multiple Modernities'." *Millennium* 29 (3) (2000): 591-611.

Ellingsen, Tanja. "The Relevance of Culture in UN Voting Behavior." Paper presented at the International Studies Association annual conference in New Orleans, March, 2002.

————. "Colorful Community or Ethnic Witches' Brew? Multiethnicity and Domestic Conflict During and After the Cold War." *Journal of Conflict Resolution* 44 (2) (2000): 228-249.

Esposito, John L., *The Islamic Threat: Myth or Reality?* 2nd ed., Oxford: Oxford University Press, 1995.

————. "Religion and Global Affairs: Political Challenges." *SAIS Review* Summer-Fall, (1998): 19-24.

Fawcett, Liz. *Religion, Ethnicity, and Social Change.* New York: St. Martins, 2000.

Fearon, James D. and David D. Latin. "A Cross-Sectional Study of Large-Scale Ethnic Violence in the Postwar Period." Unpublished paper, Department of Political Science, University of Chicago, September 30, 1997.

Feierabend, Ivo and Rosiland Feierabend. "Systemic Conditions of Political Aggression: An Application of Frustration=Aggression Theory." in Ivo

Feierabend ed., et al. *Anger, Violence and Politics*. New York: Prentice-Hall, 1973.

Fein, Helen. "Genocide: A Sociological Perspective." *Current Sociology* 38 (1) Spring (1990): 1-126.

Ferguson, Yale H. and Richard W. Mansbach. "Global Politics at the Turn of the Millennium: Changing Bases of 'Us' and 'Them'." *International Studies Review* 1 (1) (2000): 77-107.

Fields, Echo E. "Understanding Activist Fundamentalism." *Sociological Analysis* 52 (2) (1991): 175-190.

Foster-Carter, A. "The Sociology of Development." in M. Haralambos ed., *Sociology: New Directions*. Ormskirk, Lancashire: Causeway, 1985.

Fox, Jonathan, "State Failure and the Clash of Civilisations: An Examination of the Magnitude and Extent of Domestic Civilisational Conflict from 1950 to 1996." *Australian Journal of Political Science* 38 (2) (2003): 195-213.

————. *Ethnoreligious Conflict in the Late 20th Century: A General Theory.* (Lanham, MD: Lexington Books, 2002a)

————. "Ethnic Minorities and the Clash of Civilizations: A Quantitative Analysis of Huntington's Thesis." *British Journal of Political Science* 32 (3) 2002b: 415-434.

————. "Civilizational, Religious, and National Explanations for Ethnic Rebellion in the Post-Cold War Middle East." *Jewish Political Studies Review* 13 (1-2) Spring, 2001a: 177-204.

————. "Islam and the West: The Influence of Two Civilizations on Ethnic Conflict." *Journal of Peace Research* 38 (4) July, 2001b: 459-472.

————. "Are Middle East Conflicts More Religious?" *Middle East Quarterly* 8 (4) Fall 2001c: 31-40.

————. "Religion: An Oft Overlooked Element of International Studies." *International Studies Review* 3 (3) Fall, 2001d: 53-73.

————. "Religious Causes of International Intervention in Ethnic Conflicts." *International Politics* 38 (4) December, 2001e: 515-531.

————. "Clash of Civilizations or Clash of Religions, Which Is a More Important Determinant of Ethnic Conflict?." *Ethnicities* 1 (3) December 2001f: 295-320.

————. "Is Islam More Conflict Prone than Other Religions? A Cross-Sectional Study of Ethnoreligious Conflict." *Nationalism and Ethnic Politics* 6 (2) 2000a: 1-23.

————. "Religious Causes of Ethnic Discrimination." *International Studies Quarterly* 44 (3) September 2000b: 423-450.

————. "The Effects of Religious Discrimination on Ethnic Protest and Rebellion." *Journal of Conflict Studies* 20 (2) Fall, 2000c: 16-43.

————. "Do Religious Institutions Support Violence or the Status Quo?." *Studies in Conflict and Terrorism* 22 (2) 1999a: 119-139.

————. "The Influence of Religious Legitimacy on Grievance Formation by Ethnoreligious Minorities." *Journal of Peace Research* 36 (3) 1999b: 289-307.

————. "The Effects of Religion on Domestic Conflict. *" Terrorism and Political Violence* 10 (4) Winter (1998): 43-63.

————. "The Salience of Religious Issues in Ethnic Conflicts: A Large-N Study." *Nationalism and Ethnic Politics* 3 (3) Autumn (1997): 1-19.

Fox, Jonathan and Josephine Squires, "Threats to Primal Identities: A Comparison of Nationalism and Religion as it Impacts on Protest and Rebellion." *Terrorism and Political Violence* 13 (1) (2001): 88-102.

Fukayama, Francis. "The End of History." *The National Interest* 16 (4) 1989.

Fuller, Graham E. "The Next Ideology." *Foreign Policy* 98, (1995): 145-158.

Fuller, Graham E. and Ian O. Lesser, *A Sense of Siege: The Geopolitics of Islam and the West*. Boulder Colo: Westview, 1995.

Geertz, Clifford. *The Interpretation of Culture*. New York: Basic Books, 1973.

Gill, Anthony. *Rendering Unto Caesar: The Catholic Church and the State in Latin America*. Chicago: University of Chicago Press, 1998.

Girard, Rene. *Violence and the Sacred*, trans. Patrick Gregory, Baltimore Md.: Johns Hopkins University Press, 1977.

Glasner, Peter E. *The Sociology of Secularization: A Critique of a Concept*. London: Routledge, 1977.

Goldstone, Jack A. Ted Robert Gurr and Farrokh Moshiri eds. *Revolutions of the Late Twentieth Century*, Boulder Colo.: Westview, 1991.

Gopin, Marc, *Between Eden and Armageddon: The Future of World Religions, Violence, and Peacemaking*. Oxford: Oxford University Press, 2000.

Gray, John. "Global Utopias and Clashing Civilizations: Misunderstanding the Prosperity." *International Affairs* 74 (1) (1998): 149-164.

Green, David M. "The End of Identity? The Implications of Postmodernity for Political Identification." *Nationalism and Ethnic Politics* 6 (3) (2000): 68-90.

Gregg, Donald P. "A Case for Continued U.S. Engagement." *Orbis* 41 (3) (1997): 375-384.

Gungwu, Wang. "A Machiavelli for Our Times." *The National Interest* (46) 1997a: 69-73.

————. "Learn from the Past." *Far Eastern Economic Review* 160 (18) May 1 1997b: 37-38.

Gurr, Ted R. *Peoples Versus States: Minorities at Risk in the New Century*. Washington, D.C.: United States Institute of Peace Press, 2000.

————. "Peoples Against the State: Ethnopolitical Conflict and the Changing World System." *International Studies Quarterly* 38 (3) (1994): 347-377.

————. *Minorities At Risk: A Global View of Ethnopolitical Conflict*. Washington, D.C.: United States Institute of Peace, 1993a.

————. "Why Minorities Rebel." *International Political Science Review*. 14 (2) 1993b: 161-201.

————. "War Revolution, and the Growth of the Coercive State." *Comparative Political Studies* 21 (1) April (1988): 45-65.

————. *Why Men Rebel*. Princeton: Princeton University 1970.

Gurr, Ted R. and Barbara Harff. *Ethnic Conflict in World Politics*. Boulder, Colo.: Westview, 1994.

Gurr, Ted R., Barbara Harff, and Monty G. Marshall. "Internal Wars and Failures of Governance, 1954-1996." http://www.cidcm.umd.edu/inscr/stfail (Accessed May 19, 1997).

Hadden, Jeffrey E. *Islam and the Myth of Confrontation: Religion and Politics in the Middle East*. New York: St. Martin's Press, 1996.

————. "Religious Broadcasting and the Mobilization of the New Christian Right." *Journal for the Scientific Study of Religion* 26 (1) 1987a: 1-24.

————. "Toward Desacralizing Secularization Theory." *Social Forces* 65 (3) 1987b: 587-611.

Halliday, Fred."A New World Myth." *New Statesman* 10 (447) (1997): 42-43.

Halpern. "Toward Further Modernization of the Study of New Nations." *World Politics* 17 (October 1964): 157-181.

Hardacre, Helen. "The Impact of Fundamentalisms on Women, the Family, and Interpersonal Relations." in Martin E. Marty and R. Scott Appleby eds., *Fundamentalisms and Society: Reclaiming the Sciences, the Family, and Education*. Chicago: University of Chicago Press, (1993): 129-150.

Hardjono, Ratih. "The Clash of Civilizations and the Remaking of World Order." *Nieman Reports* 51 (1) (1997): 87-88.

Harris, Fredrick C. "Something Within: Religion as a Mobilizer of African-American Political Activism." *Journal of Politics* 56 (1) (1994): 42-68.

Harris, Robin. "War of the World Views." *National Review* 48 (20) (1996): 69.

Hasenclever, Andreas and Volker Rittberger. "Does Religion Make a Difference? Theoretical Approaches to the Impact of Faith on Political Conflict." *Millennium* 29 (3) (2000): 641-674.

Hassner, Pierre. "Morally Objectionable, Politically Dangerous." *The National Interest* (46) Winter 1997a: 63-69.

————. "Clashing On." *The National Interest* (48) Summer 1997b: 105-111.

Haynes, Jeff. *Religion in Third World Politics*. Boulder, Colo.: Lynne Rienner, 1994.

Heilbrunn, Jacob. "The Clash of Samuel Huntingtons." *The American Prospect* (39) (1998): 22-28.

Henderson, Errol A. "The Democratic Peace through the Lens of Culture, 1820-1989." *International Studies Quarterly* 42 (3) September (1998): 461-484.

————. "Culture or Contiguity: Ethnic Conflict, the Similarity States, and the Onset of War,1820-1989." *Journal of Conflict Resolution* 41 (5) October (1997): 649-668.

Henderson, Errol A. and J. David Singer. "Civil War in the Post-Colonial World, 1946-1992." *Journal of Peace Research* 37 (3) (2000): 275-299.

Henderson, Errol A and Richard Tucker. "Clear and Present Strangers: The Clash of Civilizations and International Conflict." *International Studies Quarterly* 45 (2) (2001): 317-338.

Heraclides, Alexis. "Secessionist Minorities and External Involvement." *Interna tional Organization* 44, (1990): 341-378.

Hill, Stuart and Donald Rothchild."The Contagion of Political Conflict in Africa and the Third World." *Journal of Conflict Resolution* 30 (4) (1986): 716-735.

Hill, Stuart, Donald Rothchild, and Colin Cameron. "Tactical Information and the Diffusion of Peaceful Protests." in David A. Lake and Donald Rothchild eds., *The International Spread of Ethnic Conflict.* Princeton: Princeton University Press, 1998: 61-88.

Hoffman, Bruce. "'Holy Terror': The Implications of Terrorism Motivated by a Religious Imperative." *Studies in Conflict and Terrorism* 18, (1995): 271-284.

Howell, David. "East Comes West." *Foreign Affairs* 76 (2) (1997): 164.

Hunter, Shirleen T. *The Future of Islam and the West: Clash of Civilizations or Peaceful Coexistence?* Westport, Conn.: Praeger, with the Center for Strategic and International Studies, Washington, D.C., 1998.

Huntington, Samuel P. "Osama bin Laden Has Given Common Identity Back to the West." *New Perspectives Quarterly* 19 (1) (2002): 5-8.

————. "Try Again: A Reply to Russett, Oneal, and Cox." *Journal of Peace Research* 37 (5) (2000): 609-610.

————. *The Clash of Civilizations and the Remaking of the World Order.* New York: Simon & Schuster, 1996a

————. "The West: Unique, Not Universal." *Foreign Affairs* 75 (6) 1996b: 28-46.

————. "The Clash of Civilizations?" *Foreign Affairs* 72 (3) 1993a: 22-49.

————. "If Not Civilizations, What? Paradigms of the Post-Cold War. " *Foreign Affairs,* 72 (5) 1993b: 186-194.

————. *Political Order in Changing Societies.* New Haven, Conn.: Yale University Press, 1968.

Iannaccone, Laurence R. "Voodoo Economics? Reviewing the Rational Choice Approach to Religion." *Journal for the Scientific Study of Religion* 34 (1) 1995a: 76-89.

————. "Second Thoughts: A Response to Chaves, Demerath, and Ellison." *Journal for the Scientific Study of Religion* 34 (1) 1995b: 113-120.

Ibrahim, Anwar. "Terror Attacks Set Back Cause of Democracy in Islam." *New Perspectives Quarterly* 19 (1) (2002): 9-11.

Ikenberry, John G. "Just Like the Rest." *Foreign Affairs* 76 (2) (1997): 162-163.

Jaggers, Keith and Ted R. Gurr. "Tracking Democracy's Third Wave with the Polity III Data." *Journal of Peace Research* 32 (4) (1995): 469-482.

Johnston, Douglas and Cynthia Sampson eds. *Religion, the Missing Dimension of Statecraft.* Oxford: Oxford University Press, 1994.

Johnston, Hank and Jozef Figa. "The Church and Political Opposition: Comparative Perspectives on Mobilization Against Authoritarian Regimes." *Journal for the Scientific Study of Religion* 27 (1) (1988): 32-47.

Juergensmeyer, Mark. *Terror in the Mind of God: The Global Rise of Religious Violence.* Berkeley: University of California Press, 2000.

————. "Terror Mandated by God." *Terrorism and Political Violence* 9 (2) Summer (1997): 16-23.

————. "The New Religious State." *Comparative Politics* 27 (4) (1995): 379-391.

————. *The New Cold War?* Berkeley: University of California, 1993.

————. "Sacrifice and Cosmic War." *Terrorism and Political Violence* 3 (3) (1991): 101-117.

Kabalkova, Vendulka. "Towards and International Political Theology." *Millennium* 29 (3) (2000): 675-704.

Kader, Zerougui A. "The Clash of Civilizations and the Remaking of World Order." *Arab Studies Quarterly* 20 (1)(1998): 89-92.

Kaplan, Jeffrey. "Introduction." *Terrorism and Political Violence* 14 (1) (2002): 1-24.

Kaufmann, Chaim D. "When All Else Fails: Ethnic Population Transfers and Partitions in the Twentieth Century." *International Security* 23 (2) (1998): 120-156.

————. "Possible and Impossible Solutions to Ethnic Civil Wars. " *International Security* 20 (4) (1996): 136-175.

Kautsky, J. *The Political Consequences of Modernization.* New York: John Wiley, 1972.

Kegley, Charles W. Jr. and Margaret G. Hermann. "Putting Military Intervention into the Democratic Peace." *Comparative Political Studies* 30 (1) (1997): 78-107.

Kennedy, Robert. "Is One Person's Terrorist Another's Freedom Fighter? Western and Islamic Approaches to 'Just War' Compared." *Terrorism and Political Violence* 11 (1) (1999): 1-21.

Khosla, Deepa. "Third World States as Intervenors in Ethnic Conflicts: Implications for Regional and International Security." *Third World Quarterly* 20 (6) (1999): 1143-1156.

Kirkpatrick, Jeane J. et. al. "The Modernizing Imperative." *Foreign Affairs* 72 (4) (1993): 22-26.

Kirth, James. "The Real Clash." *The National Interest* (37) Fall (1994): 3-14.

Kolas, Ashild. "Tibetan Nationalism: The Politics of Religion." *Journal of Peace Research* 33 (1) (1996): 51-66.

Kuhn, Thomas S. *The Structure of Scientific Revolutions.* 2nd ed. Chicago: University of Chicago Press, 1970.

Kumar, Radha. "The Troubled History of Partition." *Foreign Affairs* 76 (1) (1997): 22-34.

Kuran, Timur. "Fundamentalism and the Economy." in Martin E. Marty and R. Scott Appleby eds., *Fundamentalisms and the State: Remaking Politics, Economies, and Militance.* Chicago: University of Chicago Press, 1991, 289-301.

Lambert, Yves. "Religion in Modernity as a New Axial Age: Secularization or New Religious Forms." *Sociology of Religion* 60 (3), (1999): 303-333.

Latin, David. "Religion, Political Culture, and the Weberian Tradition." *World Politics* 30 (4) (1978): 563-593.

Laustsen, Carsten B. and Ole Waever. "In Defense of Religion: Sacred referent Objects for Securitization." *Millennium* 29 (3) (2000): 705-739.

Layachi, Azzedine and Abdel-Kader Halreche. "National Development and Political Protest: Islamists in the Maghreb Countries." *Arab Studies Quarterly* 14 (2 and 3) (1992): 69-92.

Lewis, Bernard. *Islam and the West*, Oxford: Oxford University Press, 1993.

Lichbach, Mark I. "An Evaluation of 'Does Economic Inequality Breed Political Conflict?': Studies." *World Politics* (1989): 431-470.

Liebman, Charles S. and Eliezer Don-Yehiyah. *Civil Religion in Israel: Traditional Judaism and Political Culture in the Jewish State.* Berkeley: University of California Press, 1983.

Lijphart, Arend. "The Power Sharing Approach." in Joseph V. Montville, ed., *Conflict and Peacemaking in Multiethnic Societies.* Lanham Md.: Lexington Books, (1990): 491-509.

Little, David, Religious Militancy." in Chester A. Crocker and Fen O. Hampson eds., *Managing Global Chaos: Sources of and Responses to International Conflict*, Washington DC:United States Institute of Peace Press, 1996a: 79-91.

————. "Studying 'Religious Human Rights': Methodological Foundations." in John D. van der Vyver and John Witte Jr. eds., *Religious Human Rights in Global Perspective: Legal Perspectives.* Boston: Martinus Njhoff, 1996b: 45-77.

————. *Ukraine: The Legacy of Intolerance.* Washington, D.C.: United States Institute of Peace Press, 1991.

Luckman, Thomas. *The Invisible Religion.* New York: Macmillan, 1967.

Mahbubani, Kishore. "The Dangers of Decadence." *Foreign Affairs* 72 (4) (1993): 10-14.

Manor, James. "Organizational Weakness and the Rise of Sinhalese Buddhist Extremism." in Martin E. Marty and R. Scott Appleby eds., *Accounting for Fundamentalisms: The Dynamic Character of Movements.* Chicago: University of Chicago Press, (1994): 770-784.

Marshall, Gordon. "Which Way for the Sociology of Religion? A Review Article." *Comparative Studies in Society and History* 29, (1987): 375-380.

Marshall, Paul. "Religion and Global Affairs: Disregarding Religion." *SAIS Review* Summer-Fall (1998): 13-18.

Martin, David A. *A General Theory of Secularization.* Oxford: Blackwell, 1978.

Martin, Richard C. "The Study of Religion and Violence." in David C. Rapoport, and Yonah Alexander, eds., *The Morality of Terrorism: Religious and Secular Justifications.* 2nd ed., New York: Columbia University Press, 1989: 349-373.

Marty, Martin E. and R. Scott Appleby. eds. *Accounting for Fundamentalisms: The Dynamic Character of Movements.* Chicago: University of Chicago Press, 1994.

————. *Fundamentalisms and Society: Reclaiming the Sciences, the Family, and*

Education. Chicago: University of Chicago Press, 1993.

————. *Fundamentalisms and the State: Remaking Politics, Economies and Militance.* Chicago: University of Chicago Press, 1991.

McAdam, Doug. *Political Process and the Development of Black Insurgency 1930-1970.* Chicago: University of Chicago Press,1982.

McArthy, John D. and Mayer N. Zald. "Resource Mobilization and Social Movements: A Partial Theory." *American Journal of Sociology* 82 (6) (1976): 1212-1241.

Midlarsky, Manus I. "Democracy and Islam: Implications for Civilizational Conflict and the Democratic Peace." *International Studies Quarterly* 42 (3) (1998): 458-511.

Monshipouri, Mahmood. "The West's Modern Encounter with Islam: From Discourse to Reality." *Journal of Church and State* 40 (1) (1998): 25-56.

Murphey, Dwight C. "The Clash of Civilizations." *The Journal of Social, Political, and Economic Studies* 23 (2) (1998): 215-216.

Naff, William E. "The Clash of Civilizations and the Remaking of World Order." *Annals of the American Academy of Political and Social Science* 556, (1998): 198-199.

Nasr, Vali. "Religion and Global Affairs: Secular States and Religious Oppositions." *SAIS Review* Summer-Fall (1998): 32-37.

Neckermann, Peter. "The Promise of Globalization or the Clash of Civilizations." *The World and I* 13 (12) 1998.

Nussbaum, Bruce. "Capital, Not Culture." *Foreign Affairs* 76 (2) 1997.

Olson, Mancur, Jr.."Rapid Growth as a Destabalizing Force."*Journal of Economic History* 23, 1963.

Oommen, T.K. "Religious Nationalism and Democratic Polity: The Indian Case." *Sociology of Religion* 55 (4) (1994): 455-472.

Osiander, Andreas. "Religion and Politics in Western Civilization: The Ancient World as Matrix and Mirror of the Modern." *Millennium* 29 (3) (2000): 761-790.

Pfaff, William. "The Reality of Human Affairs." *World Policy Journal* 14 (2) (1997): 89-96.

Philpott, Daniel."The Challenge of September 11 to Secularism in International Relations." *World Politics* 55 (1) (2002): 66-95.

————. "The Religious Roots of Modern International Relations." *World Politics* 52, (2000): 206-245.

Piscatori, James. "Accounting for Islamic Fundamentalisms." in Martin E. Marty and R. Scott Appleby eds., *Accounting for Fundamentalisms: The Dynamic Character of Movements.* Chicago: University of Chicago Press, (1994): 361-373.

Randall, V. and R. Theobald. *Political Change and Underdevelopment: A Critical Introduction to Third World Politics.* London: Macmillan, 1985.

Ranstorp, Magnus. "Terrorism in the Name of Religion." *Journal of International Affairs* 50 (1) (1996): 41-60.

Rapoport, David C."Sacred Terror: A Contemporary Example from Islam." in Walter Reich ed. *Origins of Terrorism: Psychologies, Ideologies, Theologies, States of Mind.* Cambridge, Mass.: Harvard University Press, (1990): 103-130.

————. "Messianic Sanctions for Terror." *Comparative Politics* 20 (2) January (1988): 195-213.

————. "Fear and Trembling: Terrorism in Three Religious Traditions." *American Political Science Review* 78 (1984): 658-677.

Rapoport, David C and Yonah Alexander, eds. *The Morality of Terrorism: Religious and Secular Justifications.* 2nd ed. New York: Columbia University Press, 1989.

Regan, Patrick M. "Choosing to Intervene: Outside Interventions in Internal Conflicts." *The Journal of Politics* 60 (3) (1998): 754-779.

————. "Conditions of Successful Third-Party Intervention in Intrastate Conflicts." *Journal of Conflict resolution* 40 (2) 1996.

Reynal-Querol, Marta. "Ethnicity, Political Systems, and Civil Wars. " *Journal of Conflict Resolution* 46 (1) (2002): 29-54.

Robertson, Roland. "Beyond the Sociology of Religion?." *Sociological Analysis* 46 (4) 1985, 355-360.

Rosecrance, Richard. "The Clash of Civilizations and the Remaking of World Order." *American Political Science Review* 92 (4) (1998): 978-980.

Rosser, J. Barkley Jr. "Belief: Its Role in Thought and Action." *American Journal of Economics and Sociology* 52 (3) July (1993): 355-368.

Rostow, W. *The Stages of Economic Growth: A Non-Communist Manifesto.* Cambridge: Cambridge University Press, 1959.

Rubin, Barry. "Religion and International Affairs." in Douglas Johnston and Cynthia Sampson eds., *Religion, the Missing Dimension of Statecraft.* Oxford: Oxford University Press, (1994): 20-34.

Rule, James B. *Theories of Civil Violence.* Berkeley: University of California Press, 1988.

Rummel, Rudolph J. "Is Collective Violence Correlated with Social Pluralism?." *Journal of Peace Research* 34 (2) (1997): 163-175.

Russett, Bruce, John R. Oneal, and Michalene Cox. "Clash of Civilizations, or Realism and Liberalism Deja Vu? Some Evidence." *Journal of Peace Research* 37 (5) (2000): 583-608.

Sahliyeh, Emile, ed. *Religious Resurgence and Politics in the Contemporary World* Albany: State University of New York Press, 1990.

Saideman, Stephen M. and R. William Ayres. "Determining the Cause of Irridentism: Logit anlayses of Minorities at Risk Data from the 1980s and 1990s." *Journal of Politics* 62 (4) (2000): 1126-1144.

Sandler, Shmuel. "Religious Zionism and the State: Political Accommodation and Radicalism in Israel." *Terrorism and Political Violence* 8 (2) (1996): 135-154.

Schbley, Ayla Hammond. "Torn Between God, Family, and Money: The Changing Profile of Lebanon's Religious Terrorists." *Studies in Conflict and Terrorism* 23 (2000): 175-196.

Schultz, Richard H. "State Disintegration and Ethnic Conflict: A Framework for Analysis." *Annals of the American Academy of Political and Social Sciences* 541, (1995): 75-88.

Seamon, Richard. "The Clash of Civilizations: And the Remaking of World Order." *United States Naval Institute. Proceedings* 124 (3) (1998): 116-118.

Senghass, Dieter. "A Clash of Civilizations–An Idea Fixe?." *Journal of Peace Research* 35 (1) (1998): 127-132.

Seul, Jefferey R. "'Ours is the Way of God': Religion, Identity and Intergroup Conflict." *Journal of Peace Research* 36 (3) (1999): 553-569.

Shupe, Anson. "The Stubborn Persistence of Religion in the Global Arena." in Emile Sahliyeh ed., *Religious Resurgence and Politics in the Contemporary World*. Albany: State University of New York Press, 1990.

Silk, Mark. *Spiritual Politics*, New York: Simon and Schuster, 1988.

Singhua, Liu, "History as Antagonism." *Far Eastern Economic Review* 160 (18) May 1 (1997): 37.

Smith, Anthony D. "The Sacred Dimension of Nationalism." *Millennium* 29 (3) (2000): 791-814.

————. "Ethnic Election and National Destiny: Some Religious Origins of Nationalist Ideals." *Nations and Nationalism* 5 (3) (1999): 331-355.

————. *The Ethnic Revival in the Modern World*. London: Cambridge University Press, 1981.

Smith, Donald E. "The Limits of Religious Resurgence." in Emile Sahliyeh ed., *Religious Resurgence and Politics in the Contemporary World*. Albany: State University of New York Press, (1990): 33-44.

————. ed. *Religion and Political Modernization*. New Haven, Conn.: Yale University Press, 1974

————. *Religion, Politics, and Social Change in the Third World*. New York: Free Press, 1971.

————. *Religion and Political Development*. Boston: Little, Brown, 1970.

Smith, Tony. "Dangerous Conjecture." *Foreign Affairs* 76 (2) (1997): 163-164.

Sutton, Frank. "Social Theory and Comparative Politics." in Harry Eckstein and David Apter, eds., *International Encyclopedia of the Social Sciences*. New York: Macmillan, 1968.

Tarrow, Sidney. *Democracy and Disorder: Protest and Politics in Italy 1965-1975*. Oxford: Clarendon, 1989.

Taylor, Bron. "Religion, Violence, and Radical Environmentalism: From Earth First! To the Unabomber to the Earth Liberation Front." *Terrorism and Political Violence* 10 (4) (1998): 1-42.

Taylor, Maxwell. *The Fanatics*. London: Brassey's, 1991.

Thomas, Scott M. "Taking Religious and Cultural Pluralism Seriously: The Global Resurgence of Religion and the Transformation of International Society." *Millennium* 29 (3) (2000): 815-841.

Tibi, Bassam. "Post-Bipolar Disorder in Crisis: The Challenge of Politicized Islam." *Millennium* 29 (4) (2000): 843-859.

Tilly, Charles. *From Mobilization to Revolution.* Reading, Mass.: Addison-Wesley, 1978.

Tipson, Frederick S. "Culture Clash-ification: A Verse to Huntington's Curse." *Foreign Affairs* 76 (2) (1997): 166-169.

Turner, Brian S. *Religion and Social Theory.* 2nd ed. London: Sage, 1991.

Van der Vyver, Johan D. "Religious Fundamentalism and Human Rights." *Journal of International Affairs* 50 (1) (1996): 21-40.

Vasquez, John A. "Factors Related to the Contagion and Diffusion of Ethnic Violence." in Manus I. Midlarsky, ed., *The Internationalization of Communal Strife.* London, Routledge, 1992.

Viorst, Milton. "The Coming Instability." *The Washington Quarterly* 20 (4) (1997): 153-167.

Voye, Liliane. "Secularization in a Context of Advanced Modernity." *Sociology of Religion* 60 (3) (1999): 275-288.

Walid, Abdurrahman. "Future Shock." *Far Eastern Economic Review* 160 (18) 1 May (1997): 38-39.

Walt, Stephen N. "Building Up New Bogeymen." *Foreign Policy,* 106, (1997): 177-189.

Warner, R. Stephen. "Work in Progress toward a New Paradigm for the Sociological Study of Religion in the United States." *American Journal of Sociology* 98 (5) March (1993): 1044-1093.

Wayland, Sarah V. "Religious Expression in Public Schools: Kirpans in Canada, Hijab in France." *Ethnic and Racial Studies* 20 (3) (1997): 545-561.

Weinberg, Leonard B. and William L. Eubank. "Terrorism and Democracy: What Recent Events Disclose." *Terrorism and Political Violence* 10 (1) (1998): 108-118.

Weinberg, Leonard, William Eubank, and Ami Pedahzur. "Characteristics of Terrorist Organizations 1910-2000." Presented at the 25th Annual Meeting of the International Society of Political Psychology in Berlin, Germany, July, 2002.

Wentz, Richard. *Why People Do Bad Things in the Name of Religion.* Macon, Ga.: Mercer, 1987

Williams, Rhys H. "Movement Dynamics and Social Change: Transforming Fundamentalist Ideologies and Organizations." in Martin E. Marty and R. Scott Appleby, eds., *Accounting for Fundamentalisms: The Dynamic Character of Movements.* Chicago: University of Chicago Press, (1994): 785-833.

Wilmer, Franke. *The Indigenous Voice in World Politics.* Newbury Park Calif: Sage, 1993.

Wilson, Bryan R. "Aspects of Secularization in the West." *Japanese Journal of Religious Studies* 3 (4) (1976): 259-276.

————. *Religion in Secular Society.* Baltimore, Md.: Penguin, 1966.

Yamazaki, Masakazu. "Asia, A Civilization in the Making." *Foreign Affairs* 75 (4) (1996): 106-128.

Young, Robert A. "How Do Peaceful Secessions Happen?." in David Carment, and

Patrick James eds., *Wars in the Midst of Peace.* Pittsburgh: University of Pittsburgh Press, (1997): 45-60.

Index

abortion, 20, 21

Afghanistan, 13, 172, 231; and international intervention, 118

African civilization, 157-58, 171-72; and frequency of civilizational clashes, 180-83; and levels of conflict, 195-201; opponents of, 187-88

Algeria, 4, 13

Al Quaeda, 15, 21, 24. *See also* September 11, 2001

animists and opponents in conflict, 60-67

Asia, 161

Austria, 20,21

autonomy, 4. *See also* self-determination

Baha'i, 6, 172

Belgium, 20, 21

Berbers. *See* Algeria

bin Laden, Usama . *See* Al Quaeda *and* September 11, 2001

Bosnia, 172

Buddhism, 21, 126; and civilizations, 158, 170-71, 173; and opponents in conflict, 60-67

Bush, George W., 21

Cambodia, 3

Catholic church, 22-23

China, 159

Christianity, 68-69; and frequency of conflict, 47-55; and international intervention, 121-24; and level of violence, 55-59 ; and opponents in conflict, 59-67 ; and percentage of world population, 47, 133; and protest, 133-18. *See also* protest *and* rebellion

clash of civilizations, 156-57, 159-61, 237-38; and conflict, 190-201, 211-20, 227-30, 234-35; critics of, 158, 161-65, 169-70; and discrimination, 220-23; frequency of, 176-90; Huntington's defense of, 166-68; and international intervention, 224-26; and Islam, 168-70, 202-05; operationalization of, 170-73; overlap with religion, 208-11; and religion, 157-59; variables measuring, 271-72

Cold War: and international intervention, 118; and religious conflict, 32, 59-69; *See also* clash of civilizations

communications technology, 16, 162

Communism, 15

conflict resolution, 25

constructivism, 18

contagion. *See* spread of conflict

About the Author

Jonathan Fox is a Lecturer in the Political Studies Department of Bar-Ilan University in Ramat Gan, Israel and a research fellow at the Begin-Sadat Center for Strteigic Studies. He received his Ph.D. in government and politics from the University of Maryland in College Park in May 1997. He has been the recipient of an Israel Science Foundation grant and has written numerous articles on the influence of religion on politics and on Samuel Huntington's civilizations theory, including articles in *Alternatives, Australian Journal of Political Science, British Journal of Political Science, Comparative Politics, Harvard International Review, International Political Science Review, International Studies Quarterly, International Studies Review, Journal of Peace Research, Political Studies,* and *Terrorism and Political Violence.* He has also published *Ethnoreligious Conflict in the Late Twentieth Century* (Lexington Books, 2002) and *Putting Religion into International Relations* (2004).